The Battle

OF STONES RIVER

AND THE FIGHT FOR MIDDLE TENNESSEE

Timothy D. Johnson, Editor

Tennessee in the Civil War:
The Best of the *Tennessee Historical Quarterly*
Carroll Van West, Series Editor
Volume 4

The Tennessee Historical Society
Nashville

First Edition

All chapters previously published
in the *Tennessee Historical Quarterly*
a publication of The Tennessee Historical Society

This book is printed on acid-free paper.

Library of Congress Control Number: 2012949612

The Tennessee Historical Society
Telephone: 615-741-8934
Email: info@tennesseehistory.org
Website: www.tennesseehistory.org

Tennessee in the Civil War is made possible in part by a publication series planning
partnership with the Tennessee Civil War National Heritage Area and a publication
sponsorship by the Tennessee Civil War Sesquicentennial Commission.

CONTENTS

Introduction:

THE BATTLE OF STONES RIVER AND THE FIGHT FOR MIDDLE TENNESSEE

Timothy D. Johnson

A cold rain mixed with sleet came down on the two armies huddled along the bank of Stones River on the evening of December 30, 1862. When the Confederate army was settled in for the night, Drewy Spurlock, a Mc-Minnville native and captain in the Sixteenth Tennessee, left his company's camp northwest of Murfreesboro and made his way into town to visit his parents who were staying at a local hotel. Having lost one of their sons during the Kentucky Campaign in October, the parents just wanted to be close to Drewy and perhaps take advantage of an opportunity to see him before the armies locked in another death struggle. The captain arrived at the hotel and stayed with his parents until the early morning hours.

Both northern and southern soldiers knew that they were on the eve of battle that night. Union General William S. Rosecrans had marched his Army of the Cumberland out of Nashville the day after Christmas. Having taken five days to cover the twenty-five miles to Murfreesboro, the Federal camps now straddled the turnpike and the railroad back to Nashville. Their camps ran roughly north-south with their left flank (northern) resting at Stones River. Only a few hundred yards away was the Confederate Army of Tennessee under General Braxton Bragg, which had invaded Kentucky three months earlier and fought the Battle of Perryville on October 8 before retreating back into Middle Tennessee. On this cold night, the Confederate army was camped with its back to Murfreesboro and its right flank (northern) overlapping the river. The two armies' close proximity made battle certain.

Earlier that evening the musicians of each army had engaged in an impromptu competition of sorts, a battle of the bands. When the Northern band struck up tunes like "Hail Columbia" and "Yankee Doodle," the Southern musicians responded with their own favorites, "Dixie" and "The Bonnie Blue Flag." Eventually the Federal band began to play "Home Sweet Home," and soon its counterpart across the way joined in as an expression of what was obviously a universal sentiment. The scene was quite an irony, because in just a few hours all harmony between the opposing armies would be forgotten.

Rosecrans and Bragg spent the night preparing for battle the next morning. The Union army numbered about 44,000 while the Confederates had approximately 37,000, and by coincidence, both generals intended to take the offensive on the morning of the thirty-first by striking at their opponent's right flank. However, Bragg was the first to attack at dawn with two divisions from General William Hardee's corps. Soon, elements of General Leonidas Polk's corps joined the assault as the southerners slowly pushed the Yankees back all morning. The Union right gave ground all along the line, but at places like "the slaughter pen" where Union division commander, General Philip Sheridan, put up a stubborn defense, the Federal army slowed the onslaught.

By afternoon, the fighting swirled around a clump of cedars called the Round Forest that had become the linchpin of Rosecrans's bent and constricted line. Beleaguered Federals held firm and beat back piecemeal Confederate attacks for hours with such terrible slaughter that the place came to be known as Hell's Half Acre. In one Confederate assault, Captain Spurlock's Sixteenth Tennessee was pinned down along the edge of a cotton field by heavy musket and artillery fire. In a futile attempt to get his company up and moving forward, he was struck and killed by enemy fire. Despite being unable to dislodge Federal troops from the Round Forest or to cut off their line of retreat back to Nashville, Bragg nevertheless believed that the Union army was near collapse as darkness fell. That night he sent a telegram to Richmond stating that he had won a great victory. However, Rosecrans had no intention of retreating, and told his generals that he intended to hold his ground at all costs. Meanwhile, Drewy Spurlock's parents, having learned of their son's death, retrieved his body from the battlefield, wrapped it, and headed home to McMinnville.

Only minor skirmishing interrupted a relatively quiet New Year's Day as both armies rested and tried to recover from the previous day's carnage. However, on the afternoon of January 2, fighting resumed in earnest when Bragg ordered General John C. Breckinridge to seize the high ground on the east side of Stones River. The Confederates succeeded in driving the enemy off the hill, but soon came under a thunderous artillery attack from dozens of Federal cannon across the river, forcing them to retreat with heavy losses. In McMinnville, thirty miles away, as the Spurlock's buried Drewy's body, they could hear the faint rumble of artillery on that sad afternoon. Late the next day, the Confederates began their retreat to Tullahoma thus bringing the bloody Battle of Stones River to an end.

Casualties for the three days of fighting totaled 12,900 Union and 11,700 Confederate. As a percentage of the number of troops engaged, that makes Stones River the bloodiest battle of the war. However, the magnitude of the bloodshed was not all that gave significance to this often overlooked battle. The North's hard fought victory came at a time when the Lincoln administration badly needed positive news from the battlefield. The war had not been going well in the Eastern Theater in 1862 as illustrated by defeats in the Peninsula Campaign and at Second Bull Run. Robert E. Lee followed those summer victories with an invasion of Maryland that was turned back by the bloody Battle of Antietam. Lee had fought his Union counterpart to a tactical stalemate, but his withdrawal back to Virginia gave the North a slim strategic victory that Lincoln needed as a springboard for issuing his Emancipation Proclamation. A Southern victory in Tennessee just as that landmark proclamation was taking effect on January 1, 1863 would have been a major embarrassment for the administration and would have fostered an appearance of desperation on the part of the president. Lincoln's relief over news of the Stones River victory was obvious in a January 5 telegram to Rosecrans: "God bless you, and all with you! Please tender to all, and accept for yourself, the nation's gratitude...."

The battle catapulted William Rosecrans to "the edge of glory" as one biographer described. For a brief time it appeared that perhaps Lincoln had found the general he had been looking for since the beginning of the war, but the Rosecrans bubble would burst in the autumn. For the Confederate army the battle exposed the infighting and divisiveness in its high command that would prove to be its Achilles' heel. In the months that followed, Rosecrans built a 220 acre earthen fortress on the edge of Murfreesboro called Fortress Rosecrans that became a giant supply depot to support his army's advance.

In addition, the Union victory was important because it secured much of Middle Tennessee and set the stage for a major offensive a few months later. In the summer, with little fanfare or media coverage, Rosecrans executed what remains today a little-known military masterpiece called the Tullahoma Campaign. While all eyes were focused on Lee's invasion of Pennsylvania and Ulysses S. Grant's movements in Mississippi, Rosecrans skillfully maneuvered Bragg out of Middle Tennessee entirely.

Because Rosecrans secured much of the state with flank marches, small battles, and relatively little bloodshed, his accomplishment was sure to be overshadowed by the epic events at Gettysburg and Vicksburg. And so it was. The Tullahoma Campaign remains today a neglected topic for Civil War research. Indeed the significance of events in Tennessee in late 1862 and early 1863 is often overlooked. Not until major battles at Chickamauga and Chattanooga in the fall of 1863 does interest seem to be rejuvenated regarding the Army of the Cumberland and the Army of Tennessee.

This volume of the "Tennessee in the Civil War Series" serves as a reminder of those three bloody days along the banks of Stones River. Nine previously published articles in the *Tennessee Historical Quarterly* constitute the chapters in this book. Renowned Civil War historian Ed Bearss provides a detailed analysis of cavalry operations in the first chapter. He meticulously recreates cavalry movements during the Union march from Nashville to Murfreesboro from December 26 to 29, and he concludes that it was counter measures by the Confederate cavalry along with weather and road conditions that turned a twenty-five mile march into a four-day trek. Bearss next covers the operations of mounted troops during the battle, including Joe Wheeler's famous ride around Rosecrans's army on December 30-31.

Chapters two and three deal with specific aspects of the battle. Christopher Losson recounts the role of the likeable but profane Confederate General Benjamin Franklin Cheatham, who led his division of Polk's Corps in the battle's opening assault. Cheatham's normally dependable Tennesseans attacked late and in piecemeal fashion due perhaps to the division commander's rumored intoxication that morning. Next, noted Civil War scholar James Lee McDonough treats the sometimes ignored final phase of the battle. In detailing Breckinridge's January 2 attack on the east bank, the author provides extended excerpts from the letters of a Union and a Confederate soldier that graphically remind the reader of the nature of war.

The remaining chapters treat the aftermath and legacy of the battle. In chapters four and five, Robert Hartje and William M. Anderson recount the Battle of Thompson Station from the Confederate and Union perspectives respectively. In this action Nathan Bedford Forrest and Earl Van Dorn teamed up to defeat a Federal force under Colonel John Coburn that had pushed forward to reconnoiter the roads south of Franklin. This small engagement illustrated the agility of Southern cavalry and the nature of mobile war in Middle Tennessee.

Next Robert S. Brandt provides an account of the Tullahoma Campaign, which, following Stones River, was the next step in gaining complete control of the state. Miranda Fraley chronicles the role of African-Americans in a chapter that deals with the preservation and commemoration of the Stones River Cemetery. In chapters eight and nine, Lenard E. Brown recounts the post war history of Fortress Rosecrans and Bob Womack tells the story of the efforts to save the battlefield from the establishment of the National Cemetery in 1865 to the creation of the Stones River Military Park in 1927 and subsequent preservation efforts to the centennial of the battle.

The Civil War was a great national tragedy on one hand, and on the other it represented a rebirth of freedom. Its significance to the nation's history is unparalleled. Stones River was the last major battle in Middle Tennessee until Franklin and Nashville in the war's closing months, and unfortunately it remains one of the least studied and written about of the state's major battles. At the 150th anniversary of the battle, it is important to remember the role that Stones River played in helping to ensure Federal control of the state's rich mid-section and the major stride forward that the battle's outcome represented for the North. The editor of this series, Carroll Van West, Director of the Center for Historic Preservation at MTSU, along with Ann Toplovich, Executive Director of the Tennessee Historical Society, and Commissioner Susan Whitaker, Chair of the Tennessee Civil War Sesquicentennial Commission, are to be commended for their foresight in remembering and commemorating the state's great battles and campaigns.

CAVALRY OPERATIONS IN THE STONES RIVER CAMPAIGN

December 26, 1862–January 5, 1863

Edwin C. Bearss

(Editor's Note: In this study, Ed Bearss traces the cavalry operations of the Stones River Campaign day by day, from the actions during the Union approach on December 26–30, 1862, into the days of the battle, December 31–January 2, 1863, and through the Confederate evacuation of Murfreesboro, January 3–5.)

December 26, 1862, the day selected by Major General William S. Rosecrans to inaugurate his projected advance from Nashville into the heart of Middle Tennessee, found the Confederate Army of Tennessee, commanded by General Braxton Bragg, concentrated in the Murfreesboro area. Lieutenant General Leonidas Polk's corps consisting of infantry divisions commanded by Major Generals B. Franklin Cheatham and Jones M. Withers, and three brigades of Major General John C. Breckinridge's division of General William J. Hardee's corps constituted Bragg's center, and were camped in and around Murfreesboro. Brigadier General John K. Jackson's brigade, which until recently had been guarding the railroad between Murfreesboro and Bridgeport, Alabama, had also been concentrated at the former town and had been assigned by Bragg to Breckinridge's division.

The other division of Hardee's corps, commanded by Major General Patrick R. Cleburne and reinforced by Brigadier General Daniel W. Adams's brigade of Breckinridge's division, was based at College Grove, near Eagleville, some fifteen miles west of Murfreesboro. This force, with which Hardee maintained his headquarters, guarded the Confederate left. The right flank of Bragg's army rested at Readyville, twelve miles east of Murfreesboro. Readyville was garrisoned by Major General John P. McCown's division. This division was an organic part of Lieutenant General E. Kirby Smith's corps, but prior to the Stones River Campaign, McCown had been directed by the Confederate War Department to report to Hardee for orders, because at this time Kirby Smith was in Knoxville commanding the Department of East Tennessee.[1]

Bragg's once all-powerful force of cavalry had been considerably reduced at the time Rosecrans's Army of the Cumberland began its forward movement. The redoubtable Brigadier General Nathan B. Forrest with some 1,900 of his hard-riding troopers had crossed the Tennessee River into West Tennessee. At this very moment Forrest's men were wreaking havoc on the Union supply lines, which were used to funnel supplies to Major General Ulysses S. Grant's Army of the Tennessee, then operating in North Mississippi. On December 22, four days before the Army of the Cumberland had marched out of Nashville, Bragg's other thunderbolt—Brigadier General John H. Morgan—had ridden out of Alexandria, Tennessee, en route to Kentucky. With him, on his second Kentucky raid, Morgan took a force consisting of 3,100 rank and file, supported by seven pieces of artillery. The vital Louisville and Nashville Railroad, over which Rosecrans drew his supplies, was the primary objective of Morgan and his "terrible men." The departure of these two crack commands, under their able leaders, served to reduce by half the strength of the cavalry serving with the Army of Tennessee. Thus when the period of active campaigning commenced, the Federals in Tennessee, for the first time in the war, had almost as many cavalrymen present with their field army as the Confederates.[2]

After the departure of Forrest and Morgan there remained with the Army of Tennessee four cavalry brigades. Three of these, commanded respectively by Brigadier Generals Joseph Wheeler, John A. Wharton, and John Pegram were charged with the responsibility of picketing the army's front and flanks. An understrength brigade of cavalry, led by Brigadier General Abraham Buford, mustering some 600 sabers, was stationed at McMinnville.[3] General Wheeler had been placed in command of the army's cavalry by Bragg.

December 26 found Wheeler's brigade bivouacked on Stewarts Creek, alongside the Nashville Pike, some ten miles northwest of Murfreesboro. Wheeler had covered his front, extending from a point east of Stones River on his right, to a point approximately midway between the Nashville Pike and Brentwood on his left, with a strong line of vedettes. On the Nashville Pike, Wheeler had established an outpost within ten miles of Nashville.[4] General Pegram's understrength brigade was posted on Wheeler's right covering the approaches to Murfreesboro from Lebanon. At a point twelve miles north of Murfreesboro, where the Lebanon Pike crossed Fall Creek, Pegram established his headquarters. Strong patrols were thrown out daily as far as Baird's Mill, six miles north of the Fall Creek staging area.[5] General Wharton's combat-wise brigade took position on Wheeler's left, with Nolensville as its base of operation. The Texan's brigade was charged with the responsibility of screening the Confederates' left flank. Wharton's picket line tied in with Wheeler's on the right, and extended in a southwesterly direction as far as Franklin.[6]

Three infantry brigades were advanced and posted in close supporting distance of each of the cavalry brigades. The hard-hitting brigade commanded by Brigadier General George Maney, of Cheatham's division, was thrown forward to Stewarts Creek to bolster Wheeler's command.[7] A brigade from Cleburne's division, led by the Brigadier General Stirling A. M. Wood, was stationed at Triune, ready to move to Wharton's succor if the need should arise.[8] Pegram's troops were supported by Colonel John Q. Loomis's Alabama brigade, which was drawn from Withers's division.

Almost simultaneously with receipt of the intelligence that Bragg's Army of Tennessee had been weakened by the departure of Forrest's and Morgan's raiders, Rosecrans learned from his staff that sufficient war material had been stockpiled in the Nashville magazines to enable the Army of the Cumberland to assume the offensive. Rosecrans's master plan called for the following movements: Major General Alexander M. McCook's right wing, consisting of three divisions, would move out of the Nashville defenses, via the Nolensville Pike, to Triune; Major General George H. Thomas, with two divisions, would advance on McCook's right, and Thomas's command would utilize the Franklin and Wilson pikes as it pushed forward. While McCook threatened Hardee's command in front, Thomas would threaten his left flank. Major General Thomas L. Crittenden, in command of the three divisions that constituted the Army of the Cumberland's left wing, would move forward on McCook's left as far as La Vergne, using the Nashville Pike as the axis of his advance. Once Thomas's two divisions reached Nolensville, McCook was to attack Hardee at Triune. If Bragg should decide to stand and fight and should reinforce Hardee with Polk, Thomas was to rush to McCook's support. However, if McCook should defeat Hardee unaided or force him to evacuate Triune without a fight, and the Rebels should mass behind Stewarts Creek, Crittenden was to spearhead the attack. If these circumstances came to pass, Thomas was to move into position on Crittenden's right, while McCook, after detaching a division charged with the mission of pursuing Hardee, would endeavor to turn the Confederates' left and get into their rear. After drafting these orders for his subordinates, Rosecrans scheduled the morning of December 26 for the beginning of the campaign.[9]

Prior to the departure of the Army of the Cumberland from Nashville, Major General David S. Stanley, Rosecrans's hand-picked chief of cavalry, divided the 4,200 troopers assigned to his organization into three commands. The First Brigade, commanded by Colonel Robert H. G. Minty, would operate along the Nashville Pike, screening the advance of Crittenden's corps. Colonel Lewis Zahm's Second Brigade would drive directly on Franklin, covering the right flank of McCook's column, and brushing aside Wharton's Rebel troopers. A reserve force consisting of three recently organized regiments, stiffened by four companies of the Third Indiana Cavalry, would receive their orders directly from General Stanley. With this force Stanley would cover McCook's corps as it pushed toward Nolensville. Colonel Minty would receive his orders directly from Colonel John Kennett, who commanded the division of cavalry.[10]

At 6:00 a.m. on the 26th, several hours before Stanley's troopers put in an appearance at McCook's camps that were situated on Mill Creek, five miles south of Nashville, the infantry moved out. The division commanded by Brigadier General Jefferson C. Davis tramped southward along the Edmondson Pike. Davis's division would utilize the Edmondson Pike as its avenue of advance as far as Prim's blacksmith shop. Here the division would turn into a country lane, which led to Nolensville. Brigadier General Philip H. Sheridan's division trudged out of the Mill Creek staging area at the same hour as Davis's did. Sheridan used as the axis of his advance the Nolensville Pike. McCook's third division, led by Brigadier General Richard W. Johnson, followed in Sheridan's wake. By the time Stanley's command put in its appearance, the roads leading to Nolensville were jammed with McCook's troops and their trains. It was apparent to the troopers that they would not be able to reach their assigned positions in advance of McCook's right wing, until after the infantry had bivouacked for the night.[11]

The advance guard of both Davis's and Sheridan's columns quickly established contact with Wharton's outposts, which were charged with the responsibility of observing the Edmondson and Nolensville pikes. The only cavalry unit with Davis's division at this time was the general's escort—Company K, Fifteenth Illinois Cavalry. Wharton's vedettes fell back without making a stand, however, and the Illinois cavalrymen were able to push to within one mile of Nolensville before they were forced to call for help. In spite of the heavy rain that pelted the column, Davis's infantry and artillery reached Prim's blacksmith shop in good time. Here the division left the Edmondson Pike and turned into the country lane that it would follow to Nolensville. The steep hills and the road, rendered all but impassable by the downpour, served to retard the column's progress. Coming up with his advance guard, Davis was informed by the Illinoisans and residents of the area that a strong force of Confederates (Wharton's brigade), supported by artillery, was in occupation of Nolensville. Before deploying his division, Davis sent a staff officer to inform Sheridan, whose division was advancing along the Nolensville Pike and had not yet put in an appearance, that the enemy had been located. Believing that he was strong enough to deal with the situation unaided, Davis formed his division for the attack. The brigade commanded by Colonel P. Sidney Post was deployed to the left of the road. Captain Oscar F. Pinney's Fifth Battery, Wisconsin Light Artillery, was emplaced to command the town and its southwestern approaches. While Post was deploying his men into line of battle, Wharton's troopers could be seen massing on the hills southwest of Nolensville. Davis fearing that the Rebels planned to turn his right flank, issued orders for Colonel William P. Carlin to form his brigade on Post's right. Colonel William E. Woodruff's Third Brigade then moved into position on Carlin's right. While the Federals were forming for the attack the Confederates succeeded in emplacing White's Tennessee Battery. But, before the Tennesseans were able to get off more than a few rounds, Pinney's six-gun battery had roared into action.[12]

Wharton having accomplished his mission, by forcing the Yankees to deploy, gave the order to withdraw. Except for some rather brisk skirmishing between the Rebels' rearguard and Carlin's brigade, which occupied the town, Wharton's troopers succeeded in breaking contact with the foe. Having captured Nolensville, and while waiting for the remainder of McCook's corps to put in an appearance, Davis learned from his scouts that Wharton's men had fallen back only some two miles.

After evacuating the village, Wharton's rugged troopers had taken position ready to defend Knob Gap, through which the Nolensville and Triune Pike passed. In spite of the late hour and the fatigued condition of his men, due to the hard day's march through rain and mud, Davis decided to attack before the Southerners could dig in. Once the brigade commanders had mustered their units, the advance was resumed with Post's brigade in the lead. As Post's vanguard approached Knob Gap, it was fired upon by White's Tennessee Battery. In response to Post's call for artillery support, the cannoneers of the Fifth Wisconsin and Second Battery, Minnesota Light Artillery, came thundering forward. The artillerists from the "Old Northwest" quickly unlimbered their pieces, and commenced to hammering the Rebels with shot and shell. While the artillery was softening up Wharton's position, Davis formed his brigades for assault—Post to the left of the road and Carlin to the right, with Woodruff on the latter officer's right. At an order from Davis the powerful Union line of battle surged forward. Wharton's troopers were driven from the gap so rapidly that

White's cannoneers were unable to remove one of their guns, which along with its caisson was captured by Carlin's brigade. Davis, taking cognizance of the late hour and in accordance with the instructions he had received from McCook, permitted his men to bivouac for the night. Wharton's troopers fell back toward Triune, where the supporting infantry of Wood's brigade was camped.[13]

McCook's main column, spearheaded by Sheridan's division, had encountered Wharton's vedettes, several miles south of the Mill Creek staging area on the Nolensville Pike. These were quickly routed; the bluecoats captured a lieutenant and a private. In response to Davis's message, the combative Sheridan had quickened the pace of his march. But by the time the head of Sheridan's division reached Nolensville, Davis was engaged in driving the Confederates from Knob Gap. McCook then directed Sheridan and Johnson to have their troops camp for the night at Nolensville.[14]

Thomas's corps, with Brigadier General James S. Negley's division in the van, followed by Major General Lovell H. Rousseau's division and Colonel Moses B. Walker's brigade, marched out of the Nashville perimeter via the Franklin Pike. If all went according to plan the troops of Thomas's corps would camp for the night at Owen's Store, on the Wilson Pike. Reaching Brentwood, Thomas's troops left the Franklin Pike, turning into the Wilson Pike. As the head of Negley's column reached Owen's store, late on the afternoon of the 26th, the sound of heavy firing became distinctly audible from the direction of Nolensville, where Davis had engaged Wharton. Negley determined to march to the sound of the guns. Leaving his trains to follow, Negley pushed forward rapidly to Davis's support. But by the time his hard-marching column reached Nolensville, the Rebels had been hurled from Knob Gap. The men of Negley's division, considerably fatigued by their forced march, then camped for the night. The muddy condition of the roads made it impossible for the remainder of Thomas's corps to keep pace with Negley; Rousseau halted for the night at Owen's store; Walker with his brigade bivouacked at Brentwood.[15]

Colonel Zahm's cavalry brigade, 950 strong, broke camp at 8 a.m. Riding southward along the Franklin Pike, Zahm's troopers found the road choked with Thomas's troops and their immense trains. After passing through Brentwood, where Thomas's command had turned into the Wilson Pike, the mounted column picked up speed as it moved toward Franklin. Two and one-half miles north of Franklin—Zahm's point—the Third Ohio Cavalry encountered and drove in a Confederate outpost.

Franklin, at this time, was garrisoned by two of Wharton's units—the Fourth Tennessee Cavalry and Davis's Tennessee Cavalry Battalion. Deploying his brigade to the left and right of the road, Zahm pressed forward. Falling back across the Big

Harpeth River, the Tennesseans took position covering that stream. After making a hurried estimate of the situation, Zahm dismounted six of his companies, with instructions to act as skirmishers. The remainder of the brigade took position on the skirmishers' flank. Zahm then gave the signal to attack. Surging forward, the bluecoats forced their way across the Big Harpeth River. After a sharp clash, the butternuts beat a hasty retreat, leaving ten prisoners in the Yankees' hands. Due to the late hour, the Federals broke off their pursuit, after following the Confederates for about two miles. Upon interrogating the prisoners, Zahm learned that there was a strong Confederate force (Wood's brigade) stationed near Triune. Having successfully discharged his mission, Zahm retraced his steps. Reaching Owen's store about 9 a.m. Zahm's troopers halted for the night.[16]

Crittenden's corps, Brigadier General John M. Palmer's division in the lead, used the Nashville Pike as the axis of its advance on the drive toward Murfrees-boro. Shortly after taking up the march on December 26, Palmer was joined by Colonels Kennett and Minty. In accordance with the instructions received from Palmer through Kennett, Minty deployed his brigade to screen Crittenden's advance. The Third Kentucky was placed on the left of the pike, the Seventh Pennsylvania on the right, and the Fourth Michigan on the pike in reserve. A strong advance guard was pushed to the front. Near the 11-mile stone, Minty's troopers encountered one of Wheeler's outposts. A brisk skirmish ensued. In this clash the Unionists drove the Rebels from the cedar break, where they had holed up, capturing six of them. After this flurry of excitement the advance was resumed.[17]

Wheeler, upon receipt of the intelligence that the bluecoats had driven in his vedettes, left his La Vergne headquarters and rode to the front. Here a hasty personal reconnaissance served to convince Wheeler that the Federals were advancing in force. In hopes of delaying the powerful Union column, Wheeler sent a member of his staff galloping madly to the rear to order up his entire command. Once the news of the Federal advance had been communicated to the unit commanders, they mustered their men. Swinging into their saddles the hard-bitten troopers of Wheeler's brigade left their Stewarts Creek cantonment. When the cavalrymen reached La Vergne they found their general eagerly awaiting them. Wheeler then led his brigade to a point astride the pike, two miles northwest of La Vergne, where he deployed his troops into line of battle, covering the crossings of Hurricane Creek. The troopers were told to dismount and take it easy pending the Yankees' appearance. The four guns of Wiggins's Arkansas Battery were emplaced near the pike.[18]

General Maney, in command of Wheeler's supporting infantry force, also moved his brigade from Stewarts Creek to La Vergne. Upon reaching La Vergne, Maney conferred briefly with Wheeler. Convinced by what he was able to learn from the cavalry officer concerning the strength of Union column, Maney decided to advise Bragg that the foe was advancing in force.[19]

Having routed the Rebel outpost from the cedar break, Minty's troopers resumed the advance. Pushing forward, the blue-coated cavalrymen were slightly distressed to note that the butternuts, who were observing their advance, seemed to be constantly increasing in numbers. The cavalry's motion was finally brought to a sudden stop when the troopers sighted Wheeler's line of battle massed to contest the passage of Hurricane Creek. Minty, taking cognizance of Wiggins's four guns, ordered Lieutenant Nathaniel M. Newell, of Battery D, First Ohio Light Artillery, to emplace his two 3-inch Rodmans on the pike. Simultaneously a staff officer was sent racing to the rear to urge that Palmer hurry to the cavalry's help.

An artillery duel of about one-half hour's duration now ensued between Wiggins's and Newell's gunners, before the vanguard of Palmer's division arrived. Once the energetic Palmer had put in an appearance he directed Captain William E. Standart to put the six guns of Battery B, First Ohio Light Artillery, into action alongside Newell's. Brigadier General Charles Cruft was instructed to deploy his brigade to the left of the road, force a crossing of Hurricane Creek, and, if it was still daylight, occupy La Vergne. Colonel Walter C. Whitaker, who was in temporary command of Colonel William B. Hazen's brigade, would form his unit to the right of the road. A hasty reconnaissance of the Confederates' right convinced Cruft that it could be easily turned. A combat team composed of the Thirty-first Indiana and First Kentucky, led by Colonel David A. Enyart, was detailed to carry out the flanking operation. The Third Kentucky Cavalry would screen Enyart's combat team's left flank as it moved forward. In conjunction with Enyart's attack Colonel Whitaker, accompanied by the Ninth Indiana and Sixth Kentucky, would attack and turn Wheeler's left.[20]

Confronted by a powerful force to his immediate front and with both his flanks threatened by Enyart's and Whitaker's combat teams, Wheeler ordered his men to be ready to retire on an instant's notice. Enyart's men, upon debouching from the cedars, sighted one of Wheeler's combat patrols near the small frame church situated near the west bank of Hurricane Creek. Enyart roared out the order for his men to charge. With bayonets flashing the blueclads drove the Confederates across the creek. Following in the Rebels' wake, Enyart's men easily reached the stream's east bank. As it was getting quite dark, Enyart decided not to push into La Vergne. Instead he deployed his troops in a field near the village's northern outskirts. South of the Nashville Pike, Whitaker's combat team, after an animated contest, forced its way across Hurricane Creek. But Whitaker found himself confronted by the same problem as Enyart, and the advent of darkness forced him to suspend his attack.

Thus when the fighting ceased for the night the Confederates still held La Vergne, but the Yankees had succeeded in establishing bridgeheads on the stream's right hank. Crittenden's corps, except for the troops holding the bridgeheads, spent the night of the 26th camped on the left bank of Hurricane Creek. Wheeler's cavalry and Maney's infantry (which had not been engaged) bivouacked in line of battle covering La Vergne. In the fighting in front of La Vergne, Crittenden lost two killed and sixteen wounded. Wheeler made no report of his losses, hut Crittenden reported that his men had captured twelve Confederates. In a letter to Rosecrans dated the 26th, Crittenden reported, "In all these skirmishes the enemy fought with such determination as to induce the belief that there must have been a large force in the neighborhood."[21]

⚬⟪⟫⚬

On the evening of December 26, Wheeler proceeded to Murfreesboro, where he attended a meeting that had been called by General Bragg. The commander of the Army of Tennessee having decided to concentrate his forces in front of Murfreesboro reportedly asked Wheeler, "How long can you hold them on the road?" "About four days, general," Wheeler quickly replied. Bragg then issued the orders for the concentration of his army, and the conference adjourned.[22]

General Cleburne, in accordance with the instruction received from Hardee on the previous evening, turned his command out at an early hour on December 27. Realizing that McCook's Union column would probably drive down the Nolensville Pike toward Triune, the combative Cleburne planned to meet the foe on ground of his own choosing, a mile north of College Grove. While Cleburne was engaged in deploying three of his own brigades and Adams's, of Breckinridge's division, orders were received from Hardee to move to Murfreesboro. This was to implement Bragg's decision to concentrate the Army of Tennessee at that point. Wood's brigade would be left at Triune to assist Wharton's cavalry in retarding the blue-coats' advance. Drenched by a cold rain, Cleburne's troops moved over a miserable road to Versailles, and then into the Salem Pike. Nightfall found the tired and disgusted veterans encamped on the Salem Pike, one mile west of Stones River.[23]

Late on the evening of the 26th, Bragg's order calling for a concentration at Murfreesboro reached McCown's headquarters at Readyville. The general ordered reveille sounded and the men mustered. Long before daybreak, McCown had his troops on the road. Despite the disagreeable weather, McCown's division negotiated the twelve miles, which separated Readyville from Murfreesboro by 9 a.m. on December 27. Upon reaching Murfreesboro McCown's troops were posted east of Stones River, adjacent to the Nashville Pike.[24]

After having ordered Cleburne to move his command to Murfreesboro, Hardee proceeded to Triune to confer with Generals Wharton and Wood. Hardee told the two officers of Bragg's plan for a concentration at Murfreesboro, and briefed them as to their respective roles. The two generals were expected to delay the foe's advance, to the best of their ability. Hardee, accompanied by his staff, then returned to Murfreesboro. Following Hardee's departure, Wood and Wharton deployed their commands in hopes that they would be able to give McCook's advancing column a hot reception. The Forty-fifth Mississippi Infantry was posted about one and one-half miles north of Triune, on the Nolensville Pike; four companies deployed as skirmishers on the right of the road; three supporting a section of the Jefferson Flying Artillery, which was masked and emplaced to the left of the road; and one company thrown out to guard the left flank. Wood held the remainder of his small brigade in reserve, immediately south of the village. Wharton's cavalry took position astride the pike a half mile in advance of the Forty-fifth Mississippi. Having deployed their men Wood and Wharton confidently awaited the Federal advance.[25]

On the night of the 26th General Rosecrans had visited McCook's headquarters at Nolensville. While there, Rosecrans told his subordinate that on the morrow he was to move on Triune, and attack Hardee's corps which intelligence reports had indicated was quartered there.[26]

In accordance with McCook's orders his subordinates turned their men out before daybreak on the 27th. After a hurried breakfast the troops marched out—General Stanley's cavalry command in the lead, followed closely by Johnson's division. It had stopped raining, but the country was blanketed by a fog that limited visibility to about 150 yards. General Stanley, remarking that he "had understood the Third [Indiana] knew how to take these rebels," ordered the Hoosiers to take the lead. A mile south of Bole Jack Pass, as the Indianians groped their way forward, they sighted a strong force of Wharton's command drawn up in line of battle. Major Robert Klein barked out the order to charge. Digging their spurs into their horses' flanks the Hoosiers surged forward. After a spirited contest the Confederates gave way, retreating across a narrow valley. The gunners of the Jefferson Flying Artillery now opened fire on the Indianians, bringing their advance to an abrupt halt.[27]

Responding to the roar of the artillery, Stanley, accompanied by the rest of his command, joined the Indianians. A quick reconnaissance convinced the general that he would need both infantry and artillery to break the Rebel roadblock. This request was immediately relayed to General Johnson, who ordered his advance brigade, commanded by Brigadier General Edward N. Kirk, to move to the cavalry's support. Kirk deployed the Thirty-fourth Illinois and Twenty-ninth Indiana as skirmishers to the left of the road; the remainder of the brigade was to move forward in line of battle covered by the skirmishers—the Thirtieth Indiana in support of Battery E, First Ohio Light Artillery. Stanley's cavalry would cover the infantry's flanks.

McCook, fearful that the dense fog that enveloped everything would render it impossible for his men to distinguish friend from foe, ordered Kirk to wait for the atmosphere to clear before closing with the Confederates. Time would not be completely wasted, for the cannoneers of Battery E would be able to take advantage of the fog's protective mantle to emplace their guns on a hill overlooking the spot where Stanley thought the masked Confederate battery was located. Johnson also made use of this hiatus to bring forward another brigade—Colonel Philemon P. Baldwin's—which was deployed in double line of battle to the right of the pike, the First Ohio and Sixth Indiana in front, the Fifth Kentucky and Ninety-third Ohio in reserve.[28]

General Wood was troubled by the intelligence that the bluecoats were seeking to emplace a battery on the commanding elevation within 500 yards of his masked battery. Furthermore the general had learned from Wharton that the Union cavalry had appeared in considerable strength on the Confederates' flanks. Realizing that he would have to act promptly, Wood decided to withdraw the Forty-fifth Mississippi and the section of the Jefferson Flying Artillery from their advance position. Wharton's troops and the men of the Forty-fifth Mississippi would cover the artillery as it was removed to the rear. When thus reformed, Wood's main line of resistance centered on the hill immediately south of Triune. The Sixteenth Alabama took position behind a stone wall southwest of town, near the Franklin Road. Six cannons (four served by the men of the Jefferson Flying Artillery and the others by White's men) were massed near the Eagleville Pike. The cannoneers trained their pieces on the approach to Nelsons Creek, which lay athwart the Yankees' line of advance. Wharton's cavalry would cover Wood's flanks, while the Thirty-third Alabama Infantry was stationed on the Eagleville Pike, several miles south of Triune, to keep open the Confederates' line of retreat.[29]

By 1:00 p.m. the fog had partially lifted. McCook ordered the advance resumed. Skirmishing constantly with Wharton's troops and the men of the Forty-fifth Mississippi, the Federals drove forward. Within a short time the bluecoated line of battle seized the ridge overlooking the village of Triune. Once the men of the Forty-fifth Mississippi had retired across Nelsons Creek, Wood had the bridge demolished. This assignment was carried out by a demolition team commanded by Captain J. W. Green.

From their vantage point the boys in blue could easily pinpoint the Confederates' main line of resistance. In hopes of silencing the six Rebel guns covering the approaches to Nelsons Creek, Kirk ordered the cannoneers of Battery B, First Ohio Artillery to put four of their James rifles in position. The Union gunners then opened fire on the Confederates with shot and shell. Lacking any rifled artillery with which to reply to the Union bombardment, Wood ordered his artillerists to limber up their pieces and retire behind the crest of the ridge overlooking Triune. Hardly had the grayclad gunners reached their supposed haven of safety than they learned that a strong force of Union cavalry was approaching from the west. Fortunately for the Southerners it now started to sleet. McCook decided that an advance at the moment would be most hazardous, and ordered Johnson not to attack until the storm had abated.[30]

The mounted force that the Confederates had sighted approaching from the west was a combat patrol, consisting of four companies of the Third Indiana and a company of the Fifteenth Pennsylvania. Crossing Nelsons Creek to the west of Triune, undetected by Wharton's troopers, the blueclads sought to turn the Confederates' left flank. The Federals ran into a hornet's nest, however, when they encountered the detachment of the Sixteenth Alabama posted behind the stone wall. Moving across an open field to attack the Alabamans, the Yankees drew the fire of the Confederate artillery. This proved too much for the cavalrymen and they fell back in confusion.[31]

While the storm was still raging Wharton and Wood conferred briefly. The two officers realized only too well that with their limited force it would be impossible to check the advance of McCook's powerful mile-long line of battle when it should resume its forward movement. Accordingly the artillery was ordered to the rear. And not a moment too soon for the storm suddenly stopped. McCook gave the word. The Union line of battle started forward. Only sporadic resistance was encountered. But the pace of the Union advance was greatly retarded by other factors—the muddy condition of the terrain, and the sodden state of the men's uniforms. On reaching Nelsons Creek, the infantry found it no barrier, and easily forded the stream. But for the artillery, it was different; a mile detour was necessary before a suitable ford was found. The Rebel brass used this delay to a good advantage, and Wood's infantrymen, covered by Wharton's cavalry, made good their escape down Eagleville Pike.[32]

Since it was starting to get dark, the bluecoats quickly gave up the chase. Johnson's troops and Stanley's cavalrymen camped for the night a mile south of Triune.

McCook's two other divisions, Sheridan's and Davis's, had followed in close support-ing distance of Johnson during the day, and by nightfall on the 27th Sheridan was in occupation of Triune and Davis was in position at Bole Jack Pass.

Wood kept his men on the road until dark, by which time they had reached a point three miles north of Eagleville. Here he permitted them to bivouac. During the night, Wood received orders from Hardee to rejoin Cleburne's division, at Murfrees-boro, on the morrow. Wharton's troopers spent the night of the 27th, midway be-tween Triune and Eagleville.[33]

Rosecrans, satisfied by the intelligence received from McCook that Hardee had retreated, ordered Thomas to join Crittenden on Stewarts Creek. The heavy rainfall had rendered the Wilson Pike all but impassable on the 27th. Therefore it took one of Thomas's divisions, Rousseau's, the entire day to move from Owen's store to Nol-ensville. Negley's division, which had reached Nolensville on the previous evening, remained in the village until 10:00 a.m., when its supply train arrived. The division then moved eastward over a terrible road, reaching Stewartsboro late in the evening and going into position on Crittenden's right. Thomas, deeply perturbed by Rous-seau's snail-like progress, decided it would be best to keep Walker off the Wilson Pike. Orders were therefore drafted directing Walker to retrace his steps toward Nashville from Brentwood. Upon reaching Nashville, Walker would then utilize the Nolens-ville Pike as his line of advance.[34]

During the day Colonel Zahm's brigade, which for the moment was operating with Thomas's corps, was quite active. A strong combat patrol composed of the First Ohio and a detachment of the Fourth Ohio, led by Colonel Minor Milliken, left the Wilson Pike campground to make a forced reconnaissance in the direction of Triune. Establishing contact with one of Wharton's outposts five miles northwest of Triune, the Federals scattered the Confederates, captured six of them, and then returned to camp.

Shortly after the departure of Milliken's command, Zahm had sent out a bat-talion of the Third Ohio to see whether the Confederates had reoccupied Frank-lin. North of the Big Harpeth River the Yankees encountered an enemy picket line, which was driven in. The Union advance was quickly checked, however, when it encountered the grayclads' main line of resistance. Satisfied that the Fourth Tennes-see Cavalry and Davis's Tennessee Battalion had again occupied Franklin, the Feder-als returned to their base. Except for sending out these two strong combat patrols, Zahm's brigade remained in its camp on the 27th.

The men of Crittenden's corps were mustered an hour and a half before daybreak on the 27th. After a hasty breakfast the troops were formed under arms and in order of battle. As soon as it was light enough to see, the Confederate artillery near La Vergne began to shell the left bank of Hurricane Creek, where the Federal officers were marshaling their units. Crittenden, having been advised by Rosecrans that his corps had advanced more rapidly than the Army of the Cumberland's other corps, decided to postpone his forward movement until late forenoon.[35]

At 11:00 a.m. Crittenden decided he had waited long enough. The corps commander gave the order to move forward. Several minutes before the attack was scheduled to commence the troops of Brigadier General Thomas J. Wood's division moved to the right bank of Hurricane Creek, into the bridgeheads which Palmer's soldiers had established the previous evening. Wood formed his division as follows: Brigadier General Milo S. Hascall's brigade was in the lead; the brigades of Colonels George D. Wagner and Charles G. Harker followed, moving forward on either side of the Nashville Pike—their mission to sustain Hascall's brigade and cover its flanks. Colonel Kennett, accompanied by Minty's brigade, had reported to Wood for orders, but since the general was satisfied that the wooded undulating terrain was not conducive to cavalry operations, he instructed the cavalry officers to form their men on the flanks of Hascall's brigade. The Third Kentucky and a company of the Second Indiana took position on the infantry brigade's left, and the Fourth Michigan covered its right.[36]

Upon moving into position, Hascall formed his brigade in double line of battle. His initial line had the Fifth-eighth Indiana on the right and the Twenty-sixth Ohio on the left, the Hoosiers being supported by the Third Kentucky and the Buckeyes by the 100th Illinois. The Eighth Indiana Battery was flanked by the Fifth-eighth Indiana and Twenty-sixth Ohio.

These dispositions having been made, Hascall prepared to carry out his instructions, which were to drive down the Nashville Pike, reach Stewarts Creek, and capture the bridge before it could be destroyed by the retreating Rebels. Covered by a strong skirmish line, Hascall's brigade moved forward toward its initial objective—La Vergne. Emerging from the woods into the large open fields fronting the town, Hascall's battle line encountered a brisk fire from Maney's and Wheeler's sharpshooters, who were sheltered behind trees, fences, and in buildings. In an effort to escape the enemy's fire Hascall's men hit the ground. The general, realizing that it would probably be less costly in the long run if he assaulted immediately, barked out the command to charge. The bluecoated infantrymen sprang to their feet, fixed bayonets, and surged forward, shouting wildly. Within five minutes' time they had driven the Confederates from the town, and occupied the ridge beyond. In the very successful attack Hascall had lost twenty-seven men, all wounded.[37]

After pausing briefly to let his men catch their breath and readjust their lines, Hascall pushed on, leaving the care of his wounded and the mopping-up operations to his supporting units. Hascall's pursuing Yankees hung close to the heels of the picked detachments covering Wheeler's and Maney's retreating brigades. About one and one-half miles beyond La Vergne, Hascall discovered his initial battle line was becoming badly fagged out. In addition many of the men of the Twenty-sixth Ohio had thrown away their knapsacks. Hascall then ordered his second line to take the lead, while sending a detail to collect the knapsacks. Before gaining the ridge overlooking Stewarts Creek, Hascall's forward progress was brought up short at least half a dozen times by Confederate roadblocks, supported by Wiggins's battery. Whenever this happened, Hascall called for artillery support. And this was readily furnished by the dependable Eighth Indiana Battery. Since they were fighting a delaying action, the Confederates would break off these sporadic engagements and fall back before being too deeply committed.[38]

Nearing Stewarts Creek, Hascall's men were first exposed to the fire of Smith's Mississippi Battery, which was assigned to Maney's brigade. A section of 6-pounder guns belonging to the Eighth Indiana Battery was brought forward to return the Confederates' fire. Badly out-ranged by the Rebels' four 12-pounder guns, the Hoosiers were forced to withdraw their pieces. Taking cognizance of the fact that the Eighth Indiana did not have any rifled artillery, Hascall sent to the rear for another battery, and in response to the general's plea several 10-pounder Parrott rifles belonging either to the Tenth Indiana Battery or the Sixth Ohio Battery were put into action. These long- ranged hard-hitting pieces quickly neutralized the gray-clads' fire.[39]

While the artillery duel was in progress, Hascall's scouts discovered that the Confederates had packed the covered bridge that spanned Stewarts Creek with fence rails and other combustibles, and had applied the torch to it. A call was made for volunteers to extinguish the blaze. This call was eagerly answered by the men of the Third Kentucky's skirmish line and Company B, Twenty-sixth Ohio Infantry, who dashed forward in spite of the fire of Confederate snipers, and put out the fire. The vital bridge was saved.

Since it was beginning to get dark, Hascall stationed the Third Kentucky at the bridge. He then posted the other units of his hard-fighting brigade in close supporting distance. While Hascall was doing this, his left flank was attacked by a detachment of the Fifty-first Alabama Cavalry, led by Lieutenant J. J. Seawell. These Southerners, isolated by the capture of the bridge, were endeavoring to cut their way through the Union lines. But it was vain hope. Hascall quickly alerted his command, and the twenty-four Confederates were driven into a fence corner, where they surrendered. After this brief flurry of excitement, Hascall permitted his men to camp for the night.[40]

꧁꧂

Several miles southeast of La Vergne, the Jefferson Pike diverged from the Nashville Pike. The Union brass, not knowing whether or not Hascall would be able to seize the Stewarts Creek bridge before the Confederates could destroy it, decided to send a force to capture the bridge that carried the Jefferson Pike over Stewarts Creek. Colonel Hazen was placed in charge of a force consisting of his own brigade, Battery F, First Ohio Light Artillery, and a battalion of the Fourth Michigan cavalry, and was ordered to carry out this assignment. Two brigades of Brigadier General Horatio P. Van Cleve's division—Colonels Samuel Beatty's and James P. Fyffe's—would camp at the junction ready to move to Hazen's help if the need should arise.[41]

Screened by the cavalry, Hazen's task force moved off at noon. About one and one-half miles east of the junction the Michiganders encountered a detachment of grayclads covering the retreat of the Fifty-first Alabama Cavalry, which was in the process of retiring down the Jefferson Pike. After firing a harmless volley the pickets retreated. The troopers then dug spurs into their horses' flanks and set off in rapid pursuit. A regular steeplechase ensued as the Northerners thundered along in pursuit of the fleeing Rebels. The Confederate rearguard soon overtook its parent unit, the Fifty-first Alabama. The panic proved to be contagious, quickly spreading through the column which stampeded across the bridge spanning Stewarts Creek. Company L, Fourth Michigan Cavalry, swept across the bridge in the wake of the fleeing Confederates. (Later, Colonel Hazen expressed certainty that had the Michiganders been armed with sabers instead of rifles, many of the Confederates would have been cut-off and captured.)

Having secured the bridge, Mix sent a messenger dashing to the rear to acquaint Hazen with the situation. The captain then deployed his ninety men to resist the inevitable Confederate counterattack, pending Hazen's arrival. But Colonel John T. Morgan had considerable difficulty in rallying the Alabamans, and when they made their initial counterthrust it was easily beaten back. Before the Confederates could organize a second attack, Hazen reached the bridge with the remainder of his task force. The cannoneers of Battery F, First Ohio Light Artillery, unlimbered their six pieces, and quickly forced the Confederates to withdraw from the immediate area. With the bridge thus secured, Hazen permitted the men of his task force to bivouac for the night. In the clash at the bridge the bluecoats had suffered three casualties, all missing. In addition to several killed and wounded the Alabamans had ten of their number captured in the engagement.[42]

Nightfall of the 27th found all of Crittenden's corps, except for the two brigades posted at the junction of the Jefferson and Nashville pikes, massed along the left bank of Stewarts Creek. Furthermore, Crittenden's force had been augmented by the arrival of Negley's division. Especially satisfying to the Federal brass had been their success in capturing intact the two bridges which spanned Stewarts Creek, and in the establishment of bridgeheads on the stream's right bank.

Wheeler's cavalry and Maney's infantry, following the retreat across Stewarts Creek, had taken position covering the approaches to Overall Creek. So rapid had been the Confederate evacuation of the Stewarts Creek line that they had left behind a considerable amount of equipment (tents and arms) that fell into the Federals' hands.[43]

To determine whether Hardee had retreated toward Shelbyville or Murfreesboro, McCook, on the 28th, ordered Johnson to have one of his brigades make a forced reconnaissance down the Shelbyville Pike. Johnson detailed the brigade, commanded by Brigadier General August Willich to carry out this mission. Stanley's cavalry accompanied Willich's troops as they trudged southward from Triune. At College Grove, the bluecoats found that the large Confederate force formerly stationed there had made a hurried departure. The Federals then followed Cleburne's line of march to the vicinity of Eagleville, where the Union officers found unmistakable signs that the grayclads had turned into a country road that gave access to the Salem Pike. Satisfied that Hardee had moved his command to Murfreesboro, the Northerners retraced their steps. Reaching Triune, Stanley and Willich relayed this information to McCook. During the course of the forced reconnaissance, the Federals had encountered no organized resistance, but had bagged forty-one prisoners—stragglers from Wharton's and Wood's command.[44] Save for the activities of this task force the remainder of McCook's corps spent a quiet Sabbath in their camps.[45]

Wharton's cavalry brigade, which was covering Wood's march to Murfreesboro, moved to Salem on the 28th. Colonel Baxter Smith, with the Fourth Tennessee and Davis's Tennessee Battalion, moved from Franklin to Eagleville. Wharton had delegated to Smith the responsibility of keeping tab on McCook's movements. Smith's scouts quickly spotted the movement of the Stanley-Willich task force. Wharton, upon learning from Smith that the force had returned to Triune, decided that Rosecrans's master plan did not call for a flanking movement against Bragg's army, then in the process of concentrating on Murfreesboro. Unless he received orders to the contrary from Bragg, Wharton informed Polk on the night of the 28th, he would establish his headquarters on the Wilkinson Pike, with his left resting on the Salem Pike and his right on Wheeler's left. Since Bragg raised no objection to Wharton's plan, the Texan proceeded to implement it on the morning of the 29th.[46]

Thomas on the 28th endeavored to concentrate his corps at Stewartsboro. Both Negley's wagon train and Rousseau's division, overcoming the "exceedingly rough" roads, succeeded in reaching the Stewarts Creek staging area from Nolensville during the day. However, Rousseau's train and Walker's brigade, as a result of the terrible marching conditions, were unable to get beyond Nolensville.[47] Zahm's cavalry brigade, which had been operating with Thomas's corps, left its Wilson Pike encampment and proceeded to Triune. Upon reaching Triune, Zahm reported to General Stanley and then permitted his men to camp for the night.[48]

Crittenden's corps, except for the troops occupying the two bridgeheads, remained in position throughout the day along the left bank of Stewarts Creek. The corps was marking time while Thomas's and McCook's men were being moved into position. Only when these two corps had reached their assigned jumping-off points would the Army of the Cumberland resume the offensive. Several times during the day sporadic skirmishing developed between the Union outposts and the combat patrols drawn from Wheeler's and Maney's brigade. But since neither side wished to goad the other into a full-fledged fight, these fire fights were of short duration. During the day the Union brass relieved Captain Mix's battalion, which was serving with Hazen's task force, with a battalion drawn from the Seventh Pennsylvania. About dusk a reconnaissance patrol from the Third Kentucky headed southward from the Stewarts Creek staging area to see if the Confederates were covering the Bole Jack Road, which would serve as McCook's line of advance toward Murfreesboro, but before they had gone very far the Kentuckians encountered one of Wharton's patrols. Judging it unsafe to proceed any further, the patrol returned to camp.[49]

On Sunday morning Bragg issued instructions directing the three infantry brigades that were supporting his cavalry to rejoin their divisions. By dark the designated units, commanded respectively by Wood, Maney, and Loomis, had reached Murfreesboro. Bragg now had all his army, except for the cavalry, concentrated in front of Murfreesboro, ready to accept the gage of battle.[50]

⁂

McCook's troops felt considerably refreshed after a day's rest. The absence of any rainfall during the previous thirty-six hours would serve to greatly improve the roads to be used in the advance on Murfreesboro. According to instructions received from Rosecrans, McCook left Baldwin's brigade and a section of artillery from the Fifth Indiana battery at Triune. He then moved out with the remainder of his corps toward Murfreesboro, using the Bole Jack Road as his line of advance. Since Davis's division had camped at the point where the Bole Jack Road diverged from the Triune Pike, his division took the lead as the corps drove eastward. Davis's division was followed, in order named, by Sheridan's and Johnson's. Since the Bole Jack Road was not macadamized, the soldiers found the going difficult, for the road had not completely dried.[51]

Stanley, whose cavalry command would screen McCook's advance, divided his force as follows: Colonel Zahm's brigade moved due east from Triune using the Franklin Road as the axis of its advance and the general, accompanied by the reserve cavalry, moved along the Bole Jack Road. At Stewarts Creek the two cavalry commands were to communicate with each other before moving on. Before leaving Triune, Zahm divided his brigade into three columns: his right regiment, the Fourth Ohio, to move via the Franklin Road; his left, the First Ohio, to be within view of the troops advancing on the Bole Jack Road; and his center, the Third Ohio, to be separated from the other two regiments by from one to one and one-half miles, depending on the terrain. Scouts and flankers were thrown out and the advance commenced.[52]

Nothing out of the ordinary happened until the Union cavalry had penetrated to within a mile of Stewarts Creek. Here the Third Ohio encountered one of Wharton's outposts. After a brisk skirmish the Confederates beat a hasty retreat, and the Union troopers quickly secured the bridge across Stewarts Creek. Before pushing on, Stanley sent a messenger to advise Davis that the cavalry had contacted the foe. Davis's vanguard soon reached Stewarts Creek, and he was ordered to halt his division there until Sheridan and Johnson had closed up.[53]

Meanwhile the troopers had continued to push onward. Several miles beyond Stewarts Creek, Zahm again contacted the foe. This time all three of his columns became engaged, more or less simultaneously, with roving patrols sent out by General Wharton. These were driven in, and the Federals continued to press forward. Approaching the north-south road connecting Wilkinson's Cross-Roads with the Franklin Road, the bluecoated troopers encountered Wharton's main line of resistance. Attacking down the Wilkinson Pike, Stanley's command drove the Rebels across Overall Creek.

Cheering wildly, the Yankees—the Fifteenth Pennsylvania Cavalry in the lead—crossed the creek close on the heels of the retreating Southerners. The reckless Pennsylvanians spurred their horses to within one-half mile of Bragg's infantry's line of battle. Here the bluecoats encountered a combat patrol drawn from the Tenth and Nineteenth South Carolina Consolidated Infantry, of Colonel Arthur M. Manigault's brigade. The sturdy South Carolinians opened a devastating fire on the Pennsylvanians. Six of the bluecoats, including the regimental commander, Major Adolph G. Rosengarten, were killed, and another half-dozen wounded. Panic-stricken by this sudden turn of events, the Pennsylvanians bolted for the rear. The regiment was so disconcerted by this experience that it was valueless during the remainder of the campaign.

Following this repulse Stanley used the reserve brigade to feel for Crittenden's corps on his left. Before nightfall the Second Tennessee had established contact with Minty's brigade, and the Army of the Cumberland had once again established contact between its wings.[54]

South of the Wilkinson Pike, Zahm's troopers forced Wharton's thinly spread brigade to retire to the east side of Overall Creek. The Federals then forded the stream and, in a series of sharp clashes, drove the Rebels on across Puckett Creek. As they ascended the rise that lay to the east of Puckett Creek, Zahm was forced to concentrate his brigade to resist a counterattack launched by the vigorous Wharton. This was repulsed, but Zahm sighted McCown's and Withers's powerful lines of battle and, believing discretion the better part of valor, he ordered his men to retire. After picketing the crossing of Overall Creek, Zahm's brigade bivouacked for the night near the Begsley Lane Church, on the road which connected the Franklin Road with Wilkinson's Cross-Roads.

Wharton, after checking Zahm's advance, concentrated his brigade near Salem, where he permitted his men to bivouac for the night. He felt that Salem would be a good base from which to operate against McCook's rear, and at the same time to cover the left flank of Bragg's main line of resistance.[55]

After McCook had received word from General Stanley that the cavalry was approaching Wilkinson's Cross-Roads, he told Davis to move out. The Union infantry, without incident, reached Wilkinson's Cross-Roads, and here McCook deployed his command with Sheridan to the left of the Wilkinson Pike, Davis to the right, and Johnson in reserve. Davis's division moved forward, and took position overlooking Overall Creek, with Woodruff's brigade guarding the bridge. As a precautionary measure, the troops bivouacked for the night in line of battle. But before retiring for the night, McCook sent a staff officer scurrying toward Triune, with orders for Baldwin to rejoin the corps on the morrow.[56]

Having received instructions from Rosecrans to resume the advance, Crittenden turned his men out at an early hour on the 29th. In accordance with the plan of operations, Wood's division would move forward on the left of the Nashville Pike,

Palmer's on the right, and Van Cleve's in close supporting distance. Negley's division, of Thomas's corps, would ford Stewarts Creek at a point two miles south of where the Nashville Pike crossed the stream, and would support the right flank of Crittenden's division as it drove toward Murfreesboro.

Since there was the possibility of a heavy engagement with Bragg's army, the cavalry would not screen the Union advance. Instead it would cover the flanks of Crittenden's corps as it drove forward. Therefore Minty, in accordance with Kennett's instructions, placed the Seventh Pennsylvania on the left, the Third Kentucky on the right, and the Fourth Michigan in reserve. The Second Indiana was detailed for courier duty.[57]

Before crossing Stewarts Creek in force, Crittenden decided to first soften up Wheeler's position. The eight guns of Batteries H and M, Fourth U. S. Artillery, commanded by Lieutenant Charles C. Parsons, were wheeled into position on the ridge overlooking Stewarts Creek. After several shells had been dropped into the woods on the opposite ridge, the Confederate pickets could be seen deserting their places of concealment and scampering for the rear. Parsons then ordered his battery to cease firing.

Once the artillery had fallen silent, Wood and Palmer waved their men forward. Covered by a strong skirmish line, the blue-clad battle lines advanced. As the bridge was to be kept open for the use of the artillery and supporting units, the infantry waded the waist-deep creek. Reaching the right bank, the Federal line of battle pushed forward. Palmer's troops moved faster than Wood's and Negley's, and by the time his command had pushed to a point one and one-half miles beyond the creek, Palmer realized that he was unsupported on both the left and right. He therefore called a halt. Meanwhile, Wheeler's troops, supported by Wiggins's battery, had commenced to contest Grose's advance. Parsons's battery now put in an appearance, and opened fire with their four 3-inch rifles. Badly outranged, the Confederate artillerists quickly withdrew their pieces. Wood's division now drew abreast of Palmer's, and the advance was resumed. In spite of several brisk clashes with Wheeler's troops, the Union infantry moved steadily and cautiously forward.[58]

With only sporadic and scattered resistance from Wheeler's rearguard, the Federal line of battle waded across Overall Creek, and pushed on toward Murfreesboro. On emerging from the clump of cedars, which within forty-eight hours would gain fame as the Round Forest, the Union skirmishers sighted the Rebel battle line dug in along a ridge one-half mile to their immediate front. The bluecoats surmised, from the increased tempo of the skirmishing, that they were no longer opposed by cavalry. And they were correct.

Wheeler, on reaching the proximity of the Confederate main line of resistance, had assembled his brigade, passed through the Rebel lines, and forded Stones River. Proceeding out the Lebanon Pike to a point some three-quarters of a mile in front of Breckinridge's main line of resistance, Wheeler deployed his troopers into line of battle, to the right of the road. The skirmishers the Yankees were now contending with were the hard-bitten men of the Ninth Mississippi Sharpshooter Battalion who had taken up positions near the Cowan house.[59]

By the time they sighted Bragg's powerful line of battle both Wood and Palmer had learned that Negley's division, unable to work its way through the cedar breaks, had been forced to move along the pike. Considerable time had been lost in reaching the pike, and at the moment Negley's vanguard was several miles to the rear. Van Cleve's division, which was following Negley's, was even farther from the front. Furthermore the two generals had been unable to obtain any information concerning the location of McCook's corps. Therefore Palmer and Wood decided to hold their troops where they were, until they had checked with Crittenden.

Until this moment all the signs had seemed to indicate to the Union brass that the Army of Tennessee would give up Murfreesboro without a fight. But the sight of the Confederate army drawn up in imposing battle array served to disenchant Palmer and Wood. Wood, as the ranking officer, did not deem it proper to precipitate an engagement with the foe, while the other units of the Army of the Cumberland were so far in the rear that they would be unable to render support in case of a serious reverse. Furthermore, it was about 4:00 p.m., and it would have been most hazardous to attempt to advance over ground that had not been reconnoitered, in the face of a vigorous and entrenched foe. Crittenden, on his arrival at the front, concurred in Wood's decision.[60]

Rosecrans having received a message from Palmer sent at 3:00 p.m. stating that he was in sight of Murfreesboro, and that the enemy was running, replied to Crittenden's dispatch: "Occupy Murfreesborough, if you can, with one division. Encamp main body of troops on this side, as before directed." Upon receipt of Rosecrans's order, Crittenden directed Wood to occupy Murfreesboro with his division. Palmer's division would keep pace with Wood's unit pending the establishment of a bridgehead on the east hank of Stones River. After having received Crittenden's order, Wood reiterated his opinion, that as it was getting quite dark it would he most dangerous to cross the river. The division commander then suggested that Crittenden "ought to take the responsibility of disobeying the order." Crittenden agreed with Wood that the operation would be most hazardous, "but as the success of the whole army might depend on the prompt execution of orders by every officer, it was my duty to advance." Immediately after Wood had ordered his division forward, both he and Palmer again approached Crittenden, and urged him to suspend the order to attack. Crittenden refused to rescind the order, but consented to hold it in abeyance until General Rosecrans could be acquainted with the situation. Shortly thereafter Rosecrans rode up. After listening to Crittenden's explanation, he approved delaying the attack.[61]

But the initial word to move forward had already reached Wood's division. This division was deployed in double line of battle as follows: Wagner's brigade in the wood, subsequently known as Round Forest, its right flank resting on the Nashville Pike; Harker's brigade on Wagner's left, its right flank extending into the woods and the remainder of the unit in an open field, fronting a ford; Hascall's brigade posted on Harker's left, with his left resting on Stones River, near McFadden's Ford. Palmer's division was massed in double line of battle to Wood's right—Grose on the left, Cruft on the right.[62]

Harker's brigade, covered by a strong skirmish line, had moved forward before the arrival of Crittenden's orders suspending the attack. Reaching the ford the bluecoated skirmishers, without a moment's hesitation, waded across. With a bridgehead established, Harker issued instructions for the Fifty-first and Seventy-third Indiana, and Thirteenth Michigan to cross simultaneously. When they reached the east bank these units quickly formed into a line of battle, and pressed forward, their objective to seize the commanding heights beyond. After covering the crossing of their comrades-in-arms, the remainder of Harker's brigade—the Sixty-fourth and Sixty-fifth Ohio, accompanied by the Sixth Ohio Battery—forded the river.[63]

The commanding elevation against which Harker had launched his attack was known as Wayne's Hill. This strategic hill had been unoccupied until mid-afternoon on the 29th. Following the withdrawal of Wheeler's cavalry, one of Breckinridge's brigade commanders, Brigadier General Roger W. Hanson, had placed Colonel Thomas H. Hunt in charge of a special task force composed of the Sixth and Ninth Kentucky, Forty-first Alabama, Cobb's Kentucky Battery, and a section of the Fifth Battery, Washington Light Artillery, and with this force Hunt moved forward and took possession of Wayne's Hill. Eight Confederate guns were posted on the crest of the hill, with the Sixth Kentucky on the battery's right, the Ninth Kentucky on the left, and the Forty-first Alabama in support. Skirmishers were thrown forward, taking position behind a rail fence flanking the river.[64]

After the Northern skirmishers had crossed the river they drew the fire of Confederate snipers, ensconced behind the fence and hidden in the thickets to their front. Undaunted the bluecoats surged forward, driving the grayclads before them. The Confederates retired on their main line of resistance atop Wayne's Hill, and soon the Union line of battle emerged from the woods into the cornfield that lay at the base of Wayne's Hill. It seemed to Harker that his bold crossing of Stones River had completely disconcerted the foe, as their outposts had fallen back in confusion before his advance. But from a prisoner, Harker learned that Breckinridge's entire division was massed within close supporting distance of the Confederates on the hill. Harker relayed this interesting bit of intelligence to General Wood, advising him that he could hold his position until reinforced. By this time the bluecoats had succeeded in establishing their forward positions within thirty paces of the Confederate's main line of resistance; indeed the Northerners claimed they were close enough to hear the Southern officers exhorting their men "in the name of their 'country and their rights' to make" a counterattack. It seems this appeal fell on deaf ears, for no sortie was made. Orders soon arrived directing Harker to recross the river, and this the Federals did without difficulty, occupying the same ground they had before the attack. Union casualties in this limited attack were two killed and three wounded; the Confederate commanders reported they had lost "not less than 10 wounded."[65]

By the time Harker's brigade had retired to the left bank of Stones River, the remainder of Crittenden's corps, and Negley's division of Thomas's corps, had arrived on the scene. Except for Hazen's brigade, which camped for the night in rear of Grose's, the men of Wood's and Palmer's divisions slept in line of battle. Negley's and Van Cleve's divisions bivouacked for the night in close supporting distance of Crittenden's main line of resistance. Minty's cavalry brigade camped immediately in rear of Crittenden's line of battle.[66]

On the 29th Thomas remained at Stewartsboro with Rousseau's division. The withdrawal of Hazen's task force from the Jefferson Pike bridge across Stewarts Creek would leave the Union rear exposed to Confederate cavalry raids, and the Union brass theorized that if the Confederate cavalry should strike at the Army of the Cumberland's supply lines, it would probably cross Stones River at Jefferson. Therefore, Thomas directed Rousseau to send one of his brigades to that point. Accordingly, Colonel John C. Starkweather's brigade was transferred from Stewartsboro to Jefferson. Walker's brigade and train, meanwhile, were delayed leaving Nolensville, having to wait while the men of the First Regiment of Michigan Engineers and Mechanics completed a bridge across Mill Creek. But by 11:00 a.m. the bridge was completed, and Walker's command was able to resume the march to Stewartsboro, where it arrived about dark.[67]

⟨ornament⟩

Nightfall on the 29th found both the Army of the Cumberland and the Army of Tennessee concentrated northwest of Murfreesboro, prepared for battle. During the Union approach march, only two of Bragg's four cavalry brigades—Wheeler's and Wharton's—had engaged the foe. Pegram's brigade, which had been posted on Fall Creek covering the Lebanon Pike, was recalled by Bragg on the afternoon of the 29th. Bragg had decided, also, that with a powerful enemy host concentrating northwest of Murfreesboro the strong Union force stationed at Gallatin did not pose an immediate threat to the Army of Tennessee. Falling back, Pegram's troopers took position east of the Lebanon Pike, and several hundred yards in advance of Breckinridge's main line of resistance, and patrols were thrown out to picket the various crossings of Stones River that lay to the north and west of Bragg's line of battle.

Upon learning of the Yankees' advance, Bragg had ordered Buford's brigade from McMinnville to Rover. Here Buford's brigade would be in an excellent position to watch the Union force that had occupied Triune. If Rosecrans's master plan called for McCook to turn the Army of Tennessee's left, Buford from his base at Rover would be able to pinpoint the movement immediately. Since Buford's brigade did not have any attached artillery, a section of the Eufaula Artillery, commanded by Lieutenant W. J. McKenzie, was sent to Rover on the 29th.[68]

In his official report of the Stones River campaign submitted on February 23, 1863, Bragg wrote:

> On Sunday, [December] the 28th, our main force of infantry and artillery was concentrated in front of Murfreesborough. While the cavalry, supported by three brigades of infantry and three batteries of artillery, impeded the advance of the enemy by constant skirmishing and sudden and unexpected attacks. To the skillful manner in which the cavalry, thus ably supported, was handled, and to the exceeding gallantry of its officers and men, must be attributed the four days' time consumed by the enemy in reaching the battle-field, a distance of only 20 miles from his encampments, over fine macadamized roads.[69]

To the dispassionate observer it would seem that Bragg went slightly overboard in his report of the Confederate cavalry's activities during the Army of the Cumberland's advance upon Murfreesboro. It would appear that a number of other factors, besides the resistance offered by Wheeler's and Wharton's troopers and their supporting infantry and artillery, were responsible for the cautious pace of the Union advance. First, there were the heavy rains that fell on the 26th and 27th, which made marching conditions most difficult. Second, Hardee's presence in the Triune area made it necessary for Rosecrans to divide his force as it moved out of the Nashville defenses. To prevent one of his corps from being isolated by the Rebels, and his army defeated in detail, it was necessary for Rosecrans to carefully regulate the advance of his respective columns. While the Nashville and Nolensville pikes were macadamized, a number of the side roads (Edmondson Pike, Wilson Pike, and Bole Jack Road, etc.) utilized by the Federals as they pushed forward were not. And these secondary roads were quickly turned into quagmires by the heavy rains. At no time during the Army of the Cumberland's approach march did the resistance of the Confederate cavalry prevent any of Rosecrans's units from reaching its assigned objective. "General Mud" succeeded where Bragg's weakened cavalry force could not. The Union commanders were delayed by Mother Nature more than they were by the Confederate cavalry, in reaching their assigned objectives.

ᏬᎢᎢᎥᎧ

Wheeler's brigade had hardly moved into position east of the Lebanon Pike, late on the afternoon of December 29, when the general received a message from General Bragg directing him to move his badly jaded command across Stones River and attack Rosecrans's supply lines. One of Pegram's regiments, the First Tennessee Cavalry, was detailed to accompany Wheeler as he fell upon the enemy's rear. Wheeler alerted his unit commanders to have their men ready to march by midnight.[70]

By the designated hour the various unit commanders had mustered and inspected their hardy troopers. Wheeler then gave the order to mount up, and the men swung into their saddles. It had started to rain again on the evening of the 29th, and it was therefore a thoroughly dampened column of grayclads that rode northward on the Lebanon Pike during the early morning hours of the 30th. About daybreak the van of Wheeler's column reached a point several miles east of Jefferson, on the Jefferson Pike. Here, while his men fed their horses, Wheeler closely questioned his scouts, and from them learned that Jefferson was occupied by a strong force of Union infantry.

Hoping to avoid a head-on collision with this force, Wheeler conferred briefly with several members of his command who hailed from the immediate area. Guided by these, the raiders abandoned the Jefferson Pike in favor of little used country lanes south of the main pike. A circuitous detour enabled Wheeler's command to by-pass Jefferson by crossing Stones River near Neal's Mill. Once across the river, the Confederate column turned north in order to get astride the Jefferson Pike. About 9:00 a.m., as the Rebel vanguard approached the Jefferson Pike, the scouts informed Wheeler that they had spotted a large wagon train moving eastward along the road toward Jefferson. Wheeler moved to attack.[71]

The supply train sighted by Wheeler's scouts was enroute from Stewarts Creek to Jefferson. This train belonging to Starkweather's brigade consisted of sixty-four wagons, loaded with camp equipage, stores, officers' baggage, knapsacks, etc., and was all but unguarded. Its escort consisted of a few convalescents seeking to rejoin their units, and a small detail sent to guard the ten wagons loaded with rations, which rolled along in the train's rear. The lead wagons had reached the Union camp at Jefferson, and were in the process of being parked, when Wheeler's grim raiders struck. A hard-hitting detachment of Wheeler's command attacked the portion of the train that had not reached the haven of safety. Simultaneously Wheeler dismounted the remainder of his brigade, deployed the men on either side of the pike, and pressed forward toward Jefferson in order to drive in Starkweather's brigade and destroy the entire train. The Union outposts were alerted in time, however, and succeeded in holding the Confederates at bay long enough to allow Starkweather to form his brigade for battle.[72]

While the wagoners hurriedly parked the wagons already in camp Starkweather deployed his brigade. The Twenty-first Wisconsin, the first unit formed, moved out on the double along the Jefferson Pike, to see whether it could save any of the wagons that Wheeler's eager men had set on fire. The Twenty-fourth Illinois and a section of artillery drawn from Battery A, First Kentucky Light Artillery, was sent to guard the bridge across the East Fork of Stones River. Starkweather proposed to support his "flying column"—the Twenty-first Wisconsin with the remainder of his brigade. The First Wisconsin was deployed as skirmishers to the left and right of the pike moved out. Colonel Starkweather, at the head of the Seventy-ninth Pennsylvania and two sections of Battery A, First Kentucky Light Artillery, followed closely behind the Wisconsin skirmishers.

Before these reinforcements could arrive, the Twenty-first Wisconsin had collided head-on with Wheeler's troopers. In the ensuing clash the Wisconsinites were badly beaten. Falling back, they took cover near a log house on a hill north of the pike, and from this commanding position the regiment was able to hold its own against the attacking Confederates.

Starkweather, observing that his "flying column" had been unable to cut its way through to relieve the wagon train, ordered a detachment of about fifty men to detour south of the pike, and try to break through the Rebel cordon, which surrounded the isolated portions of the wagon train. However, the grayclads discovered the patrol in plenty of time, and easily repulsed it.

By this time Starkweather had reached the hill held by the Twenty-first Wisconsin. The First Wisconsin took position on the Twenty-first's right, while the Seventy-ninth Pennsylvania was massed in rear of the former unit's left wing. Cannoneers manning the two sections of Battery A, First Kentucky Light Artillery, emplaced their four guns on the hill, and opened fire. Wheeler then brought up from the reserve the two guns of Wiggins's battery, and the Arkansans returned the Yankees' fire.[73]

Wheeler was satisfied that he could not drive the Union infantry from their stronghold, and remembering his orders from Bragg to raise havoc with Rosecrans's supply lines, decided to suspend the attack and move on. Therefore, two hours and ten minutes after the attack commenced the Confederates swung into their saddles, having destroyed twenty heavily loaded wagons and taken some fifty prisoners. Starkweather's brigade followed the butternuts westward for about one and one-half miles, and then returned to his base. His command had lost one killed, eight wounded; 104 missing; and nine prisoners, he reported, but Starkweather reported that one of the eight Confederate prisoners had told him that eighty-three members of Wheeler's command had been slain in the fight. This figure was greatly exaggerated for while Wheeler made no report of his losses in the clash, he subsequently reported that the total casualties in his brigade, exclusive of the First Tennessee, for the entire campaign were twenty-two dead, sixty-one wounded, and eighty-four missing.[74]

Intelligence of Wheeler's attack on Starkweather's brigade caused Rosecrans to modify his master plan slightly. Immediately before the attack, orders had been drafted directing Starkweather to rendezvous with Rousseau's division, which would then evacuate Stewartsboro and rejoin the Army of the Cumberland in front of Murfreesboro. A mounted force drawn from General Stanley's cavalry force would then assume responsibility for the protection of the Jefferson bridgehead. But because of news of Wheeler's attack, Starkweather was told to remain at Jefferson for the time being.[75]

In an effort to intercept Wheeler's raiders before they could wreak additional havoc on his supply lines, Rosecrans directed General Stanley to proceed from Wilkinson's Cross-Roads to La Vergne. By 11:00 p.m. Stanley had mustered two of his reserve cavalry regiments—the Fifteenth Pennsylvania and Fifth Tennessee, and set out in pursuit of Wheeler. But the Confederates eluded the northern pursuers, except for a brief and uneventful brush between a rebel patrol and a detachment of Pennsylvania cavalry midway between Stewarts Creek and La Vergne.[76] Early in the morning of December 31 the Federals gave up the pursuit.[77]

Following their successful attack on Starkweather's train, the Rebel raiders rode westward via the Jefferson Pike toward La Vergne, Wheeler's bagging two small Union detachments along the way—one of them composed of "bummers" out stealing stock, and the second a small, well-organized foraging party. Approaching La Vergne about 1:00 p.m. Wheeler was advised by his scouts that the village was filled with bluecoats, and that a large train was parked in the fields surrounding the village. Wheeler divided his command into three columns, and on the order to charge these converged on the town from the southeast, north, and northwest. Taken by surprise the Yankees surrendered after only a few shots had been exchanged, and Wheeler's hard-riding troopers found themselves in possession of a very large wagon train loaded with ordnance, quarter-master and commissary supplies.[78] Wheeler paroled the prisoners and then ordered the immense train and stores destroyed. The train and its contents, the general roughly calculated, were worth "many hundred thousands of dollars."[79]

Captain George K. Miller, of the Eighth Confederate Cavalry, in a letter written after the raid, described the scene in succinct terms:

> The officers went quickly to work paroling the prisoners while the men burned the wagons. It was a sight to make all rebeldom glad. Mules, stampeding with burning wagons hung to their traces, Yankees running, all appliances for our subjugation.[80]

In all, Wheeler's command, before its departure from La Vergne, paroled about 500 prisoners, captured 200 stand of arms, and destroyed McCook's reserve wagon train. Subsequently a member of Crittenden's staff estimated that the grayclads in their raid on La Vergne had destroyed nearly a million dollars worth of public property.[81]

Wheeler soon learned from his scouts that a strong force of Union infantry was approaching from the direction of Stewartsboro. He ordered his men to remount, and the cavalry force evacuated La Vergne and moved southward toward Rock Springs.[82]

At the time Wheeler's troopers descended upon La Vergne, Walker's Union infantry brigade was at Stewartsboro, preparing to begin its march to join the Army of the Cumberland in front of Murfreesboro. Just as the brigade was preparing to move out, a messenger galloped into camp, and informed Walker "that a body of rebel cavalry, numbering from 1,000 to 2,000 men... [had] attacked and were burning the supply train belonging to General McCook's corps, at... [La Vergne]." Walker immediately issued instructions for the Seventeenth, Thirty-first, and Thirty-eighth Ohio Regiments, supported by a section of the Fourth Battery, Michigan Light

Artillery, to hasten to the train's relief, leaving the Eighty-second Indiana and two sections of the Fourth Michigan Battery to guard the camp in the absence of the main body of troops.[83]

Since Walker's "flying column" had to cover about four miles, the Rebels had destroyed nearly all the wagons and their contents before its arrival. Scaling a hill about one-third of a mile southeast of La Vergne, Walker was cheered to note that a portion of Wheeler's command was still there, but he was shocked to see the havoc that the Rebels had wreaked on McCook's train. The fields surrounding the town were jammed with burning wagons. Disarmed men and broken-down horses and mules were seen wandering aimlessly about the country side. Walker quickly ordered his artillery to open fire.

At the time the artillery went into action, detachments from Wheeler's command were endeavoring to round up the mules belonging to the captured train. The shelling quickly put a stop to this, and, forgetting the mules, the butternuts scampered for cover in the woods flanking the road. In hopes of flushing the foe from the cedars, Walker ordered the Thirty-first Ohio, screened by twenty troopers of the First Ohio Cavalry, to move forward. However, the Yankees quickly discovered it was futile to chase cavalry with infantry. They quickly gave up the pursuit after capturing five Confederates.

The Seventeenth and Thirty-eighth Ohio, now put in their appearance, and these two units were detailed to police the area, which was littered with all the debris of a captured and looted army train. Two unburned wagons, many of the mules, a considerable quantity of the harness, and a considerable amount of camp and garrison equipage, were salvaged. The blueclads found that the Rebels had even broken into and rifled the trunks and valises belonging to the officers of McCook's corps, and apparently had made off with most of the clothing, and any other items which happened to excite their fancy.[84]

Wheeler's men continued their work. Entering Rock Spring they surprised and captured another wagon train. After applying the torch to the wagons and paroling the prisoners, the column headed westward and "dropped like a tornado upon quiet Nolensville." Here they discovered another large supply train, guarded by about 200 bluecoats. Taken by surprise, the Federals laid down their arms without offering any resistance. They were immediately paroled. Besides a large number of wagons loaded with ammunition and medicine, the Southerners found themselves in possession of several "fine ambulances." The torch was applied to the former, but the latter the Confederates took with them when they evacuated the village. Upon their departure from Nolensville, late on the afternoon of December 30, Wheeler's column moved

off in a westerly direction toward Franklin. As they jogged along, the grayclads encountered several Union foraging parties—their wagons loaded with "corn, bedcloth-
ing, poultry, house-furniture, eggs, butter, etc.... "The Unionists were eagerly relieved
of their plunder, their wagons burned, and they, as prisoners of war, were mounted
bareback on mules. Wheeler's command bivouacked for the night about five miles
southwest of Nolensville.[85]

◇᪥◇

Before daybreak on December 31, Wheeler again had his men in the saddle.
Detouring around Triune, Wheeler's column gained the Bole Jack Road. As the
Southerners pushed eastward, sounds of a major battle grew steadily louder, and by
the time that Wheeler's command had reached Wilkinson's Cross Roads, where contact was established with Wharton's outposts, the two divisions of the Union right
wing were in wild retreat toward the Nashville Pike. In a little more than thirty-six
hours, Wheeler not only had completed his circuit of the Army of the Cumberland's
rear, but had also destroyed several large supply trains, thus greatly compounding
Rosecrans's logistical problems. Furthermore, Wheeler's activities had diverted the
two crack infantry brigades commanded by Walker and Starkweather from joining
Rosecrans in front of Murfreesboro, and had thus kept these two hard-fighting units
from being present on the field of battle on the 31st, when the Rebels launched their
all-out attack on the Union right flank.

While Wheeler's cavalry was engaged in cutting up the Federal supply lines,
the Northern army of General Rosecrans moved closer to the Confederate lines at
Murfreesboro. On the 30th McCook's corps crossed Overall Creek, drove in the
Confederate outposts, and established itself in close proximity to Bragg's main line
of resistance. Zahm's cavalry brigade, reinforced by the Second Tennessee, covered
the right flank of McCook's corps. The troopers' mission was to ward off the forays
of Wharton's cavalry, as the infantry pushed forward. At first there were only minor
skirmishes, but Zahm's scouts soon reported that Wharton was in the process of rein-
forcing his outpost with both cavalry and artillery.[86]

Adjacent to the Begsley Lane church there were a number of large open fields,
well adapted for cavalry movements. Here Zahm formed his brigade into line of
battle. Wharton's grayclads soon emerged from the woods south of the church, and
Union and Confederate skirmishers quickly were briskly engaged. Wharton shifted
his command from left to right several times in an effort to turn Zahm's flanks, but
every time the butternuts made a feint in search of an opening, Zahm successfully

countered it. Frustrated in their efforts to outflank the Yankees, the Southerners retired in the direction of Salem. Once the foe had withdrawn Zahm reassembled his command preparatory to rejoining McCook.[87]

Before Wharton's withdrawal, General Stanley had received word that Zahm was being pressed by a superior force. Having only two cavalry regiments (the Fifteenth Pennsylvania and Fifth Tennessee) available with which to reinforce Zahm, Stanley asked McCook for help. McCook ordered Baldwin's brigade, of Johnson's division, to report to Stanley. When McCook's order arrived during the mid-afternoon, the men of Baldwin's command were resting in the woods which lay to the south of the Wilkinson Pike.[88]

Led by General Stanley, Baldwin's infantry, accompanied by the Fifth Indiana Battery, moved out of the woods and into the open fields lying to the north of the Franklin Road. They were soon joined by Zahm's brigade, whereupon Stanley ordered Baldwin to hold his brigade near the Franklin Road, while the remainder of the command made a forced reconnaissance toward the Salem Pike with the cavalry and one infantry regiment.

Before they had proceeded very far, the bluecoats encountered a few of Wharton's scouts, with whom they clashed briefly. The Federals advanced through several cotton and cornfields, and a large meadow and after moving about one and one-half miles were halted and formed into line of battle—the infantry in the center, the cavalry on the flanks. Resuming the advance, the bluecoats pushed forward another half mile, but now their advance was brought up short by Wharton's powerful brigade, massed in line of battle. The Federal infantry opened fire on the Confederates, but the range was too great. Stanley therefore had his men fall back to the Franklin Road. Since darkness was rapidly approaching Wharton made no effort to pursue. Zahm's troopers returned to their camp adjacent to the church, and Baldwin's brigade camped for the night in the woods south of Wilkinson Pike, where they had left their excess gear before participating in the reconnaissance in force.[89]

On the 30th, while Wheeler's brigade was raiding Rosecrans's supply line and Wharton's was threatening McCook's right flank, the two other Confederate cavalry brigades operating in the Murfreesboro area took it relatively east. Pegram's command, in addition to covering the approaches to Breckinridge's main line of resistance north of Murfreesboro, picketed the various fords across Stones River below the town. Buford's brigade remained at Rover throughout the day. About midnight Buford received orders from Bragg, to have his brigade ready to move for Murfreesboro at daybreak, on the 31st.[90]

CRYTO

Shortly after daybreak on December 31, Bragg launched his all-out assault on the Army of the Cumberland's right flank. General Hardee's powerful and combat-wise corps was to spearhead the thrust. At daybreak his wing would fall upon the foe. While the infantry and artillery was assailing the bluecoats in front, Wharton's cavalry was to detour around the Union right, and fall upon "their flank and rear."

For ease of handling, Wharton divided the 1,950 rank and file constituting his brigade into three combat teams, and before day-break these teams had quietly slipped into position, approximately midway between the Salem Pike and the Frank-lin Road.[91] Realizing that the Union picket line extended to a point some 600 yards south of the Franklin Road, silence was the watchword as Wharton's eager men wait-ed for Hardee's infantry to move forward. Suddenly the attack was begun. McCown's division, closely supported by Cleburne's, fell upon McCook's right flank, and within a matter of minutes Willich's and Kirk's brigades had been scattered by the attacking Rebel infantry. These two scattered brigades, minus their commanders (Willich had been captured and Kirk wounded), retired rapidly in a northwesterly direction toward the Wilkinson Pike, with four Confederate infantry brigades close on their heels. In hopes of staying the rout, Baldwin formed his brigade in the field south of the woods in which his command had bivouacked for the night. Colonel Joseph B. Dodge suc-ceeded in reforming part of Kirk's brigade on Baldwin's right. The Union command-ers hoped this hastily formed line, would check the butternuts' terrible onslaught.

So overpowering was the attack by Hardee's corps that Wharton's troopers, as they trotted forward, found it difficult to keep pace. Wharton therefore ordered his men to apply their spurs, and they soon drew abreast of the extreme left flank unit in Hardee's line of battle. Forging ahead of the hard-driving infantry, Wharton's troop-ers, after advancing two and one-half miles, discovered their way barred by a Union cavalry brigade deployed in line of battle.[92] This was Zahm's brigade, whose leader had quickly moved his men to oppose the threatened flanking movement.[93]

The Buckeyes easily beat off Wharton's initial thrust, which could be best de-scribed as a reconnaissance in force. Wharton then ordered White's battery into ac-tion, and since the Federals were without any artillery support for the moment, they retired. The bluecoats, with Wharton's troopers in pursuit, retired across the corn-field in the direction of the Wilkinson Pike, and near the pike, they made good use of their carbines, turning back Wharton's hard-charging troopers three times before they were forced to give ground. In hopes that they would be able to prolong their delaying action until reinforcements arrived, the Northern troopers took up positions covering the Wilkinson Pike.[94]

As Wharton's determined troopers approached the Wilkinson Pike, they saw that Zahm's cavalry had been augmented by both infantry and artillery. Wharton fully realized the necessity of preventing the foe from organizing a new line of battle, and ordered White's battery to unlimber. He also ordered Colonel Cox to mass "his command for a charge."[95]

With wild yells J.T. Cox's men advanced against formidable, but disorganized and discouraged, remnants of northern units that had fled before the massive Confederate attack.[96] The Yankees were quickly overwhelmed by the Southern horsemen. Their artillery piece was captured, and Colonel Gibson prepared to surrender his brigade. But a vigorous counterattack, sparked by Zahm's cavalry, threw the grayclads into momentary confusion, and Gibson and most of his men made good their escape. Not so fortunate was a detachment of the Seventy-fifth Illinois, which was surrounded and captured by Cox's command.[97]

Having rescued Colonel Gibson and a portion of his command, Zahm's troopers fell back across the open field that bounded the Wilkinson Pike on the north, then passed through a strip of woods, and emerged into a large cornfield lying to the southeast of Asbury Church. Throughout this retreat, the cavalrymen were continually harassed by the fire of and by combat patrols from Wharton's brigade.[98]

Immediately after his brigade had reached the cornfield, one of McCook's aides told Zahm that the corps' ammunition train was retiring along the road flanking the right bank of Overall Creek, and that it must be saved at all hazards. Accordingly Zahm formed his brigade to protect the train.

Wharton soon sighted the train, now guarded by Zahm's troops, withdrawing toward the Nashville Pike. By the time the grayclads had crossed the Asbury Pike, the head of the train had reached the Nashville Pike and Wharton noted that the Union cavalry had been reinforced, for now two commands instead of one stood between him and the train.[99] In addition to Zahm's men, there was now a detachment of six companies of the Fourth U.S. Cavalry, which had been sent by Rosecrans to help prevent the flanking of the Union right.[100]

Wharton ordered his artillery (White's battery) to open fire on the Union cavalry, and it did so with "considerable effect." When informed that his men were ready to charge, the general ordered White's cannoneers to cease firing. The troopers then surged forward—Ashby's Tennesseans engaging the regulars of the Fourth U.S., while Harrison's combat teams, spearheaded by the Eighth Texas, moved against Zahm's brigade. The regulars, commanded by Captain Elmer Otis, did not wait to receive the

Tennesseans' attack, but charged out to meet it. In the ensuing melee, the regulars vanquished the Tennesseans, capturing about 100 of them. Otis then reformed his brigade, preparatory to moving against White's two guns, which were guarded by about 125 Confederates.

Even before Harrison's combat team had closed with Zahm's brigade one of the latter officer's regiments, the Second Tennessee, had bolted for the rear. The First and Fourth Ohio and one battalion of the Third Ohio likewise gave way before Harrison's onslaught. Only one of Zahm's units—the Second Battalion, Third Ohio Cavalry—held firm. One of McCook's staff officers galloped up and told the battalion commander, Major James W. Paramore, he would have to hold on for a little longer if the ammunition train's safety was to be insured. Grudgingly yielding ground, the Buckeyes retired toward the Nashville Pike. Otis, realizing that if his attack on White's battery was to succeed, he would have to have more men, rode to the right and asked Major Paramore for help. The major refused stating "that he was placed there to protect a train, and would not change with me [Otis]."[101]

Wharton, desirous of exploiting the gains already made by his force, decided to by-pass the regulars and Paramore's battalion in an effort to cut his way through to the Nashville Pike. His entire brigade, except for White's battery and the Fourth Tennessee and Twelfth Tennessee Cavalry Battalion, were hurled against Zahm's badly battered command. At a word from the general, the Rebel troopers (almost 1,500 strong) thundered forward. The gentle rolling open terrain in this sector of the battlefield was very suitable for cavalry operations. After a brief hand-to-hand clash, in which the revolver was used with deadly effect, Zahm's troopers fled. In his report of the battle Zahm wrote:

> At this juncture the First and Fourth [Ohio] retired pretty fast, the enemy in close pursuit after them, the Second East Tennessee having the lead of them all. Matters looked pretty blue now... I was with the three regiments that skedaddled, and among the last to leave the field. Tried hard to rally them, but the panic was so great that I could not do it. I could not get the command together again until I arrived at the north side of the [Overall] creek....[102]

But trouble lay ahead for Wharton's men. The Ninth Michigan Infantry, attached to Thomas's corps as provost guards, had camped on the night of December 30 near the bridge that carried the Nashville Pike across Overall Creek. Some two hours after the battle had commenced, the Michiganders had sighted the first stragglers from

McCook's corps making their way to the rear, and patrols were sent out by the Ninth Michigan's tough commander, Lieutenant Colonel John G. Parkhurst, to roundup the skulkers. Shortly thereafter, the colonel observed several cavalrymen approaching very rapidly from the direction of the front. Within a few minutes a large force of cavalry, accompanied by infantry and a large wagon train, hove into view. The men were seen to be throwing away their arms and accouterment, many of them having even lost their hats. When the Michiganders inquired as to what had caused the rout, the panic-stricken soldiers replied, "We are all lost." Parkhurst, in hopes of checking the stampede, formed his regiment astride the pike. Bayonets were fixed, and the troops alerted to be on the lookout for the enemy's cavalry. Without firing upon the frightened men, Parkhurst succeeded in checking many of them in their flight. Inside of half an hour Parkhurst had collected about 1,000 cavalry, seven pieces of artillery, and nearly two regiments of infantry. The infantry belonged to Johnson's division and the cavalry to Zahm's brigade.[103] From the information obtained from the refugees, Parkhurst was unable to ascertain either the strength or composition of the pursuing force. Consequently the colonel organized the force which he had collected and formed it into line of battle, on the crest of the ridge, overlooking Overall Creek.[104]

While the pursuit of Zahm's shattered brigade was in progress, Wharton learned that Ashby's Tennesseans had been unable to hold their own against the regulars. Otis, having failed to obtain Paramore's help, had rejoined his command, and the regulars were now formed, ready to move against White's battery. Wharton, realizing that it would not only be foolish but impossible to recall his men, decided to give his personal attention to saving the battery. When the general, accompanied by two of his staff, rode up he found that, in addition to the cannoneers, there were only some twenty men of the Fourth Tennessee with the battery. Since Otis's regulars were only 400 yards away, the battery's position was most desperate. Deploying the few men available, Wharton ordered the artillerists to open fire on the bluecoats. Before very many shells had exploded in the ranks of his command, Otis received an order from Rosecrans directing him to retire to the Nashville Pike. Reluctantly the captain suspended the order to attack, and the regulars, taking their prisoners with them, withdrew.[105]

While the general was saving the battery, his troopers had reached the Nashville Pike. Here they fell upon and captured a large wagon train belonging to Thomas's corps (estimated to contain several hundred wagons), including five guns and the caissons of the Fifth Wisconsin Battery, and about 650 infantry. The Confederates acting under Colonels Cox and Harrison, quickly started the booty and prisoners toward the Wilkinson Pike, and, under the mistaken idea that they had driven all the

Union cavalry across Overall Creek, the two colonels covered only the right flank and rear of their column with patrols as they headed southward.[106]

Rosecrans, on learning of the disaster that had befallen McCook's corps, ordered Colonel Kennett to collect all the cavalry at his command, and try to rally the right wing. Leaving two battalions of the Seventh Pennsylvania to continue to serve as vedettes and couriers, Kennett, accompanied by two battalions of the Third Kentucky, started for Wilkinson's Cross-Roads. Finding the roads jammed with refugees from the front, the Kentuckians moved forward slowly. As they emerged from the woods the Kentuckians sighted the Union train being escorted to the rear by Wharton's troops.

About this time Paramore's battalion had reached the Nashville Pike at a point southeast of where the Rebels had bagged Thomas's train. The Buckeyes had saved McCook's ammunition train, except for several wagons which had broken down and could not he moved. Learning that Colonel Eli H. Murray, of the Third Kentucky, was about to attack in hopes of recovering Thomas's train, Major Paramore sent two companies to his support.

Since the Rebels did not expect a counterattack from the east, they had neglected to cover their left flank with patrols. The Confederates were thus caught by surprise, and before Cox and Harrison were able to rally their men, the Yankees had recaptured the guns of the Fifth Wisconsin battery, the wagons, and enabled some 250 of their comrades-in-arms to effect an escape. So unexpected and vigorous was the Union thrust that the Rebels decided that the attacking force must be the regulars reinforced by Zahm's brigade. Wharton, who had now arrived on the scene, decided it would be best to secure the prisoners and public property that remained in his command's possession before seeking new adventures. He therefore ordered his troopers to retire in the direction of the Wilkinson Pike, bringing their booty with them. The greatly outnumbered Union cavalry, satisfied with their success, wisely made no effort to pursue.[107]

It was not yet past noon, hut Rosecrans had succeeded in fashioning a new main line of resistance fronting the Nashville Pike, with his refused left flank resting on Stones River. Hardee's attack, while not stopped, had been materially slowed, and during the afternoon the Confederate brass were to throw in a fresh division—Breckinridge's which would fritter away its strength in a series of piecemeal attacks directed against Round Forest—that covered the salient angle in Rosecrans's line.

Once the prisoners had been turned over to the provost marshal, and the captured public property to the quartermaster and commissary officers, Wharton mustered his command in the fields adjacent to the Gresham house. Rolls were called, and Wharton found that during the morning's activities, his command had suffered about 150 casualties. "Boots and Saddles" was then sounded, and the grayclads again headed for the front.[108]

Colonel Walker's brigade, in accordance with the orders from Rosecrans received on the night of the December 30, broke camp at Stewartsboro at 7:30 a.m. While preparing to cross Stewarts Creek, Walker received orders from Rosecrans "to take up a strong position and defend the trains at the creek." The Fourth Michigan Battery was placed on a commanding hill east of the pike, the infantry being formed in line of battle in support. Hardly had Walker's men taken position than they encountered a large number of fugitives, "fleeing to the rear, and spreading most exaggerated reports of disaster to the right wing of our army." Walker's grim soldiers put an abrupt stop to this flight. Men who had thrown away their guns were compelled to pick them up again and return to the field. Walker had not been in position at Stewarts Creek for very long when orders arrived from Thomas, directing him to move to the front, where he would report to General Rousseau.[109]

Meanwhile orders from army headquarters reached General Stanley, at La Vergne, at 9:30 a.m. ordering him to move to McCook's support. Accompanied by Minty's brigade and the Fifteenth Pennsylvania and Fifth Tennessee, Stanley moved out, leaving a detachment of the Fourth Michigan and Newell's section Battery D, First Ohio Light Artillery, to guard the junction of the Nashville and Jefferson pikes. Stanley reached Stewarts Creek, just as Walker's brigade was preparing to resume the advance, and he told Walker that his troopers would screen the infantry's right flank. Walker, after covering his front with a strong line of skirmishers, passed the word to move out. These skirmishers would serve a twofold purpose: besides helping to round up the fugitives, they would give the brigade timely warnings, if the enemy should suddenly appear.[110]

Approaching Overall Creek, Walker learned that, but a short time before, a strong Confederate mounted force (Wheeler's brigade) had threatened to cut the Union lifeline west of the creek. To guard against such a catastrophe, Walker deployed his brigade in the cornfield south of the pike, and since it was a cavalry attack that was threatened, the colonel formed his troopers into squares, a section of artillery in the center of each.[111]

When the reported Confederates failed to appear, Walker alerted his men to be ready to resume the advance. However, before the colonel could form his command on the road "another stampede of mules, negroes, fugitives, and cowards of every grade" was sighted. A member of General Thomas's staff galloped up, and asked Walker to check the panic-stricken mob. The brigade was quickly formed into line of battle athwart the road. The sight of Walker's combat-ready brigade served "to re-assure and give confidence to the runaways." Frightened men were calmed, rearmed, and escorted back to their units. Once the stampede had been checked, Walker mustered his brigade, and the many-times-interrupted march to the front resumed. Reaching Overall Creek, Walker was informed by Colonel Parkhurst that the Rebel cavalry (Wharton's brigade) had returned and was again menacing the Nashville Pike. After crossing the creek, Walker took position south of the pike. Parkhurst's command continued to guard the western approaches, to the bridge spanning Overall Creek.[112]

General Buford's small brigade, acting in accordance with instructions from Bragg, had left Rover at daybreak, and reached the battlefield about noon. Here Buford received orders to proceed to Wilkinson's Cross-Roads and report to General Wheeler.

Upon reaching the crossroads, Buford was informed by Wheeler, that their combined brigades would move northward, striking the Nashville Pike west of Overall Creek, while simultaneously Wharton would be wreaking havoc on the Union trains, plying the pike east of the stream. With Buford's brigade in the van, the hard-riding Confederates moved northward toward their objectives. As Buford's brigade neared the pike, the troopers sighted a strong force of the foe, consisting of artillery, cavalry, and infantry, guarding a large wagon train. The Union infantry—Parkhurst's command—was occupying a strong position. Buford hastily deployed his brigade preparatory to attacking—the Third Kentucky Cavalry on the right, the Sixth Kentucky Cavalry on the left. One company of the Sixth Kentucky was thrown forward as skirmishers.[113]

The bluecoats were well aware of the Confederate advance. While General Stanley's troopers moved forward to engage the foe, the guns of the Fourth Michigan Battery, emplaced east of Overall Creek, raked the approaching Kentuckians with shot and shell. Fearful lest he had stirred up a hornet's nest, Wheeler ordered Buford to withdraw. Before receiving this order to retire, the Southerners had lost one killed and three wounded. In partial compensation, some thirty stragglers from McCook's corps had been captured and paroled by Buford's troopers before they had received the order to retreat. Following their repulse, the grayclads retired to Wilkinson's Cross-Road. The Federals apparently were satisfied with their local success; at any rate they did not follow it up.[114]

The morning's activities had evidently sapped the combat effectiveness of Wharton's brigade. The brigade's early afternoon thrust toward the pike, made in conjunction with Wheeler's attack, was most lethargic. Wharton's feeble stabs were easily parried by Kennett's troopers, reinforced by Zahm's reorganized brigade that had again crossed to the east side of Overall Creek. Frustrated in their half-hearted efforts to reach the Nashville Pike, Wharton's troopers retired to the Wilkinson Pike.[115]

Wheeler's thrust having been turned back, Stanley's troopers crossed Overall Creek. Moving southward from the pike, along the lane flanking the right bank of Overall Creek, the troopers drove a number of stragglers from Wharton's brigade before them. Upon reaching a point three-quarters of a mile south of the pike, Colonel Minty dismounted and deployed the troopers of the Fourth Michigan as skirmishers. The Michiganders took position in the edge of the wooded area adjacent to Asbury Church. A detachment drawn from the Fifth Tennessee, also dismounted, was placed in support of the men of the Fourth Michigan. Captain William H. Jennings's battalion, Seventh Pennsylvania Cavalry, reinforced by the two companies of Third Kentucky Cavalry, was posted in the woods to the Michiganders' right and rear. The Fifteenth Pennsylvania was massed in the rear of Jennings's command. All told the Federals had approximately 950 troopers concentrated in the woods near Asbury Church.[116]

Wharton's attack having failed to materialize, Walker again assembled his brigade on the pike. Taking up the march, the brigade moved forward a little over a mile before again halting. The unit had stopped this time in front of Rosecrans's GHQ. Here Walker received orders to report to General McCook. In accordance with instructions from McCook, Walker placed his men in position, guarding the point where Asbury Pike joined the Nashville Pike.[117]

Meanwhile Wheeler was afraid that Stanley's advance toward Asbury Church presaged an attempt to turn the Confederate left, and he determined to beat the bluecoats to the punch by attacking first. Evacuating Wilkinson's Cross-Roads, the grayclads followed the pike eastward to Overall Creek, where Wheeler divided his command. Buford's brigade would push northward along the left bank of the creek, while Wheeler's unit advanced on the opposite side. A strong force of dismounted skirmishers would cover the advance. At a prearranged signal from Wheeler, the two brigades moved off.[118]

It was almost 4:00 p.m. before the Confederate vanguard reached the vicinity of Asbury Church. Sighting the long line of skirmishers, General Stanley feared that he was about to be attacked by infantry. Within a few minutes, the remainder of Wheeler's brigade hove into view, however, and Stanley was cheered to observe that they were mounted. The general felt that his command would be better able to cope with a cavalry unit.

Pressing forward eagerly, the grayclads forced the Fourth Michigan to fall back on the Fifth Tennessee. These two regiments succeeded in momentarily checking

Wheeler's advance. In the meantime Buford had arrived at the scene, on the other side of the creek. Finding only a few scattered Union patrols operating on the west bank of Overall Creek, Buford prepared to launch a powerful attack on the Union right. Spearheaded by the Sixth Kentucky, Buford's brigade charged across the stream. The Fifteenth Pennsylvania gave way, and with his right flank laid bare, Stanley realized it would be suicidal to have his troopers remain where they were. Accordingly he ordered a retreat, and the Yankee troopers fell back rapidly in the direction of the Nashville Pike, regrouping behind the topographic crest of a ridge adjacent to the pike.[119]

Since they were approaching an area strongly held by Union infantry, Wheeler's and Buford's troopers followed the retreating Yankees cautiously. In the open field in front of the ridge behind which Stanley was marshaling his bluecoats, Wheeler reformed his command. A double line of Confederate horsemen took position immediately in front of the ridge, while a strong force sought to turn the Federals' left.

Stanley decided to beat the butternuts to the attack, however, and galloped forward leading two companies of the Fourth Michigan and some fifty men of the Fifteenth Pennsylvania. Jennings's battalion, of the Seventh Pennsylvania, lent its support to Stanley's thrust. Taken by surprise, the Southern column that had been assigned the mission of turning the Union left quickly gave way. Inspired by Stanley's example, Colonel Minty led the remainder of the Fourth Michigan and Fifteenth Pennsylvania, and Fifth Tennessee against the Confederate force massed to his immediate front. The first Confederate line quickly gave way, and Minty's troopers soon closed with the second, which also retreated.[120]

Dusk was approaching, and the Union cavalry was glad to close this unhappy day on a cheerful note. It bivouacked for the night in the fields north of Asbury Church, and a line of outposts, manned by detachments from the Fifth Tennessee, Fourth Michigan, and Fifteenth Tennessee, patrolled Asbury Pike.

Wheeler's and Buford's brigades camped for the night in the fields north of Wilkinson Pike. Upon Wheeler's retirement, Wharton's brigade again moved forward, taking position on Liddell's left. To insure against surprise, and provide for the security of the army's left flank, Wharton's troopers established and manned a strong picket line in the fields immediately to the south of Asbury Pike.[121]

Having learned that Wheeler's troopers had routed the Union cavalry from the area adjacent to Asbury Church, Rosecrans determined to bolster his mounted arm with infantry. Two infantry brigades, both badly mauled in the morning's fighting, were sent to the support of the hard-pressed cavalry. Colonel Nicholas Greusel's brigade, of Sheridan's division, and the brigade of Negley's division, led by Colonel Timothy Stanley, were soon tramping northwestward along the Nashville Pike. But by the time the two infantry brigades had reached the bridge across Overall Creek, the Union cavalry had turned back Wheeler's and Buford's butternuts. Greusel therefore formed his brigade west of the creek, in support of the Fifth Wisconsin Battery, and three companies of the Twenty-fourth Wisconsin were thrown forward to reinforce the picket line that the cavalry had established. Stanley's brigade was deployed east of the stream. Just in case the Rebels should launch a surprise attack during the night, the men of Greusel's and Stanley's brigades slept upon their arms.[122]

⟨≈≈≈⟩

While three of the cavalry brigades then operating with Bragg's army had been very active on the 31st, the fourth, Pegram's, had spent a relatively quiet day keeping under constant observation the various crossings of Stones River below Murfreesboro.

During the morning, Pegram's scouts had discovered Van Cleve's division crossing Stones River at McFadden's Ford. News of this development had been forwarded immediately to General Breckinridge, and a combat patrol had been thrown forward to support the cavalry. Evidently Pegram's troopers were not very vigorous in their scouting and patrolling. For Rosecrans, upon learning of the disaster that had overtaken McCook, ordered Van Cleve's division recalled.

Long after Van Cleve's division had recrossed the river, Breckinridge received a message from General Bragg directing him to reinforce Hardee. Not knowing that the Federals had withdrawn, Breckinridge based his plans on the latest information from Pegram, which indicated the foe was moving toward him. He therefore determined to hold Bragg's order in abeyance, and sent a staff officer to acquaint Bragg with the situation. Bragg then issued instructions for Breckinridge not to await attack, but to advance and meet it. Accordingly Breckinridge's powerful line of battle moved forward, ready to engage the supposedly oncoming foe. After advancing about one-half mile, it became all too apparent to the grayclads that the Federals had recrossed the river. Breckinridge then suspended his advance. Thanks to the lack of initiative displaced by Pegram's troopers, afternoon had arrived before Breckinridge's hard-fighting men could join their comrades-in-arms on the west side of Stones River, and by this time the Federals had stabilized their newly established main line of resistance. Bragg's chance for scoring a smashing victory had evaporated.[123]

Shortly after the noon hour, a large Union foraging party crossed Stones River at McFadden's Ford. Pegram's troopers, reinforced by Spence's combat patrol, moved forward to attack the foragers, who retired rapidly toward the ford. One of Van Cleve's brigades, commanded by Colonel Samuel W. Price, had been detailed to guard the ford, however, and Price ordered the Third Wisconsin Battery into action. The artillery's fire served to check, for a moment, the Rebel's ardor.

But, the Southerners recovered their poise in time to make off with eighteen wagons and 170 prisoners. Afraid that this raid presaged an attempt by the enemy to force a crossing at McFadden's Ford, Price threw forward the Eighth Kentucky as skirmishers, covering the ford. The Confederates were fully committed elsewhere, however, and the attack on the foraging party, Price's fears to the contrary, was just a small scale raid. But the Union brass did not know this. Several regiments were therefore pulled out of the Round Forest contest, and rushed to Price's support. Following their successful attack on the foraging party, Pegram's troopers and Spence's combat patrol returned to their camps, adjacent to the Lebanon Pike. Darkness soon descended and the day's hostilities east of the river came to an end.[124]

⚜

The opposing armies utilized the hours of darkness to fortify and strengthen their respective positions. Many of the Confederate officers felt that daybreak on January 1, 1863, would find them in possession of the field, and the Army of the Cumberland in full retreat toward Nashville. At dawn, patrols were sent forward to reconnoiter the bluecoats' position. These soon returned with the unwelcome information that the Federal army was still massed to the Rebels' immediate front. Bragg, hoping his cavalry would be able to break Rosecrans's supply line and force him to retire, sent for General Wheeler, and ordered him to proceed with three brigades (his own, Wharton's, Buford's) to the enemy's "rear, to cut off his trains and develop any movement."[125]

Once the unit commanders had mustered their troops, Wheeler's formidable striking force rode westward along the Wilkinson Pike. Turning northward at Wilkinson's Cross-Roads, the Rebel raiders moved to strike the Nashville Pike at Stewards Creek.

On the 1st, as on the previous day, the Stewards Creek bridge was guarded by the Tenth Ohio Infantry, commanded by hard-boiled Lieutenant Colonel Joseph W. Burke. Immediately before the Confederates put in their appearance, the Buckeyes had been joined by the detachment of the Fourth Michigan Cavalry and Newell's section, Battery D, First Ohio Light Artillery. These two units had been garrisoning the junction of the Nashville and Jefferson pikes. Warned by his scouts that a strong force of Rebels was approaching, Burke ordered the "long roll" sounded.

After his men had made several thrusts against Burke's fully-manned line of outposts, Wheeler decided it would be wiser, and less costly, to look elsewhere for less alert game. Recalling his vanguard, Wheeler decided to strike for La Vergne. Over seldom frequented lanes lying to the south, and out of sight of the Nashville Pike, the Confederates pushed rapidly on toward their next objective. Colonel Burke divined the Southerners' intentions, however, and sent a staff officer to warn the commander of the La Vergne garrison to be on guard.[126]

Long before daybreak on the 1st, the Federals had commenced to organize hospital trains to evacuate thousands of wounded to hospitals in Nashville. At 4:00 a.m., a large train guarded by the Ninth Michigan Infantry started for Nashville, and five hours later, a second convoy consisting of ambulances and ammunition wagons started for the rear. This train, made up of between 200 and 300 wagons, was escorted by two mounted regiments, the Third Ohio and Fifteenth Pennsylvania, commanded by Colonel Zahm. La Vergne was reached without mishap, and before pushing on to Nashville, Zahm decided it would be wise to permit his men and horses to take a break. While the men were resting in the fields adjoining the village, Zahm's scouts sighted a strong force of Rebels rapidly approaching from the southeast. After issuing orders for the trains to get under way, Zahm marshaled his command in line of battle.[127]

On reaching the vicinity of the Nashville Pike, Wheeler's troopers had sighted a wagon train. This convoy, escorted by detachments drawn from the Second Tennessee Cavalry and Twenty-second Indiana Infantry, had left Stewarts Creek shortly after Zahm's departure. Wheeler quickly matured his plan of attack. The general with his own brigade and Buford's, struck directly for the train while Wharton's eager horsemen thundered toward La Vergne. Attacked by Wheeler's and Buford's men, with Wharton's between them and the village, the Tennessee Unionists fled. The infantry and teamsters were left to fend for themselves. Ninety-five disgusted members of the Twenty-second Indiana immediately threw down their arms, and surrendered to Buford's command. After plundering the thirty-odd wagons that they had captured, the Rebels, advised of the presence of Zahm's convoy, started after it.[128]

The presence of Colonel Innes's command, the First Regiment of Michigan Engineers and Mechanics, at La Vergne probably saved Zahm's convoy. Innes had heeded Burke's warning and had completed his dispositions before the Confederates put in their appearance. Discovering Innes's Michiganders holed-up in a cedar break, Wheeler decided to let Wharton deal with them, while he and Buford bagged the convoy.

Wharton, after reconnoitering the Union strongpoint, realized its reduction would require artillery. Accordingly, he emplaced a section of White's Tennessee Battery within 400 yards of the cedar break in which Innes's regiment had taken "refuge." The cannoneers hammered away at the Yankees for about an hour before Wharton began the attack. Three units—the Fourteenth Alabama Battalion, First Confederate, and Fourth Tennessee—hurled themselves against Innes's stronghold, but the thrust was easily repulsed. Three more attacks were launched against the engineers but each, in its turn, was beaten off. In despair Wharton sent two staff officers forward, covered by flag of truce. The officers demanded that Innes immediately surrender; the hard-bitten colonel refused. Wharton next requested that the Confederates be allowed to collect and bury their dead. Innes likewise refused this request, stating that he would bury their dead and succor their wounded. Completely checkmated Wharton called off the attack and withdrew. The Federals had lost two killed, nine wounded and five missing; Wharton's casualties, he said, were "very considerable."[129]

Meanwhile, having left Wharton's troopers to mop up, Wheeler's and Buford's men galloped off in pursuit of Zahm's convoy. The Confederate vanguard soon came up with Zahm's line of battle, deployed athwart the pike a short distance beyond La Vergne. While their skirmishers engaged the bluecoats, the remainder of the Rebel force moved forward in column of fours, their line of march paralleling the pike. Zahm, sensing that the grayclads were seeking to separate him from the wagon train, collected his command, and set off in grim pursuit. Fortunately for Zahm, he overtook the train just as Wheeler's column drew abreast of it.

Checkmated in their efforts to interpose between the bluecoats and the train, the butternuts decided to shadow the convoy. After following the train for about two miles, Wheeler, in hopes he might catch the Federals' napping, ordered his vanguard to attack. With a wild yell the grayclads came thundering up the pike. The Yankees had anticipated just such a move on the Confederates' part, and were fully prepared to meet the charge—all that is, but the troopers of the Fifteenth Pennsylvania Cavalry who broke and scampered off in all directions. The men of the Third Ohio held firm, though, and the Rebel thrust was turned back. Urged on by their officers, the butternuts made a second dash toward the train. This was no more successful than the first. This time, moreover, the repulse was followed by a savage Union counterattack. Stung by this setback, Wheeler decided it would be best to let the wagon train go in peace. Except for five wagons that broke down, and were abandoned and burned, Zahm's convoy, without further adventure, reached Nashville at 9:00 a.m.[130]

Evidently a number of the teamsters had panicked, along with the men of the

Fifteenth Pennsylvania, when Wheeler's troopers attacked Zahm's wagon train. Colonel Parkhurst, whose convoy preceded Zahm's by several miles, was shocked and disturbed when his command was overhauled by these frightened people. The colonel halted his train and formed his regiment athwart the pike, after he learned from the fugitives that Zahm's train had been attacked near La Vergne. But after stopping the stampede and calming the cavalrymen, teamsters, and Negroes who had been doing the running, Parkhurst pushed on to Nashville.[131]

Colonel Burke, on learning that Colonel Innes's regiment was under attack, ordered Lieutenant William H. Dickinson to lead a detachment of the Fourth Michigan Cavalry and Newell's section of Ohio artillery to the hard-pressed Michiganders' support. Three-fourths of a mile southeast of La Vergne, the Federal troopers came upon the Confederates industriously engaged in plundering and burning the wagon train captured from the Second Tennessee. After a brisk fire fight of about one-half hour duration, the bluecoats forced the Rebels to retire.[132]

Some two hours after Dickinson's departure Burke received from Innes a request for reinforcements. Burke decided to march to Innes's aid, entrusting the security of the Stewarts Creek bridge to a regiment of casuals. But while enroute to Innes's succor, the colonel encountered Dickinson's unit returning to Stewarts Creek. Although his men had driven the butternuts from the ruined wagons, Dickinson had despaired of being able to cut his way through the Confederates to relieve Innes and was returning to Stewarts Creek for reinforcements. Burke ordered his troopers to fall in behind his infantry, and the column then pushed resolutely on toward La Vergne. Approaching the area where the train had been attacked Burke found the scene "indescribable":

> Teamsters had abandoned their wagons and came back mounted on their mules and horses; wagons were packed across the road, and many capsized on the side of the pike; horses ran wild through the woods, and, although men were allowed by me to pass as wagon guards, there were none at their posts. They had left the road and were bivouacking in small parties in the woods, evidently careless of the fate of the trains.[133]

By the time Burke's command had reached La Vergne, Innes's engineers had repulsed Wharton's butternuts. The only Confederates encountered by Burke's men were several small groups of stragglers lurking in the woods. These were easily flushed and put to flight by the bluecoated infantry.[134]

Following the escape of Zahm's convoy and the failure to reduce Innes's stronghold, the Confederate troopers rendezvoused south of La Vergne to begin the return march to join the main army. By 2:00 a.m., the exhausted cavalrymen had reached Overall Creek. Buford's brigade camped west of the stream, and Wheeler's and Wharton's troopers, after crossing the stream, bivouacked in the fields adjacent to the Wilkinson Pike. In addition to the material damage inflicted on the Union convoys, Wheeler then informed Bragg that the Army of the Cumberland was not retreating, even though material damage had been inflicted on the Union convoys. Indeed, the Federals were digging in, and bringing up fresh supplies of food and ammunition.[135]

On January 1, the few Confederate cavalry units that had been left behind on the departure of Wheeler's powerful raiding force, patrolled the area between Cleburne's left flank and Overall Creek. The small number of troopers present insured a passive role. The Union cavalry, except for the organizations detailed to guard the trains, likewise spent a quiet day guarding the Army of the Cumberland's right flank. The vigorous scouting and patrolling carried on in this section during the day, was done by the opposing infantry.

General Stanley, who had seen to it that his troopers were under arms at an early hour on the 1st, received word about 9:00 a.m. that a strong Rebel skirmish line had emerged from the woods into the open fields south of Asbury Pike. (This was Liddell's brigade, sent out by Cleburne to make a forced reconnaissance toward the Nashville Pike). Noting that the infantry was supported by a battery (the Warren Light Artillery), Stanley ordered the troopers manning his line of outposts to withdraw, leaving the difficult problem of coping with Liddell's powerful force to the Union Infantry. Throughout the remainder of the day as Federal and Rebel combat patrols slugged away at one another, the cavalry remained aloof from these savage scraps.[136]

Shortly after daybreak on the 1st, Brigadier General Samuel Beatty, who was now in command of Van Cleve's division, sent his unit across Stones River at McFadden's Ford. Pegram's patrols covering the ford melted quickly away from Beatty's resolute advance, and Beatty's troops quickly carved out a bridgehead east of the river.[137] But once the bluecoats had halted and established their main line of resistance covering the ford, Pegram's troopers, reinforced by some patrols drawn from Palmer's infantry brigade, pressed forward. The Yankees caught an occasional glimpse of these patrols, as they filtered through the woods to their immediate front, and to deal with these grayclads, Beatty ordered the Third Wisconsin Battery to cross the river. Placing their guns in position the artillerists opened fire on the Southerners, who soon dispersed. Whenever Pegram's troopers appeared to their front during the day, the Union brigade commanders would call for artillery support, and each time they did so the Third Wisconsin Battery would go into action, sending the Rebel horsemen scurrying for cover. At nightfall Pegram's men retired, and shortly thereafter, Beatty ordered the Third Wisconsin Battery to recross to the west side of Stones River.[138]

☙〰❧

After listening to Wheeler's report of the previous day's raid on the Army of the Cumberland's supply lines, Bragg on the morning of January 2 decided to grant the cavalrymen a few hours in which to rest and feed their horses. Later in the day, Bragg ordered Wharton to cross Stones River, and take position on the army's right flank. Upon Wharton's arrival, Pegram would report to the Texan for orders. Wheeler with his own and Buford's brigade was sent again to the enemy's rear, where he was to remain until he could definitely determine whether the Army of the Cumberland's commander planned a retrograde movement.[139]

By late afternoon Wharton had established his headquarters near the Lebanon Pike. In the meantime Bragg had decided that the Union bridgehead must be destroyed, and Breckinridge had massed four of his hard-hitting brigades preparatory to accomplishing that objective. Feeling somewhat anxious about his right, Breckinridge sent two staff officers to acquaint Wharton with the situation. These officers soon returned to Breckinridge' s headquarters, with the information that they had been unable to locate either Wharton or Pegram. Breckinridge could not delay longer, however, and while continuing his efforts to establish liaison with the cavalry, he ordered his men forward.[140]

The cavalry officers were completely surprised by Breckinridge's onslaught, but the combative Wharton quickly collected a small force with which to support the attacking infantry. Accompanied by three companies of the Eighth Texas Cavalry and Huwald's Tennessee Battery, Wharton and Pegram hurried to the front, arriving shortly after Breckinridge's grayclads had crushed Beatty's main line of resistance. While the eager Rebel infantry was in full pursuit of the bluecoats, who were falling back in confusion toward the ford, Wharton ordered Huwald's battery emplaced on a commanding hill, 500 yards east of the Hoover house. Learning that Pegram had forbidden the cannoneers to open fire, for fear that they would hit their own men, Wharton took personal command of the battery and opened fire on Grose's brigade, which had rallied near the Hoover house. The artillerists cut down a color bearer, and threw the brigade's line of battle into confusion.[141] Just at this junction Wharton's horse was shot from under him, and by the time the general had procured another the tide of battle had turned. Breckinridge's infantry had been caught in a terrible artillery barrage and cut to pieces, and now the Yankees launched a massive counter-attack. Fresh troops were poured across the river, to reinforce the two brigades holding out near the Hoover house.[142]

Wharton held his brigade ready to cover Breckinridge's retreat, deploying it in the edge of the woods, fronting the cornfield where the Federal line of battle had been posted before the attack. The cannoneers of White's battery were instructed to be ready to open fire on the onrushing bluecoats. Wharton's force was soon augmented by the remnants of General William Preston's brigade, which was re-formed alongside Wharton's troopers. The dismounted cavalry and infantry, supported by Robertson's battery, held their position in the edge of the woods until ordered to retire by General Breckinridge. The men of Wharton's and Pegram's brigades, fearful that the Federals might seek to press their advantage, and reach the open country adjacent to the Lebanon Pike, spent the night of the 2nd in the saddle.[143]

Over on the Union right the opposing cavalrymen took it easy during the daylight hours on the 2nd. As on the previous day, Stanley saw that his subordinates kept their men under arms in order to be prepared for an emergency. He also had two regiments thrown forward to keep the Confederates under constant surveillance. Wheeler and Buford welcomed this passive attitude, because it would allow their troopers to recoup some of their strength before launching a new strike against Rosecrans's supply line. To deter the Federals from becoming too aggressive, the Fifty-first Alabama was drawn up in line of battle near the Wilkinson Pike. With the approach of darkness Stanley, after checking to see that his picket line was manned, allowed his men to bivouac.[144]

As soon as it was dark enough to hide their movements from the foe, Wheeler and Buford mustered their commands. Last-minute instructions were given and the long column moved quietly out. The Confederates followed the pike as far as Wilkinson's Cross-Roads. Here the butternuts turned into a dirt road, which led in a northwesterly direction. Many miles had been covered, and the hour was late, before Wheeler decided to call a halt. The officers were told to let their dead-tired troopers get some sleep.

⌘

At daybreak on January 3, the march was resumed. At Antioch Church, the raiders surprised and captured a Union foraging party. After a short break to allow the command to catch its second wind, Wheeler ordered the men to remount. Wheeler's next objective would be the Union convoys moving along the Nashville Pike, and the cavalry leader planned to strike the pike at Cox's Hill, seven miles southeast of Nashville.[145]

About the time Wheeler's command was leaving Antioch Church, a convoy of ninety-five wagons loaded with hospital supplies and ammunition had left Nashville for the front. This wagon train was strongly guarded by eight companies of infantry led by Colonel Daniel McCook, and a detachment of cavalry under Colonel Zahm.[146] The march was routine until about 2:00 p.m. when the head of the convoy reached Cox's Hill, near where the state insane asylum was located. Here the convoy was attacked by Wheeler's brigade, with Buford's brigade being held in reserve. McCook ordered the Sixtieth Illinois and part of the Tenth Michigan to take position on a wooded hill south of the pike, and sent to the rear for reinforcements. But Wheeler's rugged troopers had already scattered a patrol of Union cavalrymen covering the convoy's right flank, and about sixty of the butternuts had reached the train. Leaping off their horses they started to cut loose the teams and upset wagons. McCook, unable to rally the patrol, singlehandedly engaged these grayclads, wounding at least one of them with his pistol. Before the Confederates could kill or subdue him, Colonel Zahm, accompanied by some twenty men, came to his aid and drove off the Confederate detachment. Meanwhile, McCook's infantry detachment opened a destructive fire upon Wheeler's main column, from the wooded hill, holding the Confederate cavalry at bay.[147] By the time reinforcements arrived from the rear the Confederates had begun to retire. The convoy again started for the front, where it arrived at 1:00 a.m. on the 4th.[148]

At Antioch Church, Wheeler was met by a messenger with orders for him to return to Murfreesboro immediately. Bragg had decided to evacuate Murfreesboro, largely because Wheeler's reports indicated that the Federals instead of retiring were rushing reinforcements to the front. The heavy rain that pelted down with little intermission throughout the 3rd added to the urgency of the situation, for it presaged a rapid rise in Stones River, which would render the stream unfordable. Along the road, which had been turned into oceans of mud, Wheeler's and Buford's troopers rode on the night of the 3rd. By 4:00 a.m. on the 4th, the cavalrymen reached their camps adjacent to Overall Creek. The Army of Tennessee had already retired across Stones River, but Wheeler, taking cognizance of the exhausted condition of his men, decided to permit them to get some rest before crossing the river.[149]

If Bragg were to disengage his army successfully, under the cover of darkness, the cavalry would have to man the outposts held by the infantry; and these posts would have to be held until daybreak on January 4, if the Army of Tennessee was to steal a march on the foe. Before evacuating their positions Cheatham's outposts were relieved by the troopers of the First Tennessee Cavalry, Withers's by Wharton's cavalry-men, and Breckinridge's by Pegram's. Once the infantry and artillery had been pulled hack from the front, Hardee and Polk marshaled their respective corps and began the retreat, Polk along the Shelbyville Pike and Hardee along the Manchester Pike.[150]

The rapidly rising water in Stones River also worried the Union command, which feared that high water would isolate their troops holding the bridgehead. These troops were therefore withdrawn on the night of the 3rd; but so intent was their concentration on this operation that they failed to discover that the Army of Tennessee had fallen back, until after the Confederates had stolen the march on them.

◈⟩⟩⟩⟩⟩◈

At daybreak on January 4, the Rebel cavalry evacuated the line of outpost and fell back. Before leaving Murfreesboro, Wharton detached three of his regiments under Colonel Cox to remain behind and observe the enemy's advance. When finally forced to retire, Cox was ordered to destroy the bridge that carried the Shelbyville Pike across Stones River. Meanwhile Pegram's brigade and the remainder of Wharton's rode out of town, Pegram's to cover the rear of Hardee's retreating corps and Wharton's to screen Polk.[151] Wheeler allowed his dog-tired cavalrymen to get a few hours extra rest before he ordered the unit commanders to rouse them. About 9:00 a.m. the troopers crossed Stones River, and Wheeler decided to remain, for the time being, in Murfreesboro with his own brigade and Cox's combat team. Buford's brigade was directed to join Wharton's command on the Shelbyville Pike.[152]

Union patrols cautiously feeling their way forward on the morning of the 4th found the Confederate rifle pits evacuated, and word of the Army of Tennessee's retreat was quickly sent to Rosecrans. Since the grayclads had evidently made good their escape, the Union general decided to collect and bury the dead before moving forward and occupying Murfreesboro. It was late in the afternoon before this task was completed, and Rosecrans then began regrouping his forces preparatory to crossing the river. Colonel Stanley's brigade, of Negley's division, was moved into position near the point where the railroad bridge formerly spanning Stones River had stood, and was soon joined by the First Pioneer Battalion, whose task it was to build a trestle bridge across the river. A brigade of Rousseau's division was held in close supporting distance of Stanley's. In the late afternoon Stanley's infantry engaged in some very light and harmless skirmishing with Wheeler's and Cox's troopers, ensconced on the opposite side of Stones River. During the day the Union cavalry officers concentrated their units at Wilkinson's Cross-Road, ready to move against the foe, upon a moment's notice.[153]

❧

At daybreak on January 5, General Thomas ordered Negley "to take command of the advance and pursue the enemy toward" Murfreesboro. Stanley's troops then crossed the river at the ford, below the damaged railroad bridge, and encountering no opposition quickly established a bridgehead on the east bank of Stones River. Wheeler's and Cox's commands had fallen back the previous evening, Wheeler's brigade taking position three miles from town astride the Manchester Pike, and Cox's, after destroying the Shelbyville Pike bridge, moving to Christiana. With the bridgehead established, Negley detailed Colonel John F. Miller's brigade to assist the pioneers in throwing a new bridge across Stones River, while two regiments of Brigadier General James C. Spears's brigade—the First and Sixth Tennessee—began making repairs on the railroad bridge. By 9:00 a.m. two bridges across Stones River were in operation, and Negley's division, reinforced by Walker's brigade, had occupied Murfreesboro. Here the infantry was joined by General Stanley's cavalry.[154]

Learning from civilians that the Confederates had retired from the area, via the Shelbyville and Manchester pikes, Stanley prepared to pursue. Colonel Zahm's brigade, supported by Colonel Stanley's infantry brigade, would follow the grayclads reportedly retreating toward Shelbyville, while General Stanley, accompanied by the remainder of the cavalry, would endeavor to overtake the ones seeking to escape via the Manchester Pike.

In the course of its advance to a point some four and one-half miles south of Murfreesboro, Zahm's column bagged a number of Confederate stragglers. Here Zahm halted his command, and a patrol was thrown forward to locate any organized Confederate force. It advanced another three miles to a commanding hill, from which a good view of the surrounding countryside could be obtained. Unable to spot any of the foe, the patrol rejoined Zahm, and the column then returned to Murfreesboro, arriving at 7:00 p.m.[155]

After evacuating Murfreesboro, Wheeler had retired down the Manchester Pike about three miles and camped. For security's sake an advance picket line was established within a mile of Murfreesboro. As Stanley's troopers pushed forward, his advance guard clashed with Wheeler's vedettes. Colonel Minty, who was in charge of the vanguard, informed Stanley of this development, and the general immediately hastened to the front. Placing himself at the head of the Fourth U. S. Cavalry,

Stanley led a charge which scattered the grayclads. By this time Wheeler had alerted and deployed his troopers in a thick woods covering Lytle Creek. The Confederates held their fire until the Union vanguard had forded the stream, the bridge having previously been destroyed. Wiggins's cannoneers then commenced to hammer the Federals with shot and shell. The blue-coats failed to panic, however, and held their position. Minty quickly deployed his command—the Third Kentucky to right of the pike, the Seventh Pennsylvania to the left—with three regiments held in reserve.

After first sending a messenger to ask General Negley for infantry support, Stanley ordered the attack. In this formation the bluecoats moved forward, and Wheeler's troopers retired before them. The heavy growth of cedars and dense underbrush caused the Yankees more trouble than did their foe.[156]

Skillfully disengaging his brigade, Wheeler retired to a better defensive position, athwart the Manchester Pike about five miles from Murfreesboro. Here he was reinforced by Pegram's brigade. This position was so strong that Stanley decided to postpone his attack until his infantry and artillery arrived. When these reinforcements arrived on the scene Stanley used cannon to soften up the Confederates' position and neutralize the fire of Wiggins's cannon. After a vigorous contest of about one hour's duration, the Confederates evacuated their position, taking up a new one a mile further to the rear. The Federals, satisfied with their success and taking into account the late hour, returned to Murfreesboro; and with these clashes on the Manchester Pike on January 5, 1863, the bloody Stones River Campaign drew to a close.[157]

⟨⟨⟨⟩⟩⟩

During the eleven day campaign the Confederate cavalry, except on a few occasions, had given a good account of itself. At the same time, the Federal mounted arm had, as a rule, been of small assistance to General Rosecrans. Cavalry operations in the campaign fell into four phases: the Union approach march, the raids, the battle, and the Confederate retreat.

Hardly had the Union troops left the protection of the Nashville defenses before contact was made with Wharton's and Wheeler's troopers. These Confederate cavalrymen, supported by Maney's and Wood's infantry and artillery, harassed the Yankee march. The Southerners established roadblocks at key points, and time after time the Federals were forced to halt and deploy in order to smash these roadblocks. These Confederate tactics, in conjunction with the muddy roads, compelled Rosecrans to slow the pace of his advance. It took the Federals four days to march twenty miles. Rosecrans, during this stage of the campaign, used his cavalry to screen the advance of his army.

Once the Army of the Cumberland had reached the Murfreesboro area, its supply line became a magnet that attracted the attention of the Rebel leaders. On three occasions between December 30 and January 3, General Bragg sent his troopers to prey on the Union wagon trains moving along the Nashville Pike. Of these raids, only one was a tremendous success. This was the raid begun by Wheeler on the 30th, during the course of which his troopers attacked the Union communication lines, rode completely around Rosecrans's army, and destroyed several wagon trains. The Confederate raiders forced Rosecrans to hold two infantry brigades (Starkweather's and Walker's) west of Stewarts Creek. This was of great importance, because these two units were not on the field when the Army of Tennessee launched its powerful onslaught on the Union right on the morning of the 31st.

The next Confederate raid on the Union supply lines was not nearly so successful. While the Southerners were able to destroy one train on the 1st, they failed in their attack on a second convoy. At the same time, Wharton's troopers were repulsed when they tried to capture La Vergne. On the 3rd the Confederates again moved against the Union supply line. This time a Yankee combat team charged with guarding a large train easily beat off Wheeler's raiders. Discouraged, the Rebels returned to their base.

Rosecrans's cavalry was unable to cope with Confederate attacks on the supply trains. In the clashes that accompanied these raids the grayclads emerged victorious, and finally the Union leaders, in desperation, were forced to detail infantry and artillery to escort their trains. When the Federal generals adopted this policy, the effectiveness of the Rebel raiders was reduced.

During the Battle of Stones River, Wharton's troopers performed brilliantly, while Pegram's brigade failed miserably. After Hardee's infantry had crushed the Union right, Wharton's troopers launched an effective pursuit of the retreating Yankees. Hundreds of prisoners were taken, but Wharton's men failed to capture the bridge across Overall Creek and eventually Wharton lost control of the situation. His men were unable to hold their newly gained ground in the face of a Union counterattack and were forced to fall back.

On Bragg's right, Pegram's brigade had been given the mission of watching the Union troops that had crossed Stones River at McFadden's Ford. The sweeping gains scored by Hardee's troops had forced Rosecrans to recall the soldiers who had reached the right bank of the river, but Pegram failed to detect this movement. Thus, when Bragg ordered Breckinridge to ford the river and attack the bluecoats at Round Forest, he was unable to obey because Pegram had failed to keep track of the Yankees. When Breckinridge was finally able to ascertain the Federals' whereabouts, it was too late. As a result of Pegram's dereliction, the Confederates lost a great opportunity to score a smashing victory. In the fighting on the 2nd, the Confederate cavalry played a minor role in Breckinridge's attack.

Rosecrans's cavalry was unable to hold its own against Wharton's troopers in the fighting on the morning of the 31st. Zahm's brigade was quickly knocked out of action by the hard-charging Confederates. Before the day was over, General Stanley had succeeded in putting some fight into the Union cavalry. Encouraged by the general, the Federal troopers checked Wheeler's final effort to reach the Nashville Pike.

When the Army of Tennessee evacuated Murfreesboro on the 4th, the Confederate cavalry covered its retreat. The next day (the 5th) the Union army crossed Stones River and occupied Murfreesboro. Rosecrans sent his cavalry to harass the retreating Confederates. Wheeler's troopers were discovered on the Manchester Pike. Reinforced by Spears's infantry brigade, the Union cavalry brushed the Rebels aside. Once Wheeler's troopers had fallen back, the Federals returned to Murfreesboro.

In the Stones River campaign, the Confederate cavalry played a prominent but not a decisive role. Only on two occasions did the Rebel troopers make a contribution that had a vital effect on the spectators. On the 30th, Wheeler's raiders pinned down two Union brigades that would otherwise have been on the field when Hardee attacked on the following morning. Later in the day, Pegram's failure to report the Union withdrawal across Stones River kept Bragg from committing Breckinridge's division at a time when it might have given the Confederates total victory. The Union cavalry was completely overshadowed by the grayclad horsemen.

During the campaign, the cavalrymen had spent many hours in the saddle. But in comparison with the opposing infantry the Confederate and Union troopers had suffered relatively few casualties. Out of the 4,425 men engaged, the Union cavalry lost 357 killed, wounded, and missing. Incomplete returns for Bragg's cavalry lists 467 casualties out of an effective strength of 4,237 officers and men. The Confederate cavalry had lost 11% of the force engaged; the Federals had lost 8%. To the hard-bitten infantry of Bragg's and Rosecrans's armies these losses undoubtedly looked insignificant, and supplied grist to the Civil War infantryman's complaint, "Who ever saw a dead cavalryman?"

෴

This article first appeared as two parts in the March and June 1960 issues of the *Tennessee Historical Quarterly.*

1. *The War of the Rebellion: A Compilation of the Official Records of the Union and Confederate Armies* (69 vols. and index; Washington 1880–1901), Ser. 1, XX, Pt. I, 663, 772, 843, 911. (cited hereinafter as OR). All references are to Series 1 unless otherwise noted.

2. Ibid., 132, 154, 663; OR, XVII, Pt. I, 591–97.

3. OR, XX, Pt. I, 663, 958. Joseph Wheeler was born at Augusta, Georgia, on September 10, 1836, and was graduated from the U. S. Military Academy in 1859. Upon his graduation he was assigned to duty at Carlisle Barracks, Pennsylvania. Subsequently he was transferred to New Mexico. Learning of Georgia's withdrawal from the Union, Wheeler resigned from the U. S. Army. He was commissioned a 1st lieutenant in the Confederate artillery, and assigned to duty at Pensacola. In September, 1861, Wheeler was promoted and given command of the Nineteenth Alabama Infantry. The following July, he was advanced to the rank of brigadier general and transferred to the cavalry.

John A. Wharton entered the Confederate service as a captain in the Eighth Texas Cavalry (Terry's Rangers). In the regiment's first engagement at Woodsonville, Kentucky, on 17 December 1861, Colonel Terry was killed, and shortly thereafter Terry's successor Colonel Thomas S. Lubbock died. The regiment was then reorganized, and Wharton was elected its colonel. Wharton participated in both the Battle of Shiloh and the Kentucky campaign. On November 18, 1862, following his return from Kentucky, he was promoted to brigadier general.

John Pegram, a native of Virginia, was graduated from the U. S. Military Academy in 1854. Commissioned a brevet 2nd lieutenant in the dragoons, Pegram served on the western frontier until 1858. In that year Pegram, now a 1st lieutenant in the Second Dragoons, received a two years' leave of absence to enable him to make a tour of Europe. He remained in the U. S. Army until 10 May 1861, when he resigned. Entering Confederate service, Pegram was advanced rapidly in rank, participating in the Western Virginia Campaign in the summer of 1861, where he was forced to surrender his command to Rosecrans's at Rich Mountain. Exchanged in the summer of 1862, Pegram was assigned to Bragg's staff. Subsequently he became Kirby Smith's chief of staff. In November, 1862, Pegram was promoted to a brigadier general and placed in charge of a cavalry brigade.

Abraham Buford was born in Kentucky in 1820, and graduated from the U. S. Military Academy in 1841. He participated in the Mexican War as a 1st lieutenant in the First Dragoons. For gallantry and meritorious conduct at the battle of Buena Vista, he was brevetted a captain. Buford resigned from the army on 22 October 1854, and took up farming near Versailles, Kentucky. With the outbreak of the Civil War, Buford cast his lot with the South. On 3 September 1862 Buford received his commission as a brigadier general, and assumed command of a newly organized brigade of cavalry that had been recruited during the Kentucky campaign.

4. OR, XX, Pt. I, 958. Wheeler's brigade consisted of the following units: First Alabama Cavalry, Colonel William W. Allen; Third Alabama Cavalry, .Major F. Y. Gaines; Fifty-first Alabama Cavalry, Colonel J. T. Morgan; Eighth Confederate Cavalry, Colonel W. B. Wade;

Major D. W. Holman's Tennessee Cavalry Battalion; Major D. C. Douglas's Tennessee Cavalry Battalion, and Captain J. H. Wiggins's four-gun Arkansas Battery.

5. Ibid., 958; OR, XX, Pt. II, 450, 452. Pegram's brigade consisted of the First Georgia Cavalry, Colonel J. J. Morrison; First Louisiana Cavalry, Colonel J. C. Scott; First Tennessee Cavalry, Colonel I J. E. Carter; Sixteenth Tennessee Cavalry Battalion, Lt. Colonel J. R. Neal; Howald's Tennessee Battery, Captain G. A. Huwald.

6. OR, XX, Pt. I, 958; OR, XX, Pt. II, 455, 458. Wharton's brigade was composed of the following units: Fourteenth Alabama Cavalry Battalion, Lt. Col. J. C. Malone; First Confederate Cavalry, Colonel J. T. Cox; Third Confederate Cavalry, Lt. Col. W. N. Estes; Second Georgia, Lt. Col. J. E. Dunlop; detachment Third Georgia Cavalry, Major R. Thompson; Second Tennessee Cavalry, Colonel H. M. Ashby; Fourth Tennessee Cavalry, Colonel B. Smith; Davis' Tennessee Battalion, Major J. R. Davis; .Murray's Tennessee Regiment, Major W. S. Bledsoe; Eighth Texas Cavalry, Colonel T. Harrison; Twelfth Tennessee Cavalry Battalion, Captain L. T. Hardy; White's Tennessee Battery, Captain B. F. White.

7. OR, XX, Pt. I, 733. Maney's brigade consisted of the First and Twenty-seventh Tennessee Infantry (Consolidated), Colonel H. R. Field; Fourth Confederate Infantry, Colonel J. A. McMurry; Sixth and Ninth Tennessee Infantry (Consolidated), Colonel C. S. Hurt, and Smith's Mississippi Battery, Lt. W. B. Turner.

8. Ibid., 896. The force accompanying General Wood to Triune consisted of the Sixteenth Alabama, Colonel W. B. Wood; Thirty-third Alabama, Colonel S. Adams; Forty-fifth Mississippi, Lt. Col. R. Charlton; two companies Fifteenth Mississippi Sharpshooter Battalion, Captain A. T. Hawkins; and the Jefferson Flying Artillery.

9. Ibid., 754; OR, XX, Pt. II, 450, 189–90. Loomis's brigade was made up of the Nineteenth, Twenty-second, Twenty-fifth, Twenty-sixth, and Thirty-ninth Alabama Infantry Regiments; the Seventeenth Alabama Sharpshooter Battalion; the First Louisiana (Regulars); and Robertson's Florida Battery.

10. Ibid., 617. Minty's brigade was composed of the following units: Company M, Second Indiana Cavalry, Captain J. A. S. Mitchell; Third Kentucky, Colonel E. H. Murray; Fourth Michigan, Lt. Col. W. H. Dickinson; Seventh Pennsylvania, Major J. E. Wynkoop. The First Ohio, Colonel M. Milliken; Third Ohio, Lt. Col. D. A. Murray; the Fourth Ohio, Major J. L. Pugh constituted Zahm's brigade. The three newly organized regiments that reported directly to General Stanley were the Fifteenth Pennsylvania, Major A. H. Rosengarten; the Fifth Tennessee, Colonel W. B. Stones; and the Second Tennessee, Colonel D. M. Ray. A section of Battery D, First Ohio Light Artillery, commanded by Lt. N. M. Newell, reported directly to Colonel Kennett. David S. Stanley, a native of Ohio, graduated from the U. S. Military Academy in the class of 1852. Commissioned a 2nd lieutenant in the First Cavalry, Stanley held the rank of captain at the time Ft. Sumter was fired upon. Following the outbreak of hostilities, Stanley rose rapidly in rank, being made a major general of volunteers on 29 November 1862. Robert H. G.

Minty, a native of Ireland and a resident of Michigan at the beginning of the Civil War, entered the Federal service as a major in the Second Michigan Cavalry. Minty had been promoted to Colonel on 31 July 1862. Lewis Zahm was born in Germany, immigrated to the United States, and settled in Ohio. Zahm entered the Union service initially as colonel of the Third Ohio Cavalry.

11. OR, 253, 262, 295, 347.

12. Ibid., 262, 269, 279, 347.

13. Ibid., 262–63, 266, 269, 279.

14. Ibid., 295, 347.

15. Ibid., 372.

16. Ibid., 633, 635, 641, 644.

17. Ibid., 446, 623, 627, 631.

18. Ibid., 958, 962, 965.

19. Ibid., 733–34.

20. Ibid., 446, 520, 526, 543, 623, 627. Colonel Hazen had been detained in Nashville by the commission investigating Major General Don C. Buell, and did not rejoin his brigade until the night of December 26.

21. OR, 446, 520, 526, 543, 623, 627, 731, 958, 962, 965.

22. John P. Dyer, *"Fightin' Joe" Wheeler* (Baton Rouge, 1941), 80.

23. OR, XX, Pt. I, 843.

24. Ibid., 911.

25. Ibid., 896.

26. Ibid., 253.

27. Ibid., 253, 617, 646.

28. Ibid., 253, 318–19, 336–37.

29. Ibid., 894, 896–97, 901, 903, 906.

30. Ibid., 253, 319, 897.

31. Ibid., 646–47, 897.

32. Ibid., 253–54, 298, 302, 319, 328–29, 337.

33. Ibid., 263, 303, 319, 337, 347, 617, 897.

34. Ibid., 190, 372.

35. Ibid., 635, 639 .

36. Ibid., 448, 458, 623.

37. Ibid., 464–65.

38. Ibid., 465, 475, 480, 482, 734, 962, 965.

39. Ibid., 465.

40. Ibid., 465–66, 475, 962, 965.

41. Ibid., 447, 542–43, 629.

42. Ibid., 521, 542-45, 629–30, 962–63.

43. Ibid., 459, 734, 958, 963, 965.

44. Ibid., 254, 303, 617.

45. Ibid., 254, 263, 295, 347.

46. OR, XX, Pt. II, 467.

47. OR, XX, Pt. I, 372.

48. Ibid., 635, 639.

49. Ibid., 448, 459, 516, 623, 958, 961, 963; OR, XX, Pt. II, 261.

50. OR, XX, Pt. I, 663; OR, XX, Pt. II, 467.

51.. OR, XX, Pt. I, 254, 263, 295, 298, 337, 347.

52. Ibid., 617, 635.

53. Ibid., 254, 263, 617, 635, 639, 644.

54. Ibid., 617, 635, 648, 754.

55. Ibid., 635, 640, 643–44; OR, XX, Pt. II, 469.

56. OR, XX, Pt. I, 254, 263, 295, 347.

57. Ibid., 372, 448, 459, 501, 526, 560, 623.

58. Ibid., 459, 501, 517, 523–24, 526, 560, 958, 963.

59. Ibid., 459, 754, 958, 963.

60. Ibid., 448, 459.

61. Ibid., 190–91, 448; OR, XX, Pt. II, 263–64.

62. OR, XX, Pt. II, 459, 516. Grose's left flank rested on the turnpike, Cruft's brigade being posted in the edge of the woods that lay to the east of a country lane (today's Van Cleve Lane in Murfreesboro.)

63. OR, XX, Pt. II, 501, 511. Before crossing the river, Harker's initial line of battle was deployed from left to right as follows: Thirteenth Michigan, Fifty-first and Seventy-third Indiana.

64. OR, XX, Pt. II, 829, 832, 835.

65. Ibid., 501, 507, 509-510, 5ll, 829, 832, 835.

66. Ibid., 372, 431, 516, 623.

67. Ibid., 372, 391, 441; OR, XX, Pt. II, 272.

68. OR, XX, Pt. I, 944, 970.

69. Ibid., 663.

70. OR, Ser. 1, XX, Pt. I, 664, 958, 963; Dyer, "Fightin' Joe". Wheeler, 81.

71. OR, Ser. 1, XX, Pt. I, 958, 960, 963, 965. The other section of Wiggins's battery had been left at Murfreesboro, before the raiders' departure.

72. Ibid., 391.

73. Ibid., 391–92, 958, 960, 965.

74. Ibid., 392, 958, 960.

75. OR, Ser. l, XX, Pt-II, 286, 279. Starkweather's brigade remained at Jefferson until the next day, when it was again ordered to rejoin the Army of the Cumberland. However, the brigade did not reach the field of battle until 5 p.m., after the day's fighting had closed.

76. OR, Ser. 1, XX, Pt. I. 618, 623–24.

77. Ibid.

78. Ibid., Dyer, *"Fightin' Joe" Wheeler*, 82–83; G. C. Kniffin "The Battle of Stone's River," *Battles and Leaders of the Civil War*, Vol. III, (New York, 1884), 614.

79. OR, Ser. 1, XX, Pt. II, 275; OR, Ser. 1, XX, Pt. I, 959–60.

80. Dyer, *"Fightin' Joe" Wheeler*, 83.

81. OR, Ser. 1, XX, Pt. I, 959–60; Kniffin, "The Battle of Stone's River," 614.

82. OR, Ser. 1, XX, Pt. I, 959–60. It is difficult to arrive at the exact number of wagons destroyed at La Vergne by Wheeler's troopers. Lieutenant Colonel James D. Webb of the Fifty-first Alabama Cavalry, reports that his unit captured thirty-six wagons laden with ammunition, commissary, and quartermaster stores. Captain Miller, in his letter, states that the Rebels captured 300 heavily loaded wagons. Wheeler made no report of the number of wagons destroyed at La Vergne. Lieutenant Colonel John W. Taylor, the Army of the Cumberland's chief quartermaster, in his enumeration of public animals and transportation lost by the army in the period between December 26, 1862, and January 16, 1863, listed McCook's losses as 150 wagons and twenty-two ambulances. Since it was McCook's reserve train which Wheeler bagged his figure is too large. If we should deduct the ambulances and the wagons lost by individual units, it reduces the vehicles lost by McCook's Corps during the Stones River campaign to 103. It is probable that all or most of these wagons belonging to Davis's and Sheridan's supply trains and corps headquarters were destroyed by Wheeler at La Vergne. In addition it is quite likely that a number of wagons belonging to sutlers were travelling with the train, at the time that it was attacked and were also destroyed. OR, Ser. 1, XX. Pt. I, 226–27.

83. Ibid., 441.

84. Ibid., Kniffin, "The Battle of Stones River," 615.

85. Ibid., 959–60, 964; Dyer, *"Fightin' Joe" Wheeler*, 83. It is impossible to list the exact number of wagons burned by Wheeler at Rock Spring and Nolensville. Neither Wheeler nor the Federals made a report of the number of wagons destroyed at these points. Captain Miller in a letter after the event wrote, that the butternuts captured "some 150 wagons" at Nolensville. Colonel Webb in his official report of the attack on Nolensville stated, "After which they [the troopers of the Fifty-first Alabama] proceeded to. Nolensville, and, with other commands of this brigade, captured 20 wagons, 50 prisoners, the teams of horses and mules, late in the afternoon of that day [December 30].

86. OR, Ser. 1, XX, Pt. I, 635–36.

87. Ibid., 636; OR, Ser. 1, XX, PL II, 469.

88. OR, Ser. l, XX, Pt. I, 254, 337, 345.

89. Ibid., 337, 339, 341, 343, 345, 636, 640.

90. Ibid, 970.

91. Ibid, 966.

92. Ibid.

93. Ibid., 636, 640–41.

94. Ibid.

95. Ibid., 306, 966.

96. Ibid., 271.

97. Ibid., 271, 306, 636, 966.

98. Ibid., 636–38, 913, 939.

99. Ibid., 637, 641, 643, 966; *Map of the Battlefield of Stones River*. Survey under the direction of Capt. M. Michler (National Archives, Washington).

100. OR. Ser. 1, XX, Pt. I, 648–49.

101. Ibid., 637, 640, 646, 649, 967.

102. Ibid., 637, 967.

103. Ibid., 652.

104. Ibid., 652–53

105. Ibid., 649, 967.

106. Ibid., 967.

107. Ibid., 621, 627–28, 641–42, 652, 967–68. Wharton's brigade as it withdrew within the Confederate lines, brought along as spoils of war, five or six pieces of artillery, about 400 prisoners, 328 head of beef. cattle, and a number of mules cut from the wagons.

108. Ibid., 968.

109. Ibid., 442.

110. Ibid., 442, 618, 624.

111. Ibid., 442.

112. Ibid., 442, 653.

113. Ibid., 959–60, 970.

114. Ibid., 653, 959–60, 970.

115. Ibid., 637, 653, 968.

116. Ibid., 624.

117. Ibid., 442.

118. Ibid., 959–60, 971.

119. Ibid., 618, 624, 959–60, 971.

120. Ibid., 618, 624–25, 959–60, 964, 971.

121. Ibid., 618, 625, 960, 968, 971.

122. Ibid., 357, 359, 108. One of Greusel's regiments—the Thirty-sixth Illinois—was temporarily attached to Laiboldt's brigade, and did not accompany its parent unit to Overall

Creek.

123. Ibid., 665–66, 782–83, 789.

124. Ibid., 607–608, 804. Price had posted his brigade on the crest of the ridge overlooking McFadden's ford. The unit was massed in double line of battle. From right to left the initial line consisted of the Eighth Kentucky, Third Wisconsin Battery, Fifty-first Ohio, and Thirty-fifth Indiana. The second line had the Twenty-first Kentucky on the right and the Ninty-ninth Ohio on the left.

125. Ibid., 667.

126. Ibid., 654–55. Several units, among them the Third Alabama Cavalry, were left behind for picket duty upon the cavalry's departure. One of Wharton's regiments—the Second Tennessee—was detached on the morning of January 1 and ordered to report to General Pegram.

127. Ibid., 634, 653.

128. Ibid., 630, 959–60, 968, 971.

129. Ibid., 651, 968–69.

130. Ibid., 634, 637, 642.

131. Ibid., 653.

132. Ibid., 628–29, 655.

133. Ibid., 655–56.

134. Ibid., 656.

135. Ibid., 959·60, 969, 971.

136. Ibid., 618, 625.

137. Ibid., 575. Van Cleve had been wounded on December 31 and during the evening the general had turned over his command to General Beatty.

138. Ibid., 575, 582, 598, 608. During the afternoon of January 1, Grose's brigade had reinforced the bridgehead, but at dark the unit recrossed the river.

139. Ibid., 667.

140. Ibid., 785–86, 969.

141. Ibid., 969. Grose's brigade had recrossed the river for a second time on the morning of January 2.

142. Ibid., Grose's brigade and Colonel James P. Fyffe's brigade, of Beatty's division. were the two units holding out near the Hoover house.

143. Ibid., 813, 969.

144. Ibid., 618, 625, 964, 971.

145. Ibid., 959–60, 964, 971.

146. Ibid., 445, 628, 642.

147. Ibid., 445, 638, 959–60, 964, 971.

148. Ibid., 420, 425, 638, 959–60, 964, 971.

149. Ibid., 669, 959–60, 964, 971.

150. Ibid., 618, 625, 969; OR, Ser. I, XX, Pt. II, 479.

151. OR, Ser. I. XX, Pt. T, 265, 969; OR, Ser. I, XX, Pt. II, 482–83.

152. OR, Ser. I, XX, Pt. I, 959·60, 964, 971.

153. Ibid., 169, 374, 408, 618, 625, 959–60.

154. Ibid., 374, 408, 418, 959–60; OR, Ser. I, XX, Pt. II, 425. Spears's brigade that had joined the army on the morning of January 3, was assigned to Negley's division that evening.

155. OR, Ser. I, XX, Pt. I, 408, 618, 638.

156. Ibid., 418, 618, 625, 957–59.

157. Ibid., 409, 418, 618, 625, 957–59.

MAJOR-GENERAL BENJAMIN FRANKLIN CHEATHAM AND THE BATTLE OF STONES RIVER

Christopher Losson

The lingering merriment of Christmas 1862 faded abruptly for the Confederate Army of Tennessee when Brigadier General George Maney reported from La Vergne, fifteen miles distant from both Nashville and Murfreesboro, that Union troops were advancing from the capital. After advising Confederate chieftain Braxton Bragg of the Federal movement, Maney slowly withdrew towards Murfreesboro while Bragg sought hurriedly to draw his army together along the meandering banks of nearby Stones River. It was not until Monday, December 29, three days after he first detected the Yankees in his front, that Maney's brigade was reunited with the division to which it belonged.[1] This division, which was composed almost exclusively of Tennesseans[2] and claimed over six thousand officers and men,[3] was under the command of one of the most colorful generals in the army, Major General Benjamin Franklin Cheatham.

Cheatham was a native of Nashville and descended on the maternal side from James Robertson, founder of the city. A veteran of the Mexican War and the California Gold Rush, he returned to Tennessee in 1853 and played a prominent role in the state militia. When the debate over secession loomed, close friend and fellow Democrat Isham Harris prevailed upon Cheatham to head the supply department of the Provisional Army of Tennessee. Cheatham acceded to Governor Harris's request, and his energetic efforts were rewarded with a Confederate brigadier's commission in July 1861 after the Volunteer State seceded. By late 1862 he had already served in

Civil War engagements at Belmont, Shiloh, and in the Kentucky campaign, where his men crumpled the Union left at Perryville. His promotion to major general came in March of 1862, shortly before Shiloh.[4]

One of his troopers described Cheatham as being nearly five feet nine, "dark skin, portly looking, quite... affable in manners at all times." The description added that Cheatham wore a heavy moustache, "presents the appearance of a soldier," and was a "quite commanding" figure. Interjected into this otherwise favorable assessment was the soldier's lament that Cheatham was "one of the wickedest men I ever heard speak."[5] His talent for spewing profanity when aroused was legendary. An English visitor in 1863 remarked that the "stout, rather rough-looking" Cheatham owned a reputation as a "great fighter" but also commented on Cheatham's propensity for cursing, which did not seem in any way minimized by the fact that his division was part of a corps headed by Leonidas Polk, the former Episcopal bishop of Louisiana.[6] Cheatham's profane encouragement was especially prevalent in battle, a prospect that loomed larger as the Yankees moved forward.

The Union Army of the Cumberland that sought out Bragg's army was led by General William S. Rosecrans; it was divided into three corps, each commanded by a major general. These three corps advanced by varying routes and converged before the Confederate position. The left corps was directed by Thomas L. Crittenden, the center was led by George H. Thomas, and the right by Alexander M. McCook. Estimates of troop strength vary, but one author concludes the Yankees mustered around 44,000 men to 38,000 for the Rebels.[7]

The site selected by Bragg for the battle was a curious one. Murfreesboro was accessible by five turnpikes out of Nashville. Worse yet, Stones River bisected the southern line. To add to the hazards, the area around the river was a combination of open fields, dense cedar breaks, and rough limestone outcroppings. To contest the Union advance the North Carolina-born Bragg drew upon five divisions. Cheatham's division was included with another under Major General Jones M. Withers to comprise Polk's corps. Lieutenant General William Hardee supervised the other three divisions, under the respective commands of Major Generals John P. McCown, Patrick Cleburne, and John C. Breckinridge.

Bragg aligned his forces for a sledgehammer blow against McCook and Thomas. McCook was situated on the Triune road, with Thomas along the Franklin and Wilkinson roads. On December 30 and 31, McCown's and Cleburne's divisions were transferred from the eastern side of Stones River and placed to the left of Polk's corps. McCown's division formed the Confederate left, with Cleburne stationed behind him. To McCown's right was Withers, whose division curved along the Wilkinson and Nashville pikes. Cheatham formed a second line behind Withers and along the banks of Stones River. Only Breckinridge remained on the east side of the river.[8]

Bragg's battle plan consisted of an intricate wheeling movement from left to right. McCown was to open the battle by forcing McCook to the northeast. Cleburne would support McCown, and then Polk would have Withers and Cheatham pound McCook and Thomas as Rebel brigades successively took up the attack. The aim was to roll up the Union right flank and pin it against Stones River.[9] The plan was ambitious and required excellent coordination and timing.

McCown inaugurated the assault shortly after 6 a.m., shoving out along the Triune road and forcing the startled Federals back. He erred by not wheeling properly, so that a gap formed between his right and Withers's left. Cleburne's supporting division fell into the opening and gradually the extreme right of Rosecrans's army was knocked backwards in the direction of the Wilkinson road. Cleburne's attack stalled when the Rebel infantry on his right failed to attack as scheduled, and Union artillery began to pour in an enfilading fire. The tardy forces ostensibly belonged to Withers, but they were under Cheatham's supervision. On the eve of the battle, Polk, worried about the difficult terrain, formulated an ungainly command shuffle. Cheatham led the two left brigades of Withers's division, one commanded by Colonel J.Q. Loomis and the other under Colonel A.M. Manigault. Cheatham also directed the two left brigades of his own division, under Maney and A.J. Vaughan, who formed a line several hundred yards to the rear of Loomis and Manigault. Withers directed four brigades on the right, two from his own division under James Chalmer and Patton Anderson, along with Cheatham's reserve brigades of Daniel Donelson and A.P. Stewart.[10]

At 7 a.m., roughly an hour after the initial Confederate thrust, Loomis was belatedly sent forward by Cheatham. Loomis's Alabamians ran headlong into the left division of McCook's corps, commanded by Philip Sheridan, and a brigade from General John C. Davis's division. These units were secreted in a thick cedar grove, and concentrated Union fire shattered Loomis's soldiers as they crossed an open woods and cornfield. All element of surprise had evaporated by the time Cheatham committed the brigade, with the result that Loomis's men were forced to retreat, which they did in some disarray. Loomis himself was wounded when struck by a sheared tree limb, and Colonel J.G. Coltart assumed command. Cheatham busied himself by reorganizing the brigade as the reserve brigade under Vaughan moved to the attack. Vaughan was marginally more successful and drove Union artillerists from two cannon; but a deadly enfilading fire from the right doomed his assault, and he withdrew as well.[11]

Complicating matters was the fact that Manigault had not assaulted in coordination with Loomis, as the battle plan stipulated. Rather, an entire hour elapsed before the South Carolinian was hurled forward. Like Loomis and Vaughan, however, the lone brigade was subjected to a galling fire from the flank. Manigault's initial assault was repulsed, a second charge met the same fate, and presently Maney's Tennesseans came up on the left to help break the Union stronghold.[12] Up to this point Cheatham's performance was extremely suspect. Not only was he late in taking up the attack, but his piecemeal sorties by individual brigades inflated casualty figures while failing to carry the Federal positions. Cheatham might have been able to save some men if he had launched the two forward brigades in unison and been ready to funnel in Vaughan and Maney as required, but he did not do so. As it was, Loomis, Vaughan, and Manigault all suffered severe losses; Vaughan, for instance, lost a third of his force early in the engagement.[13] There had been some success, but the Yankees were aligned in a new defensive position along the Wilkinson road and still offered stout resistance.

Cheatham's men faced new obstacles when they renewed the attack. Two Union batteries were especially vexing and were partially responsible for breaking Manigault's previous charges. The two batteries were situated about six hundred yards apart, one near the Harding farmhouse and a nearby brick kiln, while the other was located in a wooded area to the east. The two batteries were advantageously placed so that when an attack was made against one battery the other was able to pour in a flanking fire. Maney and Manigault determined to attack the batteries together, Maney's brigade dashing for the one near the Harding house while Manigault drove for the one in the woods.

As with other developments in Cheatham's front, the venture was marked by confusion. Maney moved forward before Manigault was fully reformed, so his brigade was subjected to artillery fire from both the front and flank. Some of his men mistakenly thought the battery in the woods a Confederate one and delayed their assault until it was determined otherwise. The Union cannoneers near the Harding house used their respite to withdraw their guns across the Wilkinson Road. Maney then hastened forward a battery under Lieutenant William B. Turner, who shelled the northerners, silenced the offending battery, and drove off some infantry supports. Manigault had meanwhile assaulted the second Union battery with two regiments but was rebuffed.[14]

At this juncture, around 9 a.m., Cheatham at last decided to coordinate his attacks. Riding to Maney's line, the Tennessean repositioned Manigault, who had reformed his lines for a third time, and prepared for a new assault. About the same time he placed Coltart and Vaughan to the left. Perhaps frustrated by the stubborn resistance of the Federals, Cheatham decided personal leadership might provide the impetus required to dislodge Sheridan's tenacious defenders. Both Maney and Vaughan reported that Cheatham accompanied his units as they assailed the Wilkinson Road line, with Cheatham at the head of Maney's regiments. Sam R. Watkins, a private in the First Tennessee who later wrote an often-cited account of his wartime service, noted that Cheatham cried, "Come on boys, and follow me." Maney's men sprinted forward at Cheatham's exhortation, moving in conjunction with the other Confederate brigades. The Tennessean continued to lead the charge, prompting Watkins to recognize "the power of one man, born to command, over a multitude of men then almost routed and demoralized."[15]

Cheatham's efforts were aided by Withers, who finally plowed into the Union flank with Anderson and A.P. Stewart. Just as Withers struck, Cheatham's legions collided with two Federal batteries. While Cheatham slashed with his sword his troops overran the Union line and slaughtered the Yankees who attempted desperately to hurl them back. The cost was staggering, and four assaults were required by Cheatham's men along the Wilkinson road before they were able to batter the Federals back; but the second Union line melted away as McCook and Thomas shunted back through the forest to the Nashville road. The fighting was so severe that one Union battery lost ninety-five horses in a vain effort to hold their position, while one of the cedar groves in the vicinity was practically obliterated by the time the bluecoats gave way.[16]

The Federals were forced to form a third line, this one resting at a strong site formed by an angle of Stones River on one side and a deep cut of the Nashville railroad on the other. Thick cedar trees covered the four-acre site, which featured a sharp salient known as the Round Forest. The angle became the next target for Confederate assaults. As the afternoon wore away, Bragg dispatched brigades in sporadic attacks against the bulge. Chalmers, Donelson, Stewart, and Maney were thrown separately at the Round Forest; exhausted and weakened, they failed to break through. The charges were often repulsed with frightful cost. Some of Donelson's regiments were nearly exterminated in their attempt. When four of Breckinridge's brigades were summoned to aid Polk, they, too, were chewed up in disjointed thrusts. At sunset the incessant artillery and musketry fire mercifully diminished.[17]

The ground over which Cheatham and the rest of the Army of Tennessee had met the Yankees was strewn with dead, wounded, supplies, and wartime debris. Of 5,544 listed as engaged, Cheatham lost 1,999 killed, wounded, or missing, a stupendous 36 per cent casualty rate. Individual units were decimated in both those brigades

Cheatham directed and in those Withers led. Daniel S. Donelson's Eighth Tennessee lost 306 of 402 engaged while Vaughan's Twelfth Tennessee lost 164 out of 292.[18] Despite the high casualty lists Bragg wired Richmond that a tremendous victory had been won.[19] In actuality, the success achieved on December 31 was illusory. The Federals had been driven back several miles, but the southerners had sustained heavy losses, utilized most of their reserves, and were disorganized.

A number of miscues had caused Bragg's plan to go awry. McCown's directional error and the respective tardiness of Cheatham and Withers to attack as scheduled hampered Confederate efforts. Cheatham did not seem sure of himself in the initial part of the conflict, and the brigades he directed were hurt by his uncertainty. There is strong evidence to believe that drinking contributed to Cheatham's woes early in the morning. When Cheatham's men over-ran the Harding house, they discovered it was being utilized as a Federal hospital. An Illinois veteran who remained behind to assist his comrades related that the Confederates threw a provost guard around the buildings, and a short time later Generals Cheatham and Hardee rode up, accompanied by their staffs. The Yank was impressed by Hardee, who was "very dignified," but caustically noted that "Gen. Cheatham was more demonstrative, and answered more clearly to the character attributed to Southerners. It was the judgment of more than one that day that he was intoxicated." The Yankee also heard that when the body of Confederate Brigadier General James E. Rains was brought to the Harding house, Cheatham "wept freely" at the sight of his slain comrade.[20]

A second, less reliable source related that Cheatham lined Maney and Vaughan's brigades in battle formation at one point during the morning and attempted to encourage his men by waving his hat. As he doffed the hat, however, Cheatham ingloriously fell off his steed. While his mortified Tennesseans watched on in amazement, "Old Frank" sprawled on the ground, "as limp and helpless as a bag (of) meal."[21] At some point in the engagement Hardee conveyed to Bragg the news of Cheatham's imbibing.[22] Though Bragg did not immediately take action against Cheatham, which is somewhat curious, he used the subject of Cheatham's moral delinquency in an acrimonious dispute after the battle. In a post-war letter Bragg recounted that he understood Cheatham to have been so drunk all day on December 31 that a staff officer was required to hold him on his horse.[23]

Historians have generally accepted the charges that Cheatham was intoxicated, partly because Bragg claimed that neither Polk nor Cheatham contested the allegation.[24] Nonetheless, it is difficult to reconcile the conflicting reports. Watkins, who also mentions whiskey as a possible source of Confederate woes, witnessed Cheatham wielding his sword and taking a prominent part in the successful effort to break the Federal line along the Wilkinson road. His account does not jibe well with the Bragg and Johnston versions, which portray a commander who was stone drunk and seemingly insensible. As Bragg and Cheatham did eventually detest one another, the North Carolinian probably saw fit to place Cheatham in as poor a light as possible. Perhaps he exaggerated Cheatham's drunkenness in order to discredit the Tennessean. If Watkins's eyewitness account of the charge is to be believed and Cheatham was indeed as drunk as Bragg maintained, his recuperative powers must have been incredible. In any event, it is almost impossible to sort out the truth or ascertain exactly why Cheatham was drinking so early in the morning. He may have been continuing a Yuletime celebration, fortifying himself for the battle, or attempting to ward off the cold weather.[25] The only facts that can be stated with certainty are that his men were poorly served by their divisional commander for the early part of the battle and suffered needless casualties until Cheatham managed to rally them for a concerted movement.

On New Year's Day, Bragg was startled to learn that Rosecrans still faced him. The Union troops had abandoned only the Round Forest salient, which was occupied by some of Withers's units. Neither army commander pressed the other, and the day passed without a serious engagement. On January 2, Bragg decided to use Breckinridge's relatively fresh division to seize a ridge on the eastern side of Stones River that threatened Polk on the opposite side. Without consulting Hardee, Bragg ordered Breckinridge forward. After a short period of success Breckinridge's soldiers were rocked by three Union brigades in a counterattack, and Crittenden's massed artillery tore gaping holes in their ranks. Breckinridge's two battle lines broke and hurried for the rear. An alarmed Bragg called Patton Anderson across the river to bolster Breckinridge in case the Yankees followed up their advantage. Later during the evening McCown and Cleburne transferred their divisions to the eastern side of Stones River.[26]

As rain and sleet fell during the night, the river started to swell. Only Cheatham and Withers remained on the western side with their crippled divisions. While the rain continued and Stones River rose, the two generals met to discuss the situation. Fearful of being isolated, at 12:15 a.m. they drafted a letter to Bragg stating that only three reliable brigades remained and urged Bragg to withdraw.[27] The letter went from Cheatham and Withers via Polk, who endorsed the advice tendered by his divisional commanders. Polk remarked, "I greatly fear the consequences of another engagement," and added, "We could now perhaps get off with some safety and with some credit," provided that "the affair was well managed." Awakened by a staff officer,

Bragg read but part of the missives before replying succinctly to Polk, "We shall hold our own at every hazard."[28]

In the morning Bragg reversed himself. During the night McCook's captured papers were brought to headquarters, and as the North Carolinian read the papers he became convinced that Rosecrans had an even larger force than previously estimated. A council with Hardee and Polk cemented the inclination to retreat, though it meant abandoning hundreds of wounded men in Murfreesboro.[29] Polk led the withdrawal, with Cheatham's division moving southward en route to Shelbyville in the early morning hours of January 4.[30]

The retreat was barely concluded before discord enveloped the army. Bragg was severely criticized by disgruntled elements of the Tennessee populace. Among the critics were Senators Gustavus Henry and Henry Foote, while certain elements within the army joined in the campaign as well. These groups were disappointed by the Murfreesboro withdrawal and felt it fit into a recurring and depressing cycle. As at Shiloh and Perryville, Rebel forces had seemingly garnered success in the first part of the fighting at Stones River, only to end up in retreat. One of Bragg's most tormenting detractors was the *Chattanooga Rebel*, which falsely observed that the decision to retreat from Murfreesboro had been made by Bragg against the wishes of his high officers.[31] The allegation angered Bragg, who first read the offending article to his staff members and then drafted a circular letter to his corps and divisional commanders.

"Finding myself assailed in private and public," Bragg wrote on January 11, 1863, "... it becomes necessary to save my fair name." The North Carolinian complained that even staff officers of his generals were convinced that the withdrawal was Bragg's idea and carried out against the wishes of their commanders. Fearing the possible demoralization of his soldiers as the conflicting rumors swirled, Bragg asked his officers to report on whether they had advised the retreat. To support his position Bragg enclosed copies of the letter sent by Cheatham and Withers on January 3, as well as Polk's endorsement. Had Bragg limited his inquiry to but this point he would have spared himself a good deal of misery. Almost as an afterthought, Bragg petulantly noted that General Kirby Smith had been called to Virginia, "it is supposed with a view to supercede me." Bragg then vowed to "retire without a regret" if he discovered that "I have lost the good opinion of my Generals upon whom I have ever relied as upon a foundation of rock."[32]

The frank replies of his officers jolted Bragg. Hardee, Breckinridge, and Cleburne all responded by stating that Bragg no longer held the trust of the army and should step down. The advice echoed the recommendation of Bragg's own staff, who reached the same conclusion in an earlier meeting.[33] Polk was then absent from the army, and Cheatham and Withers wished to consult with their corps leader before re-plying. Cheatham did send a short note acknowledging that he was one of the first to counsel retreat. There was no response regarding Bragg's offer to resign, or any nota-tion as to the sentiment towards Bragg in Cheatham's division.[34] When Polk returned in late January he asked Bragg exactly what it was he wanted to know: were there two questions implicit in the circular, or one, as Cheatham claimed? Thoroughly tired of unfavorable reports, and unwilling to have Polk and Cheatham slash at him as had the officers in Hardee's corps, Bragg hastened to tell Polk he was interested in but one point, the retreat. Polk then responded that his endorsement to Cheatham and Withers's note had been "deliberately considered" and that he would tender the same advice in similar circumstances.[35]

It is hard to believe that Cheatham failed to recognize the dual questions con-tained in Bragg's circular. Hardee and his generals certainly exhibited no hesitation in recommending that Bragg resign, an indication that they indeed discovered two queries in the letter. By being less than candid with Bragg, Polk, Cheatham, and Withers all placed Hardee and his subordinates in an embarrassing position. The reticence of Polk and his divisional leaders aroused resentment in Hardee's corps. McCown, for instance, railed that Cheatham "said one thing among the officers behind Genl. Bragg's back and wrote him a totally different thing."[36] Cheatham almost certainly shared the lack of confidence in Bragg's abilities that his fellow generals espoused, and his silence is puzzling. Perhaps Cheatham's first thought was of self-preservation, and by refusing to criticize Bragg openly he hoped to escape any controversy related to his battlefield intemperance. If this was the motive for Cheatham's taciturnity, his hopes were dashed shortly after the Richmond govern-ment sustained Bragg as army commander despite the reservations of several of his high-ranking subalterns.

Stung by the denunciations aroused by his letter, Bragg resolved to punish those officers he considered offensive and to eliminate them from the army if pos-sible. He also cast about for scapegoats whom he could blame as the culprits in the battle. One of his targets was Cheatham. Cheatham was responsible for Cle-burne's heavy casualties by attacking later than ordered, Bragg charged, and he pointedly left Cheatham's name off the long list of officers commended in his of-ficial report of the battle. The omission touched off an uproar in Polk's corps, and a furious Cheatham threatened to resign. Isham Harris attempted to mollify his fellow Tennessean, and Cheatham remained with his division in spite of his disdain for Bragg.[37] Though Bragg was correct in asserting that Cheatham helped contrib-ute to Cleburne's casualty lists, it is interesting to note that Withers was warmly praised in Bragg's report. Historians have tended to downplay that Withers was also tardy in pressing the attack; Patton Anderson did not go forward until 9 a.m., by which time Manigualt had already been repelled in his third assault of the morning. Cheatham's men suffered casualties in part because of Withers's slowness, a fact Bragg was unwilling to accept. It is natural that he praised Withers, for the latter was a strong Bragg supporter and in fact published a defense of Bragg's conduct in a Mobile newspaper.[38] Nonetheless, Bragg was not exercising objectivity by the time he compiled his official report.

Eventually Bragg determined to reveal Cheatham's drinking to Richmond, perhaps in part to squash the sentiment of Cheatham's soldiers who voiced their displeasure at Bragg's version of the battle. Writing from Tullahoma on April 9, 1863, Bragg expressed surprise at Polk's Murfreesboro report, which was written March 21. In the report Polk lauded both Cheatham and Withers for "their cordial support and co-operation" during the engagement. Bragg interpreted this as undue praise for Cheatham, especially since Polk had heard of Cheatham's intoxication "from other sources," which confirmed Bragg's message to that effect. Polk assured Bragg that he had verbally admonished Cheatham; but in early January, Bragg insisted that Polk censure Cheatham in writing and averred that Cheatham's dereliction was overlooked only in light of "his previous distinguished services." Polk told Bragg that the reprimand had "the desired effect." The North Carolinian was therefore surprised and angered over Polk's complimentary remarks about Cheatham and felt compelled to write the government to justify his omission.[39]

Secretary of War James Seddon regarded the report as "very unfortunate" and added to the turmoil already brewing in the western army. Seddon also recommended that "a court of inquiry should I suppose be ordered," when he forwarded the report to President Davis.[40] If a court was convened, no evidence remains to prove its existence, and Cheatham continued as a divisional leader. His relations with Bragg, however, were decidedly strained by the incident.

Therefore, the subject of Cheatham and the Battle of Stones River ended inconclusively. Unable to secure Cheatham's removal, Bragg succeeded in his effort to tarnish Cheatham's leadership at Murfreesboro. Nevertheless, Bragg's exclusion of Cheatham reflected unfavorably on the Tennessee troops he led who had sacrificed themselves in the attacks on McCook and Thomas. Though Bragg did laud the private soldiers for their conduct, the Tennessee troops were hailed by Cheatham for their fortitude and "gallant, soldier-like bearing" during the campaign. Thus Bragg failed in his attempt to drive Cheatham and his men apart. As the spring of 1863 arrived, Cheatham remained an inspiring figure to his men, just as he had been at Murfreesboro several months prior.[41]

⊙⫘⊙

This article first appeared in the Fall 1982 *Tennessee Historical Quarterly*.

1. *War of the Rebellion: A Compliation of the Official Records of the Union and Confederate Armies*, 128 vols. (Washington, D.C., 1880–1901), Series 1, Vol. XX, pt. 1, 733–34. Hereinafter cited as OR. All references are to Series 1, Vol. XX, pt. 1 unless otherwise noted.

2. The only non-Tennessee units were the Ninth Texas Infantry Regiment and two Mississippi batteries. See OR, 658.

3. A field return for the period 28 December 1862–4 January 1863, sets the total number of officers and men in Cheatham's division engaged in the battle at 6,359. Cheatham claimed 5,859 combatants. See OR, 693, 709.

4. Manuscript Guide, Benjamin Franklin Cheatham Papers, Manuscript Section, Tennessee State Library and Archives. Hereinafter cited as Cheatham Papers, TSLA. Jon L. Wakelyn, *Biographical Dictionary of the Confederacy* (Westport, Conn., 1977), 128–29; Ezra Warner, *Generals in Gray* (Baton Rouge, 1959), 47.

5. Joe Spence Diary, 1861–1862, Confederate Collection, TSLA, 21.

6. Walter Lord, ed., *The Fremantle Diary: Being the journal of Lieutenant Colonel James Arthur Fremantle, Goldstream Guards, on his Three Months in the Southern States* (Boston, 1954), 116–17.

7. James Lee McDonough, *Stones River: Bloody Winter in Tennessee* (Knoxville, 1980), 69.

8. OR, 663–64, 686, 705, 844. General Bragg's Official Report of the Battle of Murfreesboro, William P. Palmer Collection of Braxton Bragg Papers, The Western Reserve Historical Society, Cleveland, Ohio. Hereinafter cited as Bragg's Murfreesboro Report, Western Reserve.

9. Bragg's Murfreesboro Report, Western Reserve; OR, 686, 734.

10. OR, 689, 754, 774–75, 846. Withers explained that the arrangement was made due to the topography, and was intended to help the divisional commanders determine when to commit reserve forces.

11. Ibid., 687,706, 743–44,754–55. Cheatham wrote a Murfreesboro battle report, pages 3–9 of which survive in the Cheatham Papers, TSLA. It contains minor variations from his report published in the OR, but generally the author cites the report found in the OR.

12. OR, 687, 706, 734, 755.

13. Ibid., 687, 745, 709.

14. Ibid., 688,706–07,734–35,741.

15. Ibid., 735, 744; Sam R. Watkins, *"Co. Aytch," Maury Grays, First Tennessee Regiment; or, A Side Show of the Big Show* (Reprint edition, Jackson, Tenn., 1952), 93-4.

16. Watkins, "Co. Aytch. "93–4; OR, 354,744, 755; Col. W.D. Smith, *Battle of Stones River, Tennessee* (Washington, D.C., 1932), 38–9. Smith's account was compiled for the Historical Section of the Army War College, but not published commercially. The copy cited is in the collection at Stones River National Military Park.

17. McDonough, *Stones River*, 131–37, 140–44; Thomas L. Connelly, *Autumn of Glory: The Army of Tennessee, 1862–1865* (Baton Rouge, 1971), 58–61.

18. OR, 674, 676, 707, 709. A list of casualties in the Cheatham Papers lists sixty fewer casualties, 1,939, as do some reports in the OR. This is still a heavy rate, 3.5 per cent casualties.

19. OR, 662.

20. L.G. Bennett and Wm. M. Haigh, *History of the Thirty-Sixth Regiment Illinois Volunteers* (Aurora, Ill.), 1876, 348. Rains, a Nashville native, no doubt knew Cheatham. He was killed early in the battle, while leading his men against a Union battery. Warner, *Generals in Gray*, 250–.51.

21. John Johnston to John Trotwood Moore, 9 June 1927. The story was circulated in a number of newspapers, including the *Nashville Tennessean*, 24 July 1927 (?). Both the newspaper clipping and Johnston's letter are in the Gideon Johnson Pillow Collection, TSLA. Though Johnson maintained that the incident was related by an eyewitness, an unnamed lieutenant in the Sixth Tennessee, the purpose for which he wrote Tennessee State Archivist Moore casts doubt upon the complete credibility of his account. Johnston was interested in lauding Major General Gideon Pillow, whom he felt should have received more credit than Cheatham for Confederate success at Belmont. Pillow had a checkered Civil War career and may have resented Cheatham, in part because both were commissioned brigadiers in July, 1861, although Polk recommended Pillow to the grade of major general. At one point Pillow incurred Hardee's displeasure, and the latter hinted that Cheatham might be a suitable replacement. Joseph Parks, *General Leonidas Polk, C.S.A.: The Fighting Bishop* (Baton Rouge, 1962), 173–74; Warner, *Generals in Gray*, 241; Nathaniel Cheairs Hughes, Jr., *General William J. Hardee: Old Reliable* (Baton Rouge, 1965), 78–79.

22. Braxton Bragg to Gen. Samuel Cooper (Adjutant and Inspector General), 9 April 1863, Palmer Collection of Braxton Bragg Papers, Western Reserve.

23. Braxton Bragg to Major E. T. Sykes, 8 February 1873, cited in William M. Polk, *Leonidas Polk: Bishop and General* (2 vols. New York, 1915), II, 312.

24. Bragg to Cooper, 9 April 1863, Bragg Papers, Western Reserve.

25. Cheatham was by no means a teetotaler, and one other Civil War incident is tied to a possible instance of intoxication. A Georgia colonel suspected Cheatham of being drunk on one occasion during the long trek from Tupelo to North Carolina after the disastrous battle of Nashville. Lilla Mills Hawes, ed., *The Memoirs of Charles H. Olmstead* (Savannah, 1964), 177. It is not known when or where Cheatham acquired his drinking habits, though the Mexican War is one possibility. The author thinks that it is unlikely Cheatham could have retained command

were he a habitual drunkard, no matter how powerful his political or military allies.

26. OR, 622; Hughes, William]. Hardee, 145.

27. Cheatham and Withers to Bragg, 3 January 1863, Cheatham Papers, TSLA. The original letter stated that only three brigades were trustworthy, but Cheatham and Withers corrected the wording to read divisions on 21 March 1863; OR, 702.

28. Polk to Bragg, 3 January 1863, Cheatham Papers, TSLA. Bragg's reply was inserted at the bottom of Polk's letter.

29. Bragg's Murfreesboro Report, Western Reserve.

30. Cheatham's Murfreesboro Report, TSLA; OR, 708.

31. Hughes, William J. Hardee, 147.

32. Bragg to Cheatham, 11 January 1863, Cheatham Papers, TSLA.

33. OR, 682–84, Grady McWhiney, Braxton Bragg and Confederate Defeat: Field Command (New York, 1969), 375–76.

34. OR, 684.

35. Ibid., 701–02.

36. Gideon Pillow to Maj. (Wm. Clare), 9 March 1863. Palmer Collection of Braxton Bragg Papers, Western Reserve.

37. Bragg's Murfreesboro Report, Western Reserve; OR, Vol. XXXIII, pt. 2, 624. For revealing accounts of Bragg's feuds with his generals refer to Connelly, Autumn of Glory. 73–92, and McWhiney, Braxton Bragg and Confederate Defeat, 374–88.

38. OR, 755; Pillow to Maj. Clare, 9 March 1863, Bragg Papers, Western Reserve.

39. Bragg to Cooper, 9 April 1863, Bragg Papers, Western Reserve.

40. Ibid.

41. Bragg's Murfreesboro Report, Western Reserve; OR, 708. The controversy surrounding Cheatham at Stones River apparently did not alter the popular sentiment felt towards Cheatham by men in his division. Cheatham is referred to favorably in a number of extant sources, including regimental histories, Confederate Veteran reminiscences, and in diaries and memoirs located in collections at the TSLA.

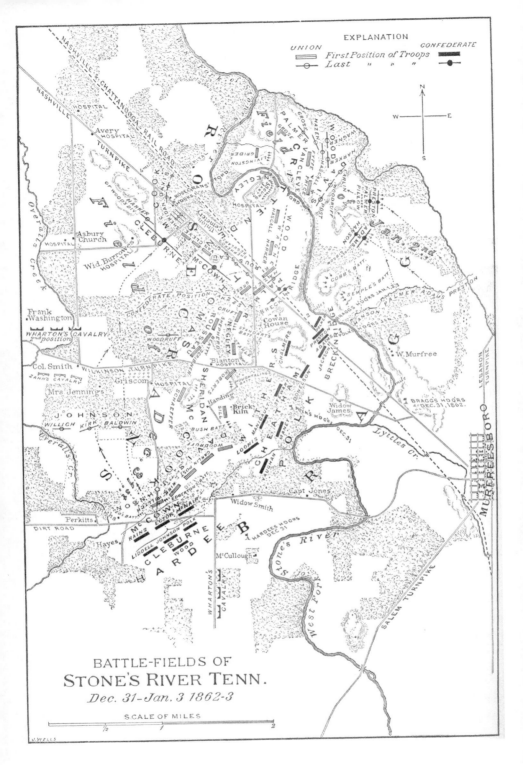

Battle of Stones River

(*Battles and Leaders of the Civil War*, Vol. III, 1884)

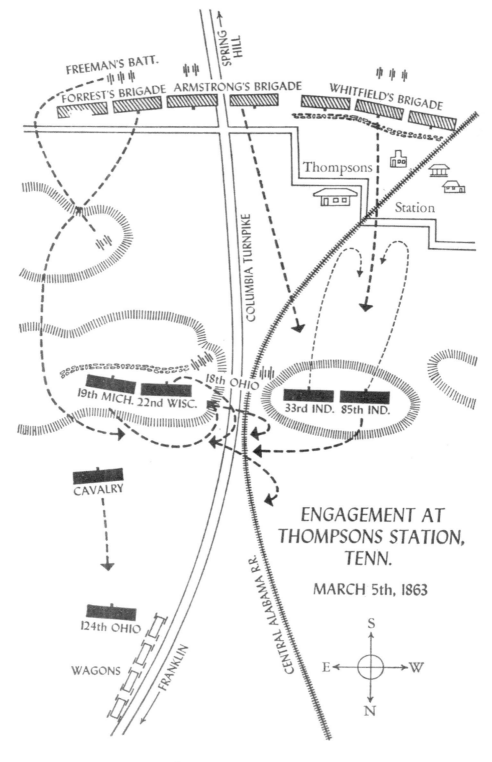

FREEMAN'S BATT.

FORREST'S BRIGADE   ARMSTRONG'S BRIGADE   WHITFIELD'S BRIGADE

SPRING HILL

Thompsons

Station

COLUMBIA TURNPIKE

18th OHIO

19th MICH.   22nd WISC.

33rd IND.   85th IND.

CAVALRY

ENGAGEMENT AT
THOMPSONS STATION,
TENN.

MARCH 5th, 1863

124th OHIO

WAGONS

FRANKLIN

CENTRAL ALABAMA R.R.

S

E   W

N

Battle of Thompsons Station

(Courtesy of William M. Anderson)

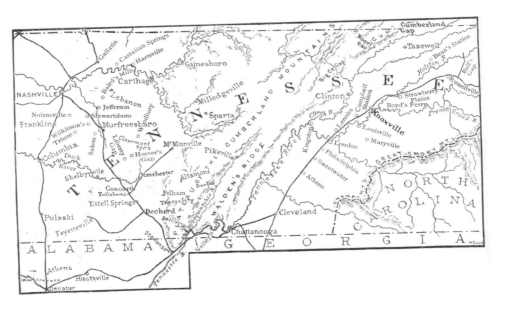

The Tullahoma Campaign

(*Battles and Leaders of the Civil War*, Vol. III, 1884)

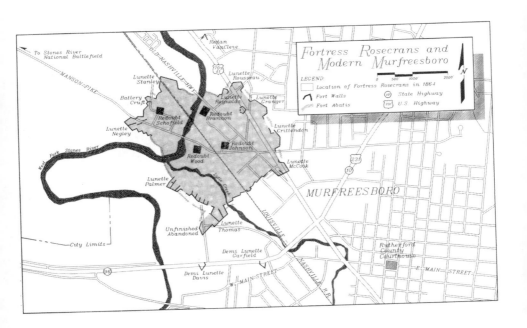

Fortress Rosencrans

(National Park Service)

Braxton Bragg
(Library of Congress)

Joseph Wheeler
(Library of Congress)

Benjamin F. Cheatham
(Library of Congress)

Earl Van Dorn
(Tennessee Historical Society)

George Maney
(Alabama Department of Archives and History)

William S. Rosecrans

(Library of Congress)

Alexander M. McCook

(Library of Congress)

James P. Fyffe

(Tennessee Historical Society)

John Coburn

(Heritage Foundation of Williamson County)

John T. Wilder

(Library of Congress)

Negley's Charge across Stones River, January 2, 1863 (Library of Congress)

Dedication of the Hazen Monument, 1863 (National Archives)

Stones River National Cemetery (Tennessee Historical Society)

THE LAST DAY AT STONES RIVER:

Experiences of a Yank and a Reb

$\text{\small ——————}\ \textit{Cmmc}\ \text{——————}$

James L. McDonough

O n a cold, gloomy, Friday afternoon in January, beside a river whose name few people outside of Middle Tennessee had ever heard, and close to a town equally obscure, one of the spectacular, breathtaking moments of the entire Civil War occurred. The determined Confederate brigades that anxiously formed for the assault east of Stones River were not as numerous as those in the famous charge at Gettysburg six months later, or the even larger, though little-known, Rebel assault twenty miles to the west at Franklin nearly two years afterward; but Brigadier General John C. Breckinridge's colorful Confederates, moving out in impressive alignment across an open field west of Murfreesboro, steadily tramping toward the Union line, possessed a pride and participated in a drama that were not surpassed by any of the war's more massive assaults.

The time was four o'clock. The date was January 2, 1863. Tense Yankees on the high ground above McFadden's Ford, their weapons tightly clutched in readiness for bloody work, watched silently as five thousand Rebels marched against them. This time there would be no surprise like the morning of the battle's first day. This time the Federals were peering down their gun sights as the Grayclads came on.

But the frontline Union forces, with Colonel Samuel Price's and Colonel James Fyffe's brigades lying in double line of battle, were less than two thousand strong. Even counting Benjamin Grider's reserve brigade and William Grose's brigade from John M. Palmer's division, the Yankees did not number four thousand soldiers east of

Stones River, while the Confederates, enjoying substantially more than a two-to-one advantage over the Union infantry in the front line, had another two thousand cavalry at hand. Some of the Federals in the front line, seeing the Rebels move unflinchingly up the rise, must have known that they were significantly outnumbered.

The first Yankee volley, fired when the Rebels were within one hundred yards, did not come close to arresting the Confederate's charge. And there was not time to reload. The Grayclads were upon them, mounting their works from end to end. The fighting was desperate, hand-to-hand, and short. Men shot their opponents at point-blank range, clubbed them with rifle butts and pistol handles, or stuck them with bayonets. Overwhelmed and demoralized, the Union infantry of Price's brigade fled to the rear while the Confederates reloaded, poured a deadly fire of musketry into their routed ranks, and screamed in triumph.[1]

There had been one chance to save the Union right wing under Price. If Grider's reserve brigade could have been brought into action earlier, Price's command might have held its ground. But Grider's unit, thinking the Rebels would not attack until the next day, had stacked their weapons and relaxed. The Confederate onslaught took the brigade by surprise. Grabbing their rifled-muskets and hastily forming into line of battle, Grider's regiments marched to the fight at the order of their division commander, Colonel Samuel Beatty. Apparently undaunted by the desperate situation, they moved eagerly toward the battle only to be met by Price's regiments, racing headlong for the rear, and running directly through their ranks.

Meanwhile, a little farther to the east, the Rebel assault was reaching high tide as calamity struck the Union brigade under Fyffe. When the Confederates launched their attack, Colonel Fyffe was back near the ford, talking with Colonel Beatty and Major General William S. Rosecrans. Their discussion was abruptly terminated as a courier galloped up with news that the enemy was about to advance; Colonel Fyffe mounted and rode to his headquarters. He arrived in time to see the advancing lines of Roger Hanson's and Gideon Pillow's brigades colliding with the Yankees under Price. Only one of Fyffe's regiments, the Forty-fourth Indiana anchoring his right flank, was close enough to give fire support to Price's line as the heavy masses of Rebel infantry bore down upon it.

Fyffe told his regimental commanders to wheel their units to the right, for he intended to take the Grayclads in their exposed right flank. Unfortunately, he had not reckoned with the oncoming second Southern battle line, composed of two brigades that now moved to the attack. Suddenly Fyffe realized that Price's whole unit had collapsed, his own right flank was thus unsupported, and, worse yet, the Rebels were closer to McFadden's Ford than he was. Fearing his brigade would be cut off, Fyffe ordered a retreat, which soon turned into a shambles. Fyffe himself was thrown from his horse and disabled. At least one of the regiments, Fyffe's own Fifty-ninth Ohio, panicked and ran right through the Twenty-third Kentucky, trampling some of its men who lay behind a rail fence. It was no more than thirty minutes since Breckinridge had launched his assault and three Yankee brigades were routed.[2]

Probably the Federals had enough manpower east of Stones River, if it had been used effectively, to have held their front line. But Grider's reserve brigade never got into action until Price's front line infantry were routed. In Fyffe's front line brigade, only one regiment supplied any effective flanking fire on the Rebel attacking columns as they drove in against Price. Then when Price was overwhelmed, Fyffe's soldiers found themselves outflanked and, trying to retreat, they panicked and went to pieces. Finally, William Grose's brigade, which was supposed to anchor the Union left, was, like Grider's reserve, never in the fight until both of the front-line brigades had gone to the rear, one overwhelmed and the other panicked.

The weight of the Rebel assault, four brigades strong, had gone in against Price's lone brigade, assisted by two regiments, the Seventy-ninth Indiana from Grider's command and the Forty-fourth Indiana from Fyffe's brigade. The Rebel force was concentrated while the Union strength was dispersed, enabling the Confederates to dispose of the Yankee infantry in piece-meal fashion. The Grayclads should not have accomplished as much as they did.

A glorious victory was at hand, or so it must have seemed to the jubilant Southerners, as the Federal line retreated before the advancing Rebels. Some of the Confederates, infantry from the Sixth and Second Kentucky and Gibson's Louisiana brigade, had even charged across the River in pursuit of the fleeing Yankees.

Actually, what seemed the forerunner of victory was a prelude to disaster. As the retreating Federals were pushed back toward the river, they drew the hotly pursuing Rebels down the forward slope and within range of some forty five cannon massed on the hill west of Stones River. The Union artillerists had the chance they had been waiting for, to shoot at the foe without harming their comrades. Unleashing a fierce cannonade, darkening the sky with smoke, and striking across the river into the ranks of the Confederates, the Federal guns dealt destruction up and down the lines.

It was suddenly, as one writer expressed it, "as if the Rebs had opened the door of hell, and the devil himself was there to greet them."[3] The soggy river bottom over which the Yankees had been driven had become a death trap as the Federal gunners blazed away with deadly effect. There was nothing reasonable to do except fall back.

When Major General Braxton Bragg was informed that Breckinridge's troops were beginning to retreat, he ordered Brigadier General J. Patton Anderson's brigade to cross the river and provide reinforcement. The battle, of course, was all over when Anderson arrived, too late for his infantry to help. Besides, the Federals had mounted a strong counterattack.

With heavy reinforcements at hand and a little daylight remaining, the Yankees acted quickly, although it was apparently an impatient brigade commander who sensed that the time was right and triggered the attack. Generals Thomas Crittenden, James Negley, John Palmer, and Rosecrans looked on from the ridge that bristled with Union artillery. Colonel John F. Miller of Negley's division, without waiting for orders from his general, moved out against the Rebels. Then Colonel Timothy R. Stanley's brigade joined him, ordered forward by Generals Rosecrans and Negley.

Cheering wildly as they surged after the retiring Grayclads, the Yankees now realized that the momentum of battle had changed. Other units joined in, as thousands of Federals splashed across the stream to the east bank. Grider's and Price's shattered commands, anxious to redeem themselves, quickly responded. There were units from Fyffe's brigade, and from other commands—all now pursuing the Rebels, forcing their artillery back from the ridge above the ford, finally compelling them to once more take up their original line along Wayne's Hill. Nothing had been changed by the short, bloody fight, the Federals regaining everything they had held before the assault took place.[4]

Colonel James P. Fyffe of Ohio, whose front line brigade was driven back in panic by Breckinridge's assault, wrote letters to his mother and wife following the battle that helped to bring alive the human element of the tragic conflict. Fyffe had been a lieutenant in the Mexican War and saw action at the Battle of Monterrey. Later he "read law" and in 1851 went to California seeking gold, keeping an interesting journal of his experiences in the gold field and his return by sea. Filled with a love for his country, a sense of duty, and an adventurous desire to participate in, as he expressed it, "the grandest events that have shaken the world since Peter the Hermit preached the Great Crusade for the rescue of the Holy Land," Fyffe went to war for the Union.[5]

There is a marked contrast between his letters written before the Battle of Stones River and those written afterward. His rather light hearted, chit-chat approach, and the continual fond and romantic references in the letters to his wife, are replaced by a more serious, brief, and matter-of-fact tone as he contemplates the crisis he has just survived.

The following are the major portions of two letters, the first to his mother and the second to his wife, both penned a few days after the battle.

Camp near Murfreesboro
January 10, 1863

My dear Mother,

I am sitting alone in my tent tonight and have been thinking about you all, away at home.... I thought the best thing I could do would be to write to my Ma, and the rest..., for this letter is for the whole family....

I was not in condition to write, and I am not much better now, for the "black Dog," got hold of me this afternoon; in other words, had a touch of the blues, originating partly from being very sore from a fall off my horse,... and partly, I suppose, from the reactions of the system after so long and sustained excitement....

In the last day of fighting, the great charge made by [Brig. Gen. John C.] Breckinridge's force just missed my brigade, where it stood in a single line, without any reserves whatever, and fell about two hundred yards to the right, where Colonel [Samuel] Beatty's troops... were posted, sweeping them backward like fall leaves before a wintry wind; one after the other the lines were swept away. If it had fallen on me, in place of where it did, I do not see how a single man could have escaped of my brigade....

I was not going to describe the battle, only allude to the narrow escape..., but as I have told this much, I will add that Breckinridge's charge was intended to cut through our lines and get to the [McFadden's] ford over Stone[s] River... They succeeded in getting to the ford, turning our right, but found themselves in what the French call a *cul de sac*. They found themselves in a bend of the river, running around them as it were, while the opposite bank was lined with fifty pieces of cannon, and dark with dense masses of infantry. I need not state what followed ....

I do not know what is to become of the people in this country. They [Confederates] force all the poor white people into the ranks, as soldiers, and have a law exempting every white man from the conscript law who owns 20 Negroes, thus forcing the poor, who had nothing to do with bringing on the war, to do the fighting, while the wealthy man who did all he could to bring it on is exempt by law from fighting.

We have been without tents or cooking utensils, nearly ever since we left Nashville until yesterday when our train came by, and I don't know when I was so glad to see a man as I was to see Tom Macaker. He had stayed back with my Head Quarter wagons, and we feared they were burned. Tom tells me [they] had a narrow escape. The train was very long and was attacked and part of it burned....

I hope Ma, you won't fret about the war. Somehow or other I have got to believe that it may all come out right, that the Great Being who rules over all things [will conclude it] for the best.

Your affectionate Son,

Perry

Camp near Murfreesboro
January 20, 1863

My Dear Wife,

I sent you a telegram the last day of the fight assuring you of my safety, to save you unnecessary anxiety, and my messenger has just returned and informed me he did not deliver it because the wires were down between Nashville and Louisville. I feel annoyed about it, and have set down to write you at once. Our tents have just come up, and are not pitched yet, and it is spitting snow so I can not write much.

You will see Gus Pems is killed before this reaches you. He was shot dead, venturing too far to get the wounded. He was a noble boy. His body was sent to Nashville to send home. William King was wounded in the arm.... John Brockhouse is missing. Leach is killed. Lieutenant A. Connor was wounded.... Lieutenant Dancer, Eleventh Kentucky, on my staff, was wounded in the last day's fight, and my horse, frightened by a shell, became frantic and threw me off, dragging me by the foot ... bruising my face and back and disabling me... right in the midst of a terrific [enemy] charge. You will see all about it in my official report. We got mail today for the brigade; hardly any letters for the 59th Regiment [Fifty-Ninth Ohio Volunteer Infantry]; none for me....

I must now close, as I am not sufficiently recovered from the exhausting effects of the terrible struggle we have gone through to pretend to write much. My love to al ....

Yours affectionately,
J. P. Fyffe

P.S. Adjt. Charles King goes to Nashville today to send Gus Pems body home. Henry Liggett is also going to take his brother's remains.... Tom Macabeer got back from Nashville yesterday. I had a hard time while he was gone—no wagon—no tent—no blankets—no cooking utensils—nothing to cook if we had; I tell you—we have had a "Bad time...."

Colonel Fyffe, in spite of his troubles, was actually fortunate, if compared to William McKay, a Tennessean in the ranks of the Rebel army. Badly wounded in the thigh during Breckinridge's assault, McKay experienced a seemingly unending nightmare of pain and anguish. "I remained helpless and partially unconscious until our command retreated," he wrote.

> I saw the Yankees coming and attempted to get up but could not. Our men
> moved up a battery of three guns and planted them just over where I lay. The
> fire from the guns was nearly hot enough to burn my face, and the Yankee bul-
> lets rattled on the gun carriages like hail.[6]

Finally the Confederates, with most of their horses killed, had to leave their
guns. As McKay lay between the lines, suddenly shrapnel and concussion from a
bursting shell, fired by the Rebels, broke his left arm and badly bruised his body. For
hours he remained in the field while a cold drizzle mixed with sleet came down and
Federal soldiers marched by him and over him. "I lay where I fell until about midnight
and received brutal treatment from some of the Yankees," McKay later recounted.

> The commanders of companies would say as they passed me, 'look out men;
> here is a wounded man' and some of them would step over me carefully while
> others would give me a kick, call me a damned Rebel, and I was covered with
> black spots from the bruises.

At last two Federals, searching the battlefield for a friend, took pity, secured an
ambulance, and had McKay taken to a Federal hospital. The horror was far from ended
however. Overworked attendants, thinking he was too near dead to waste their time,
laid him out on the ground. McKay's own words speak for themselves: "I lay all day Saturday in the rain without any attention being paid me. When I would ask for water they
would say 'you don't need water. We will take you to the graveyard after a while' ..."

McKay then felt fortunate that it was raining. He found he could suck the water
out of his rain-soaked coat sleeve. After dark on Saturday night some of the attendants, concluding that he was not going to die after all, picked him up, laying him in
a tent out of the rain. During the night two wounded Confederates died in the tent
and one of them fell across McKay's legs, where his body lay for several hours.

Sunday, at noon, McKay found himself moved to another tent where both Rebel
and Federal wounded lay. Not until Monday morning was he given breakfast, his first
food since Friday, before he was wounded. Next came the surgeons, who decided that
his wounded leg must be amputated. McKay rebelled, saying that they could not do
it, and then he begged and pleaded with them not to do it, until the chief surgeon
put an end to the matter: "If the damned Rebel wants to die let him go," was the
conclusion.

The surgeons moved on, amputated the leg of a Florida soldier near by, and the next day he died. The foul air and the sight of suffering and death were all around McKay. Two Yankee wounded were close at hand, one right beside him, and they also died. "So the three men nearest to me died," wrote McKay, "and none of them seemed to be wounded as badly as I was."

Having barely survived, and avoided the amputation of his mangled leg, it was not until January 7 or 8, 1863, that real hope was kindled when a man named Casper Freas, in company with a Mrs. Clemons, came upon McKay in the Federal hospital at Murfreesboro. The woman was in search of her husband (he was never found), whose two brothers had both been killed on the last day of the battle. Surprised to find McKay, who had been reported dead by a soldier claiming to have actually examined the corpse, Freas took an immediate interest in him. Procuring a surgeon's certificate that testified that McKay was mortally wounded, Freas secured a pass to take him to his own home. After a harsh cursing from the Provost Marshal who issued his parole, McKay found himself loaded into a wagon. The one friend he had made among the Federal surgeons packed in a pair of blankets, a bottle of whiskey, and some tea, coffee, and sugar—but the blankets, and whiskey disappeared as soon as the surgeon was out of sight, swiped by the Yankee guards.

At last McKay's wagon completed the ten-mile trip to the home of Freas. "I could not understand," McKay wrote, "why he would burden himself with a wounded man." Eventually, he realized Freas was a Union sympathizer, merely using McKay for his own interests, as he hoped to prevent the Confederates, who would know that he was caring for a wounded Rebel, from harming his property. In the meantime, Freas was planning a quick departure to Indiana. "The night he left," remembered McKay, "proved to be the most horrible of all my trials."

Freas and his family exited the house about midnight, placing McKay in the care of a big black man who promised to look after him through the night. As soon as the family had gone McKay said that the black man began bringing in fence rails to make a fire by putting one end on the fire and the other out on the floor. "I begged him to desist," wrote McKay, "but he would not obey me." Instead he kept bringing in rails, saying he was going to make a *good* fire—and then go home!

Indeed McKay soon had a tremendous fire, but, unable to move, spent part of the night in terror, fully expecting that the house would catch fire and he would be burned to death. Finally the fire died down, and then the severe cold set in, leaving McKay badly chilled and despondent when a neighbor happened to find him the next day. It would be summer before McKay, nursed by a Confederate family, eventually regained enough strength to struggle about on a pair of crutches.

Perhaps McKay was a fitting symbol of the mangled armies, with their combined total of over 24,000 casualties at the Battle of Stones River, for neither army moved again until the summer of 1863.

ᏮᎢᏦᏫᎩ

This article first appeared in the Spring 1981 issue of the *Tennessee Historical Quarterly*.

1. *War of the Rebellion: A Compilation of the Official Records of the Union and Confederate Armies*, 129 vols. (Washington, D.C., 1880–1901), Serial I, vol. XX, pt. 1, 615, 827, 833. Hereafter cited as OR. All references are to Serial I, vol. XX, part 1.

2. Ibid., 598–99, 601, 602–06.

3. Robert Womack, "The River Ran Red with Men's Blood," *Accent*, magazine of the Murfreesboro *Daily News Journal*, 26 December 1976, 10.

4. OR, 434, 408, 184–85, 451.

5. Fyffe to his wife Willa Ann Mefford Fyffe, 11 December 1862. Fyffe's letters were made available to the author by Mr. E. Gale Pewitt, Naperville, Illinois. The originals are in the Public Library, Chattanooga, Tennessee. They contain some misspelled words and improper punctuation. The spelling has been corrected and the punctuation improved in order to make the letters more readable.

6. These and other quotes from William L. McKay "Memoirs," Confederate Collection, Tennessee State Library and Archives.

THE GRAY DRAGOON WINS HIS FINAL VICTORY:

Van Dorn and Thompson's Station

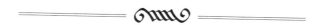

Robert Hartje

In the hills and valleys of Tennessee and northern Mississippi early in 1863 a strange quiet settled like an ominous fog. The echoes of Stones River's heavy guns and the cries of agony from that battlefield died down, but men waited, almost with impatience, for continued action. Quietness contrasted with the earlier sounds of violence, so much so that one observer suggested the possibility that "evil powers" were raising the stillness so that they might "pause to gather fresh strength" for a "fiercer and deadlier blast."[1]

Just below Nashville, Confederate General Braxton Bragg's battered army blocked the southward advance of General William Rosecrans's Army of the Cumberland. Bragg's line of defense extended from Shelbyville to Wartrace. With limited manpower and depleted resources, his Confederate veterans, still smarting from the twin humiliation of their Kentucky withdrawal and the Stones River defeat, offered the last line of resistance toward Chattanooga in the "Augean Stables of the West," as Cooper DeLeon so quaintly described the Tennessee theater of war.

Outside Bragg's main line his cavalrymen patrolled the countryside from Columbia to McMinnville. Their missions were ill-defined, their ranks were rent by chronic absenteeism and desertion, and yet they were always on the alert to the waning possibilities of discovering a supply depot to raid or an isolated Federal unit upon which to pounce. These mounted troops, commanded by some of the finest cavalry officers of the war, but with more courage than manpower, continuously harassed the blueclad army settled so firmly before them. The names of some of the cavalry leaders, Joseph Wheeler, Nathan Bedford Forrest, and Earl Van Dorn, in particular, soon became household words to Tennesseans who looked to horse and dragoon for their delivery from "Yankee aggression." The cavalry so impressed General Joseph E. Johnston during these months that he later credited them with holding the destiny of the Confederacy in their hands in early 1863.

The presence of Southern cavalry in Tennessee also impressed the Federals. At his Murfreesboro headquarters, General Rosecrans observed his enemy with obvious consternation.[2] With his own position a bit precarious because of his dependence upon a single railroad line to Louisville for his supplies, the Ohio commander viewed as premature any showdown action against Bragg's Army of Tennessee. Winter rains and floods, threatening vital roads with inundation, convinced Rosecrans that it would be unwise to undertake a campaign until thoroughly prepared. Criticism from Washington little influenced his tactical decisions as he delayed the momentous task of invasion, absorbed always "in calling for reinforcements," a game well-understood and often played by Northern commanders on several fronts.[3]

It was not a lack of physical courage that prevented the rival commanders in Tennessee from initiating the offensive operations so enthusiastically urged upon them by their respective war departments. Too often both Bragg and Rosecrans had demonstrated courage, resourcefulness, and initiative when these qualities were sorely needed in both armies. What these men lacked, as with many others thrown too quickly into total war, were certain intangible qualities of leadership, best described by Clausewitz as "inner light" and "resolution," the former which perceived the true meaning in any given situation, the latter being the courage to follow that "faint light."[4] In too many cases during the Civil War the "inner light" flickered and resolution waned as the size of the command increased. Officers who had been effective with small troop units lost their effectiveness overnight under the demands of heavier responsibilities. While troops chaffed in camps and garrisons, telegraph wires were heated with requests for more troops, more supplies, and more time. Too rapid promotion thus affected Bragg and Rosecrans, and it is not unusual that the late winter and spring of 1863 became seasons of reconnaissance, raids, and skirmishes, too often punctuated by fitful misunderstandings between field commanders and their superiors at opposite ends of telegraph lines. In both armies in Tennessee it was the cavalry that most often engaged the enemy at major times of indecision.

The extensive use of Confederate cavalry in Tennessee in early 1863 related directly to a series of events that began with President Jefferson Davis's appointment of General Joseph E. Johnston to command all the troops in the Department of the

West. Confederate authorities, thoroughly alarmed over the safety of the Mississippi River, hoped that this move would unite the divided command in the Mississippi valley and reverse the sad fortunes of summer and autumn in that important region. The new assignment for Johnston, a nebulous one at best, placed the doughty Virginian over Bragg and John C. Pemberton, the latter commanding at Vicksburg. It hopefully set the stage for better communications within Confederate lines in that far-flung theater of operations. Johnston, inactive in the field since his near-fatal wound at Fair Oaks, viewed his new assignment with misgivings, and it was with great reluctance that he accepted it.

Hampered at first by the personal intrusion of President Davis into the department, Johnston struggled to find an answer to the harassing problem of a divided army and an ever-advancing enemy. It was not by accident that he turned to cavalry; neither was it with regret. In the previous December two successful forays behind Union lines by Generals Forrest in Middle Tennessee and Van Dorn in northern Mississippi had sustained his belief in the effectiveness of mounted troops against an invading force. These cavalry raids not only proved the worth of mounted infantry to an army defending deep in its own territory, but they also successfully challenged Grant's threat toward Vicksburg. These blows and the Confederate victory at Chickasaw Bluffs hinted strongly to Johnston that his most pressing challenge had shifted suddenly from the Mississippi to central Tennessee, where Bragg held a tenuous position just south of Nashville. Early in January Johnston made an important decision. To his war department he reported: "I am preparing to send 6,000 cavalry under Van Dorn to Bragg's aid to operate upon the enemy's communication."[5]

Earl Van Dorn, the proud little Mississippian, became a hero of questionable dimensions in the drama of cavalry action that followed Johnston's decision. A tragic figure in a tragic era, bad fortune was his constant companion until his war department saw fit to return him to his first love, the cavalry. He regained a bit of his lost prestige with his successful Holly Springs raid and he was Johnston's first choice for transfer to Tennessee in the Confederacy's never-ending game of meeting the enemy with the largest mobile striking-force at his most vulnerable point.[6]

Van Dorn viewed this new arrangement with mixed emotions. The presence of General Pemberton at Vicksburg was a constant reminder to him of his own failure, the stunning Corinth defeat, where victory would have brought to his own shoulders instead of to Pemberton's the much-coveted stars of a lieutenant general. But in Tennessee the enemy was in force; and where the enemy was, there too was opportunity for glory and applause. What more could an ambitious officer ask?

Whether the transfer of Van Dorn's command from Pemberton to Bragg was a wise move is still debatable. Pemberton always contended that the loss of this cavalry cost him heavily in the summer engagement with Grant in and around Vicksburg. This is probably true, but in reality both Confederate armies were understrength. Rapid transfer of troops seemed the only possible solution to their manpower problems. When Grant halted his Vicksburg offensive, if only temporarily, Johnston had little choice but to meet the greatest threat (Rosecrans at Murfreesboro) with the largest possible number, while still maintaining a line of defense before Grant's Vicksburg force.

Van Dorn assumed his new command in mid-winter. It was no easy matter to prepare troops for the difficult trip to Tennessee, but he set to work making the necessary arrangements. He called in cavalry units scattered from southern Mississippi to eastern Louisiana and united them at Tupelo in early February. Here he made final preparations for the long ride.[7] Victor Rose, one of the riders, later remembered these preparations with some feeling:

> Before commencing the long and fatiguing march, Van Dorn issued his celebrated "Order No. 5", in which he prescribed the minutest rules for the government of his corps, whether in camp or on the march. Proper distances were prescribed to be observed on the march between companies, regiments, brigades, and divisions; a regular system of bugle calls was formulated; challenge and replies of videttes, etc... the whole concluding with the impetuous declaration: "Cavalry knows no danger—knows no failure; *what it is ordered to do, it must do.*"[8]

The tone of the directive carried a ring of the Van Dorn of an earlier and a happier day, in those first months of the war when his celebrated name had been on the lips of many throughout the Confederacy. Back of the braggadocio, though, there rang a serious note. It was Order Number Five all the way to Tennessee! Earl Van Dorn must have been reflecting back on those ill-fated campaigns in Arkansas and Mississippi, remembering how poorly-disciplined troops added to the confusion which in both instances brought tragic defeat to his armies.

It was a dreary day when the Confederates finally departed from Tupelo. Behind their commander rode approximately 7,500 troops organized into two divisions.[9] The height of the winter season was at hand and wet, disagreeable weather dogged their footsteps from the beginning of the expedition. They plodded over broken roads, they waded river swamps, and they forded swollen streams. Their bodies ached for rest, and the occasional sunshine lacked the warmth needed to dry out clothing and supplies. Men and animals suffered alike. Some grumbling appeared in the ranks, but it was never in evidence when the commanding general rode in their midst.[10]

If Van Dorn suffered, no one knew about it. Ever the youthful-looking field marshal rode ahead of his troops, his eyes toward Tennessee, the glitter of anticipation noted even in the worst of conditions. As was his custom he spoke to no one of his plans. At the evening campfire he made small talk with some of his officers, but brigadier generals and colonels learned their orders only as Van Dorn was ready to divulge them. High-ranking officers were as surprised as accompanying journalists as the exact route of their march unfolded before them.

Van Dorn directed his cavalry first to Florence, Alabama. Here they spent a day crossing the turbulent Tennessee River. Before leaving the river's banks many a young man looked back toward warmer Alabama before he reluctantly moved northward again.[11]

From Florence travel conditions worsened. Struggling horses and weary riders followed ragged, often imperceptible trails for endless hours. Sometimes roads terminated abruptly. Flooding streams blocked their paths. Outnumbered Federal cavalry outposts, their officers alerted to the unusual activity before them, reacted as best they could before the large force. They burned important bridges and threw roadblocks into expected pathways of the invading troops. This forced wearisome and time-consuming delays. To make matters worse bushwhackers offered a constant threat to lead units and stragglers. The enthusiasm so prominent at Tupelo faded as horses struggled in mud to their haunches, and men sat in their saddles, cold, wet, and disgusted.

Van Dorn watched his men anxiously, but still he continued his relentless pace. He instituted prompt disciplinary action for any violation of regimen that threatened to delay his progress. February's sun remained half-hidden in haze and foliage, but the troops pushed on. Before him, in Bragg's command, there was another chance for Earl Van Dorn, it might be his last one!

The twentieth of February was a frosty cold morning in Middle Tennessee. Confederate troops in camp near Columbia rose slowly and departed their tents reluctantly. Suddenly these early-risers were greeted with wild shouts by happy men on tired horses. To Van Dorn and his fatigued marchers the outlines of the city in the frost-covered dawn was a glorious sight. When they saw Columbia, it was impossible for them to contain their enthusiasm. A wild cheer rang through their ranks as the horsemen rode into a Confederate camp that soon took up the cheer.[12]

Columbia looked good to Earl Van Dorn, but it was only a first step. From the moment he had accepted his new assignment, he had Kentucky and Ohio on his mind. Dreams of himself as a victorious general leading a slashing, hard-charging army into the heart of the enemy territory persisted. Just before his arrival at Columbia, General Leonidas Polk, also commanding in Tennessee, had inadvertently encouraged him in his unrealistic thoughts. On February 8, while the Mississippi cavalry struggled through southern Tennessee, Polk wrote Van Dorn that he had hopes for a concerted action by the Mississippian in conjunction with General Wheeler against a Federal force then threatening Wheeler's operations against Northern supply lines.[13] Such an operation would take Van Dorn toward Kentucky and give him a start on his anticipated objective. Though he arrived in Columbia too late to participate in Polk's scheme, the proposal whetted his appetite. An incurable optimist, he never seemed to realize the problems at hand in his grandiose schemes; instead he seemed always to have his heart set on what he termed "cutting loose."

Van Dorn probably accepted the Tennessee assignment with the understanding that he would operate unfettered against the enemy. This pattern of command already had been well established in Middle Tennessee by Generals Forrest, Wheeler, and John Morgan. Morgan, in particular, impressed him. Here was the man of action that he approved. Van Dorn liked the thought of sudden, devastating blows into enemy country. This type of action not only wrecked enemy communication and supply lines, but it also brought distinction to the bold commander who conducted the raid.

The excitement of the intimacy of battle rang in his words when Van Dorn reported his arrival to General Johnston. "I am now here with my whole command," he announced, "and will be ready to make any movement you may desire."[14]

Then, as if afraid that Johnston might not place him close enough to the front, he suggested an attack on Franklin. After routing the Franklin garrison he would cross the Cumberland River and operate on the north bank of that stream and on to the banks of the Ohio, "unless General Bragg is threatened by General Rosecrans soon." It was action he sought, and there was near pathos in his plea at the conclusion of his letter to Johnston: "Let me beg of you not to make me and my command a part of the picket of any army. I can do you better service, I am sure. We are proud of being cavalry, and desire to win distinction under the title."[15]

General Johnston's reply was diplomatic but firm:

> My first object in bringing you into Middle Tennessee was to enable you to
> take part in a battle, in the event of the advance of the Federal army; the

second, that you might operate upon his lines of communications, previous to his moving from Murfreesborough, and up to the time of engagement, or, if it should appear to be expedient, battle being unlikely, that you might move into Kentucky or farther.[16]

For the moment there was no scheduled attack for Franklin. Van Dorn must await the decisions of his commanding officer before engaging in unusual maneuvers. For the time being the orthodox actions were defense and reconnaissance.

General Bragg did not keep his new cavalry commander in the wings for very long. On February 25 he placed him and General Wheeler in command of cavalry corps. Van Dorn' s corps at first consisted of two divisions, about five thousand troops. His division commanders were Brigadier Generals William T. Martin and William H. Jackson, two fine cavalry officers. Brigade commanders included Brigadier Generals Frank G. Armstrong and George B. Cosby, and Colonel John W. Whitfield. General Forrest also joined this command, and his brigade brought the effective strength to about 6,500.[17] These troops were to serve as the eyes and ears of the left wing of the Confederate line of defense. Their area of operation extended from Columbia to Spring Hill. Before them Federal cavalry commanded by two of Van Dorn's Pea Ridge opponents of a year earlier, Generals Franz Sigel and Jefferson C. Davis, offered them formidable opposition. Van Dorn temporarily shelved his Kentucky invasion plans, but new excitement loomed for him as it became his responsibility to prevent the Union force before him from moving against the center of General Bragg's line.

From Van Dorn's sector of the Confederate defense line his gaze turned always toward Franklin, one of the most active spots in the Northern line. As early as February 18, General Forrest had reported the danger of an attack from Franklin, and Bragg had hurried an investigation of the situation.[18] No action resulted, but Confederate pickets increased their vigil. Almost every day some new report circulated giving warning of unusual restlessness near the city.

Unaware that General Rosecrans's plans did not include an advance but only a strengthening of his front, each rumor of movement increased Southern apprehensions about their positions. Fearful of being caught off-balance, Confederate cavalry crowded Franklin precariously during the last week of February and the first days of March.[19] To Rosecrans this action seemed too much like an offensive, and his response was to treat these Confederate moves as such. On March 3, he issued an order through his chief of staff, Brigadier General James A. Garfield, directing Brigadier

General Charles C. Gilbert to send a "sufficient cavalry force" down the Spring Hill Road to investigate Confederate activity in that vicinity.

General Garfield made two important mistakes in planning and carrying out this mission. He first underestimated the strength of his opponents before him. His reinforced brigade was ample as a task force against outposts and overextended enemy lines. It was not adequate against cavalry divisions with mobile artillery. His second mistake related to his first. "Take a forage train along," he directed. Expecting only token resistance in the Spring Hill area, he ordered his troops to serve as a convoy for a wagon train that he hoped would gather forage from the countryside for the Franklin garrison.[20] Thus encumbered, the reconnaissance force was at great disadvantage in any large scale skirmish.

The Union commander who led the foray toward Spring Hill was Colonel John Coburn, "a brave and determined commander."[21] Gilbert later explained his choice of Coburn: "As my own troops were scattered through the town, or engaged in work which was of importance, I deemed it most expeditious to send Colonel Coburn, whose command was compact and ready to move."[22]

Although Coburn possessed wide leeway of decision making for his expedition, he, like Garfield, knew little of the details of the situation before him. He proceeded on an uncertain mission with more courage than understanding of what problems he might encounter.

Colonel Coburn, the commander of the Third Brigade of the First Division of the Reserve Corps of the Army of the Cumberland, departed from Franklin on March 4 at 9:00 a.m. With him were 2,837 troops, including the Thirty-third and Eighty-fifth Indiana Infantry Regiments, the Twenty-second Wisconsin Infantry, and the Nineteenth Michigan Infantry from his own brigade; 600 cavalry detached from the Ninth Pennsylvania, Fourth Kentucky, and Second Michigan Cavalry Regiments, and the Eighteenth Ohio Battery.[23] His line of march was toward Spring Hill, thirteen miles distant, where Coburn hoped to camp on his first night out. He marched with four wagons for each of his regiments in addition to the wagon train of eighty vehicles, strung out behind his troops in a long line. "Wait for the wagons, boys, and we'll all take a ride," Van Dorn remarked caustically when he heard of the train.[24]

The weather was "cool and favorable," and Coburn's troops marched with a light step. This was just another reconnaissance to them, and most of the men were happy to get away from routine garrison life for a few days. Coburn himself harbored no thoughts of any engagement other than mild skirmishes. His plan was to divide his command on his second day out. Then, in conjunction with troops under Phil Sheridan from Murfreesboro who he expected to meet near Spring Hill, he intended to search out and report the enemy's position and activities to his own headquarters.[25]

On the same day that Coburn began his move, Earl Van Dom initiated what he later described as a "forced reconnaissance" toward Franklin, also over the Spring Hill Road. Brigadier General Jackson, with three brigades (about 1,200 mounted men) preceding the main force, was on the road early in the day. Jackson's troops rode easily over the hard-packed road, unaware of the Federal activity before them. By mid-morning they arrived at Thompson's Station, a small village located about nine miles south of Franklin. Their arrival on the south side of the village coincided almost exactly with the arrival of Coburn's force on the northern edge of the town.

Both commanders showed surprise at the presence of the other force and for some minutes there was confusion in the two commands as to their next moves. Jackson recovered his composure first and drew his small force into a roadblock. He extended his line to the left and the right of the turnpike until it was about five hundred feet in length. Behind this position, Captain Houston King, commanding the Second Missouri Battery, quickly unlimbered two artillery pieces and began pumping shots into "the large body of enemy with [the] long baggage train."[26] In spite of the heavy fire Coburn deployed his small force effectively, sending Captain

Charles C. Aleshire's Eighteenth Ohio Battery to an excellent defensive position on a knoll just to the left of the pike. From this position Aleshire returned the Confederate fire with telling effect. For over an hour, the two units continued a brisk artillery fire across a field just east of the village, but with indecisive results. All about the troops the ground was broken and irregular, "in many places steep and precipitous," except for the open field in front of them, and it was difficult for either commander to gain an immediate terrain advantage.

With shells falling in front of his position, Coburn watched for an opening. About noon he decided he could wait no longer. Seizing the initiative, he impulsively lashed out against the Confederate position with his cavalry.

There was consternation on the faces of the Confederate officers as Jackson instinctively retreated before the new thrust. Surprise did not develop into rout, however. Jackson's troops crossed a hill in orderly formation, and Coburn's lead troops lost sight of them. Jackson then set up a longer line of defense in the hills south of Thompson's Station.[27] When the Confederates suddenly emerged from the woods in their long line in front of the two advancing Federal units, the charging bluecoats ceased their wild shouting and beat a hasty retreat back to their original position. If Jackson had any ideas of a counterattack, he shelved them in the face of well-aimed grape and canister fire from the Union position. It was in these positions that General

Van Dorn found the two forces when he arrived at the edge of Thompson's Station with the main body of his command.[28] Casualties for the first skirmish had been light. Reports seem to agree that the Confederates suffered the greater losses, with about fifteen killed and several others wounded as against only two or three Federals wounded.[29]

Sometime during the early afternoon Van Dorn must have huddled briefly with General Jackson and assessed the Confederate situation. Deceived by the Federal show of force into suspecting a larger army before them, Van Dorn decided that a counterattack for the moment was out of the question. He instead chose to hold his own line and give a display of his strength from behind the protective covering of the irregular hills behind him. This he did in a convincing fashion for several hours. Both armies settled in their positions and conducted a sporadic artillery and small arms duel until near the close of the day.

Again it was the brave and energetic Coburn who moved. This time it was that troublesome wagon train that brought on the action. Obviously the wagons had become a liability once the Federals were under fire, so when things settled down a bit, Coburn requested and received permission to return them to Franklin.[30] To divert Van Dorn's attention while the wagons were being put on the road, Coburn initiated what appeared to be an all-out offensive. Van Dorn was not caught off-guard by this action, and his artillery responded to the new threat with its heaviest fire of the afternoon. Thirty-nine of the wagons made their escape, but heavy Confederate fire forced Coburn to halt this operation short of his goal of returning all the vehicles. Coburn also terminated his offensive, realizing that any further advance would undoubtedly have brought on a full-scale engagement for which he knew his small force was inadequate. He then withdrew his troops to a line of hills north of Thompson's Station, and action ceased for the day. During the night the two armies bivouacked in hills along the Columbia-Franklin pike, about four miles apart.[31]

The night was quiet except for occasional picket firing, but it was during the night that Van Dorn made an important discovery. Confederate scouts, entering the Union lines after dark, found Coburn's force to be much smaller than they had thought. This discovery changed the Confederate planning for the coming day as Van Dorn now "determined to give them battle."[32] But first he would allow Coburn to make his move.

Coburn's night was less productive of good news. He, too, gained information of his enemy, but his news was all bad. Negroes informed him that the Confederates possessed infantry, cavalry, and artillery in depth, something that Coburn surely must have realized. Then just after dawn two Negro boys, who contended that they were refugees from the Confederate "army," informed Coburn that Van Dorn and an army of 15,000 were set to take Franklin.[33]

Coburn was in difficult situation. He knew that Van Dorn did not have 15,000 men, but he realized that the Confederates did greatly outnumber his small force. Franklin was strangely silent to his predicament. He did receive a small ammunition resupply just before dawn, "some 48 rounds of shell," but there was no word as to what he should do against the superior force before him. Reasoning to his own sorrow that his original orders meant he must push on, Coburn decided to move forward, even if Van Dorn resisted his move. Certainly Sheridan's force, expected from another direction, would arrive in time to flank the Confederates and prevent them from continuing on toward Franklin.

Coburn reflected on these matters as long as he felt time allowed. Then he quietly announced his decision to his young assistant adjutant general, Lieutenant H. B. Adams: "I am going ahead," he said, "I have no option in the matter."[34] To his other officers he was a little more emphatic: "My orders are imperative," he informed them about seven o'clock. "I must go on or show cowardice."[35] This last statement seems to reveal the key to what otherwise appears as a rash action.

The hills south of Nashville dominate the landscape for miles around. In any season their quiet beauty impresses visitor and native alike. Some are rounded and barren. More often they have pointed peaks and are well-covered with trees. Cedars often predominate. To the casual observer there is little pattern in their arrangement; they seem to have just been spattered over the countryside by some giant unseen hand. Hills, beautifying the landscape, so peaceful and majestic, they, too, felt the lusts of war.

To a military commander facing a determined enemy on the terrain between Columbia and Franklin, these Tennessee hills smacked less of beauty and more of tactical maneuvering. In a campaign, the hills could serve either as excellent defensive positions or as obstacles to an advance. An artillery piece properly placed on the rim of a hill could command a wide stretch of the valley before it. On the other hand, a costly attack would be required to remove an enemy entrenched in a line of hills.

Thompson's Station, a whistle stop on the Nashville and Decatur Railroad in 1863, is almost completely surrounded by these small irregular hills. On the morning of March 5, the Confederate position was set in a prominent line of these hills just south of the village. This range traversed the Columbia pike at right angles, with a high knob on either side of the road upon which Van Dorn had placed troops. After passing between the knobs of this range of hills, the road descended into a large open valley, then an open field, actually the eastern limits of the village. East of the road the field extended about three-quarters of a mile, and then the irregular hills again appeared. West of the road the field narrowed slightly as the range occupied by the Confederates angled slightly to the north and then faded off to the northwest. At the base of the hills on this side of the pike was the village of Thompson's Station, little more than a station house, a school, and several undistinguished buildings. These buildings were on the railroad, about three hundred yards from the turnpike.

Just south of the village, near the foot of one of the highest hills, ran a gully, about one hundred yards in length. Paralleling the gully was a stone fence of about the same length. Behind these obstacles Confederate dismounted troops faced the village, awaiting whatever action might develop within the Union lines on the other side of town. Confederate skirmishers and sharpshooters also occupied the station house and several of the buildings, hoping to warn the main line of Confederates of any attack in the direction of the village. Across the southern range of hills, the Confederates lined up as follows. On the extreme right, across the turnpike, General Forrest was on the second of two prominent knolls. Next to him, General Armstrong also held the Confederate right. Across the road Jackson's troops reached to the railroad, with Whitfield's brigade stationed behind the stone fence.[36] Since the railroad veered off toward the southwest away from the turnpike, after leaving the station, the Confederate line must have extended for over a mile.

To the north of Thompson's Station the hills are not so impressive until you cross the West Harpeth River about two and one-half miles north. Despite the absence of dominating hills, there are several prominent knolls, and all through the region the ground is irregular and broken, as near the southern position. Just beyond the West Harpeth River, about three and one-half miles north of the village, the turnpike again bisects a range of high hills. It was from their shelter that Coburn began his offensive on the morning of the fifth.

After deciding to attack the Confederates if necessary, Coburn carefully surveyed his map of the countryside about him. As he gazed at the map his first concern was for two small roads that paralleled the turnpike. These roads were perfect for an enemy flanking movement. How could he prevent such a possibility? Turning abruptly to his cavalry commander, Colonel Thomas J. Jordan, he requested him "to send a sufficient force of cavalry on each of these roads" and keep him informed of any Confederate moves on them. "I will delay my forces a sufficient length of time for them to give said information," he promised Jordan.[37]

True to his word Coburn delayed his attack until eight o'clock. He then moved slowly toward the Confederate position, his remaining cavalry in the lead. Skirmishing with advance Confederate pickets began almost as soon as the Federals began their march, but it was not until ten o'clock that the real engagement began, about a half mile north of the village.

"Here," later wrote Colonel William L. Utley, commanding the Twenty-second Wisconsin Regiment, "the booming of cannon and the howling of a shell... admonished us that there was work ahead."[38] Here, indeed, was work for the Federals. The first shell from Captain King's battery atop a knoll just east of the turnpike fell in the midst of the advance Federal cavalry and did not explode. Not so the other shells. As King zeroed in on the advancing troops, Coburn's cavalry skirmishers fell off to the side of the road to be replaced by the infantry units. Coburn quickly ordered his infantry units to take up a line of attack, the Thirty-third and Eighty-fifth Indiana Regiments on the west side of the turnpike, the Twenty-second Wisconsin and the Nineteenth Michigan on the east. Captain Aleshire's artillery was moved to "the hill to the left of the pike" behind the infantry units where it took up its gruesome task of attempting to dislodge the Confederates from their strong positions.

The Federals were not easily dissuaded from their attack. Even as Coburn organized his new line, Confederate artillery punished the Federals with 6-, 12-, and 18-pounders as well as intense small-arms fire. As the artillery barrage increased its tempo, Coburn decided quickly that removal of this obstacle was of first order. Turning to Colonel John P. Baird, commanding the Eighty-fifth Indiana, he asked if that officer could displace the artillery barrier in the hills before them. "I'll try," replied the colonel with all the confidence he could muster.

"I will send the Thirty-third Indiana with you," replied Coburn. Then as if the assignment before Baird was not enough he added, "and if you take the battery on the right, take the other close by on the left also."[39]

The attack of the Indiana troops, first against the station house and then toward the stone fence commanded much of the attention of the late morning and early afternoon. These troops attacked the depot area about 11:30 and pushed the Confederate skirmishers there back to their main positions with little difficulty. The Indianians, with Coburn in direct command, then made one of the most dramatic moves of the day. With grape and canister falling all about them, they proceeded across an open field toward the stone fence.

The sun shone bright, and the blue uniforms reflected the light as the riflemen pushed across the five hundred yards of open field. "Never on drill or parade have I seen them move with more precision," wrote the commander of the Thirty-third Indiana, Lieutenant Colonel James M. Henderson.[40] Across the field the going was rough. Some of the men stumbled over obstacles, others disappeared from the ranks, victims of sporadic firing from behind the fence. His position threatened by the large force before the fence, Jackson quickly reinforced this line with Colonel Samuel G. Earle's Third Arkansas Cavalry from Armstrong's position. The reinforced line watched the advancing Federals with muted admiration, holding their main fire until the blue line was just in front of their position.

Suddenly sharp commands sounded from behind the fence and the Confederate line exploded. Before them, the blue line melted, the survivors retreating rapidly under the heavy fire. Well-masked by the fence and gully, the Arkansans and Texans behind it continued to fire with unabated energy. Dusty, perspiring farm boys from Indiana retreated, fighting on as though possessed of demons. Instead of throwing down their weapons and fleeing, they sought shelter anywhere, among scrubby cedars, along the embankment of the railroad, in the buildings near the depot, and always they fired back at their antagonists. Still, the Confederate fire seemed to search them out of their hiding places, and again they retreated under pressure.

This was the time the impatient Confederate commanders awaited. Yelling along the line for a counterattack, the gray line moved across the stone wall. "With a shout, men and officers all rushed to the encounter, and in a moment the foe was driven from the houses in and behind which he had sought shelter, and compelled in the wildest confusion to seek refuge behind a hill a mile to his rear.... "[41]

From across the turnpike the Nineteenth Michigan moved hastily to join the Indianians on the hill. With these fresh troops the reinforced Federals took up an excellent defensive position. It was up to the Confederates now to displace them. Van Dorn had moved his men too quickly against the charging Indianians, allowing them to retreat to fight again. To displace them now would require a more courageous effort. But courage was hardly lacking in either army, and before the new Federal position some of the bloodiest fighting of the day took place.

Colonels Whitfield, Earle, and L. S. Ross, commanding the Arkansans and the Texans, delayed only momentarily before assaulting the new Federal position. Captain King's artillery prepared the way for them. From a nearby hill the Missourians poured a heavy barrage toward the new objective. The artillery was still firing when shouting rebels leaped from the valley floor near the railroad and attacked the hill in great fury. Rocks and foliage blocked their paths, but on they charged up the slope. Over the dead and wounded of both armies they painstakingly made their way until they arrived within twenty yards of the Federal line. Here they met the full force of Federal small arms' fire. Before this murderous onslaught they halted their own attack and reluctantly returned to their earlier position near the railroad.

The sun was too hot, the troops were short of water, the wounded needed medical attention, but swearing officers overlooked all that and quickly reformed their ranks. Signals echoed down the line, and the Confederates again doggedly charged up the hill. Once more they gained the summit at severe cost, only to be stopped once more by the determined defenders. This charge was even more costly to both armies than the first one. Among the Confederate dead was Colonel Earle, with a bullet through his head. He had died at the head of his regiment, leading his men across the rim of the hill when the fatal bullet struck him down.[42]

At the foot of the hill following the second repulse, Confederate officers faced the prospects of a third charge with some misgivings. Certainly they could dislodge the small enemy force atop the peculiar-shaped knoll. But where was Forrest? Why had he not joined them in their bloody assaults?

Across the turnpike Forrest had not been inactive; in fact he, too, had been seriously engaged since the early morning. Using Captain S. L. Freeman's mobile artillery to great effect, he had battled the left wing of the Union force in the hills east of the pike from the very first moments of the battle. His persistent efforts, coupled with Coburn's transfer of the Nineteenth Michigan, finally broke the Federal defenders before him. The Twenty-second Wisconsin and the cavalry detachments with them scurried toward the West Harpeth River just as the second Confederate charge failed on the other side of the road. Van Dorn was elated. Forrest was now free to engage the center of the line. Sensing a new opportunity, Van Dorn then ordered Forrest to Jackson's aid. "If possible," he instructed, "get in rear of the enemy."[43]

Forrest executed the last part of this order with dexterity, moving his army as far as possible around the Federal left to avoid other troop units that might be in the area. It was no easy matter for him to cross the valleys and cedar knobs, but his troops moved as quickly as possible. With Forrest advancing on Coburn's rear, Van Dorn delayed further activity in front of the railroad. Then after General George B. Cosby's regiment had joined the Texans and Arkansans from Armstrong's brigade, the Confederate commander ordered the third charge.

As Forrest struggled against natural elements to gain Coburn's rear, Jackson began his new attack in front of the Union position. Again shouting, firing, sweating Confederates mounted the hill toward the flaming Federal guns. Again firepower from the hill halted the impetuous Confederates short of their objective.

Suddenly there was a roar in the Federal rear. On the battlefield the scene changed abruptly, as though a writer, sympathetic to the cause of the South, had decided to end his script on a happy note. Through the trees near the base of Coburn's hill appeared Forrest and two reinforced regiments of dismounted cavalry, charging the Federal rear. Forrest's troopers had fought hard to arrive behind the lines, but they were now set to turn the tide of battle. Forrest's giant charger, Roderick, had just recently been shot from under him, but that hardy officer continued with his troops in the attack, also on foot.[44] Warning shouts alerted the battered Federals on the hill to the "fresh" attack. There was some confusion among the grime-covered defenders, but raw courage and frantic recklessness caused many of them to turn and fire into the midst of the new threat. Lieutenant Colonel E. B. Trezevant and Captain Montgomery Little, two of Forrest's bravest officers, fell, mortally wounded, in front of the new Union line, but the charge continued unabated. The surging Confederates rushed to a point within twenty feet of the exhausted defenders where a young captain, dashing from his ranks, seized the colors of the Nineteenth Michigan.[45]

There must have been a note of desperation in Colonel Coburn's voice as he ordered his men to fix their bayonets and prepare for a fight to the finish. Then the Federal commander discovered that Forrest had yet another unit in reserve, and his mood of desperation changed to one of futility. He surveyed his position quickly. His ammunition was nearly gone, his cavalry and artillery had mysteriously "disappeared," Confederates beset his position from every side, his paths of escape were blocked. There was no hope, and Coburn was not prepared to sacrifice more brave men to a hopeless cause. White flags suddenly appeared from within the Union lines. Van Dorn halted his advance and investigated. It was all over; the flags told the story. Coburn and his garrison had thrown down their guns and surrendered.

The afternoon sun was low on the horizon when the Confederates took over the field, but there yet remained time for looting and pillaging by the victorious troops, as was usual in such situations. "It was a sad and revolting sight," remarked a Federal colonel, "to witness the barbarity of the inhuman demons stripping our noble dead."[46] But Yankee shoes, guns, belts, knives, and other small articles were prizes too valuable for destitute Confederates to resist. Again the battlefield became their informal quartermaster.

Records of battle casualties vary in the different reports of the commanders involved. Van Dorn's report shows 357 killed, wounded, and missing among his own troops in the two days' action. Coburn gives the Northern losses as 378 killed, wounded, and missing in addition to 1,221 who were captured in the final moments f the action.[47] A few of the Northern soldiers escaped down the Franklin pike, having departed earlier with the last of the wagon train. But most of Coburn's original command surrendered with their colonel. After a short internment in Southern prisons, Coburn and most of his officers were exchanged and returned to duty. The enlisted men were also soon exchanged, and Coburn was able again to command the Third Brigade in late June.[48]

Thompson's Station had not been an important battle in deciding the fate of Middle Tennessee. It began no great Southern offensive. It stymied no important

Federal move. But Thompson's Station was another of the many clashes between cavalry units, and it typified a new mode of combat that dominated action in the West until the close of the war.[49]

Although both commanders showed courage and initiative in the fighting in those unnamed Tennessee hills, they were also guilty of tactical errors that were costly to their own troops and to their personal reputations as commanders. Coburn probably made the biggest mistake when he engaged the large enemy force, but part of this blame can also be laid to his own commanders. General Rosecrans took note of this when he wrote that the "unnecessary" loss at the station was caused by Coburn's "want of proper caution" plus General Gilbert's "indecision."[50] Although Van Dorn was fast proving himself a skillful tactician with mounted infantry, he, too, made important errors. He did select a fine defensive position in which to meet the enemy head on, a good move if properly conducted. But when the enemy struck his position he was both premature in striking back and slow in flanking the outnumbered force. To his own credit, he stayed with his men at the front, as did Coburn, and personally led them to victory.[51]

The Confederates won the field at Thompson's Station, but it was something of a hollow victory. The village was untenable for future operations and the Confederates departed its bounds before the day ended. Federal prisoners were hustled southward quickly to Tullahoma and on to Southern prisons, and the Confederate cavalry returned to Columbia.

Ironically, the coming fortunes of the two commanders in the battle were neatly reversed. Coburn and most of the prisoners were released at about the same time. Coburn, who then set up headquarters in Indiana and helped reorganize his old unit, later returned to Rosecrans's command, fighting mostly in Tennessee and Georgia. His brigade was among the several Northern units to occupy Atlanta in December, 1864, and he lived to fight out the rest of the war.

Not so with Earl Van Dorn. He continued to harass the Northern army in Middle Tennessee in guerilla operations, but only two months and two days following the affair at Thompson's Station, the little Mississippian died ignobly at the hands of an irate husband. He was killed at Spring Hill on May 7, 1863, by Dr. George Peters, whose defense was that Van Dorn had violated his home. The exact circumstances of the shooting remain to this day a subject of bitter controversy.

⚬⚬⚬⚬

This article first appeared in the March 1964 issue of the *Tennessee Historical Quarterly*.

1. Thomas Cooper DeLeon, *Four Years in Rebel Capitals* (Mobile, Ala. 1890), 219–20.

2. General Rosecrans replaced General Don Carlos Buell in Tennessee early in 1863.

3. Kenneth P. Williams, *Lincoln Finds a General* (5 vols.; New York, 1949–59), V, 146.

4. Karl von Clausewitz, *War, Politics, and Power* (Gateway edition, Chicago), 118.

5. *The War of the Rebellion: A Compilation of the Official Records of the Union and Confederate Armies* (69 vols. and index; Washington, 1880–1901), Ser. 1, XVII, Part II, 838. Hereinafter cited as OR. All references are to Series 1.

6. Robert Hartje, "Van Dorn Conducts a Raid on Holly Springs and Enters Tennessee," *Tennessee Historical Quarterly*, XVIII (Summer 1959), 120–33.

7. OR, XXIII, Pt. II, 43; *Mobile Advertiser and Register*, 3 March 1863.

8. Victor M. Rose, *Ross's Texas Brigade* (Louisville, 1881), 92.

9. OR, XVII, Pt. II, 844.

10 *Mobile Advertiser and Register*, 3 March 1863.

11. OR, XXIV, Pt. III, 58, 64; *Mobile Advertiser and Register*, 3 March 1863.

12. OR, XXIII, Pt. II, 641; *Mobile Advertiser and Register*, 1 and 3 March 1863.

13 OR, XXIII, Pt. II, 630.

14. OR, LII, Pt. II, 425.

15. "N'Importe," a newspaper reporter from a Mobile paper, wrote that Van Dorn's new assignment was actually to contain Federal General Franz Sigel's force near Columbia, and that this was a duty "very disagreeable and unpleasant to Van Dorn." N'Importe further stated that the Mississippian had entered Tennessee to render heavy blows against the enemy "by rapid and brilliant cavalry demonstrations" much as General Morgan had been doing. *Mobile Advertiser and Register*, 8 March 1863."

16. OR, XXIII, Pt. II, 646.

17. RobertS. Henry, *"First with the Most" Forrest* (New York, 1944), 128; OR, XXIII, Pt. II, 650, 654.

18. John Allen Wyeth, *Life of General Nathan Bedford Forrest* (New York, 154; OR, LII, Pt. II, 427–28.

19. OR, XXIII, Pt. I, 75.

20. Ibid., 77.

21 Henry, *Forrest*, 129.

22. OR, XXIII, Pt. I, 76–77.

23. This is Coburn's figure. General Rosecrans and Absalom Baird reported the number as 1,845. OR, XXIII, Pt. I, 74, 84, 86.

24. *Mobile Advertiser and Register*, 14 May 1863.

25. OR, XXIII, Pt. I, 80, 85–86.

26. Ibid., 116. Colonel Thomas J, Jordan, commanding the Ninth Pennsylvania Cavalry, reported that the Federal artillery fired first. Coburn and others say King's battery began the

engagement. Ibid., 80, 86, 97.

27. Lieutenant Colonel Edward Bloodgood of the Twenty-second Wisconsin Infantry, reported the line as "over a mile in length." OR, XXIII, Pt. I, 112. For a description of the countryside around Thompson's Station, see pages 16–17.

28. OR, XXIII, Pt. I, 80, 86, 94, 113, 116.

29. Ibid., 80, 86.

30. Ibid., 94.

31. Ibid., 86, 94, 116.

32. Ibid., 116.

33. Ibid., 86, 96, 98.

34. Ibid., 94.

35. Ibid., 98.

36. Ibid., 116. N'Importe, a newspaper reporter for the *Mobile Advertiser and Register* described these positions in his paper, 20 March 1863.

37. 81 OR, XXIII, Pt. I, 98

38. Ibid., 106.

39. Ibid., 99.

40. Ibid., 101.

41 Ibid., 124.

42. The Reverend W. T. Watson, chaplain of the force, was also killed in this charge. Descriptions of these charges are found in OR, XXIII, Pt. I, 88–89, 98–99, 101, 103, 107–108, 117, 122, 124. See also a good account in *Mobile Advertiser and Register*, 20 March 1863; and in [John Fitch], *Annals of the Army of the Cumberland* (Philadelphia, 1863), 419 ff. It was on this charge that seventeen-year-old Alice Thompson ran from her residence in the village, "raised the fallen flag and rallied the wavering regiment" of Confederate troops. Henry, *Forrest*, 130.

43. OR, XXIII, Pt. I, 120.

44. Henry, *Forrest*, 130.

45. OR, XXIII, Pt. I, 121n.

46. Report of Colonel William L. Utley, OR, XVIII, Pt. I, 109.

47. OR, XXIII, Pt. I, 75, 84, 91, 119. A Shelbyville reporter said, probably erroneously, that 2,600 prisoners from Coburn's command passed through his city on March 9. *Fayetteville Observer*, 19 March 1863.

48. OR, XXIII, Pt. II, 579.

49. A Memphis correspondent wrote an article on the effectiveness of cavalry and mounted infantry activities in Tennessee. His article directed praise at recent Northern activities, which showed Rosecrans's army developing tactics similar to those used so successfully by the Confederate forces. *Memphis Bulletin*, 16 May 1863.

50. OR, XXIII, Pt. I, 74.

51. Dr. John A. Wyeth was quite critical of Van Dorn for his handling of the battle at Thompson's Station. Of course Wyeth was writing in favor of Forrest's role, but his arguments do stand up. "General Van Dorn knew almost exactly the strength of his adversary the night before the engagement," said the doctor, "and he had troops in abundance to have interposed in Coburn's rear enough cavalry to have prevented this retreat and insured the capture of all the enemy's wagons, artillery, and practically all his force." Wyeth, *Forrest*, 162–63.

THE UNION SIDE OF
THOMPSON'S STATION

William M. Anderson

T he new year began quietly in the western theatre following the Union victory at Stones River at the close of 1862. Major General William Rosecrans, in command of the Army of the Cumberland, had halted his pursuit of the Confederates when his army occupied Murfreesboro.

As was often the case during the Civil War, Rosecrans's army was as exhausted and disorganized in victory as was the enemy in defeat. The Army of the Cumberland needed recruits to replace heavy casualties suffered at Stones River; its supply lines had been seriously disrupted and Rosecrans determinedly sought cavalry strength to match the Confederates. Amidst refitting, foraging, and healing, Rosecrans was being pressed by General in Chief Henry Halleck to begin an offensive. In early March, several Union armies began probing General Braxton Bragg's lines to determine his strength. The Confederates were launching similar tests.[1]

Rosecrans ordered Brigadier General Charles C. Gilbert, commander at Franklin, to reconnoiter the Columbia Pike as far south as Spring Hill. His advance was also to serve as a foraging expedition. Gilbert selected Colonel John Coburn's brigade to execute his mission. Coburn's brigade, consisting of the Nineteenth Michigan, Twenty-second Wisconsin, and the Thirty-third and Eighty-fifth Indiana Infantry Regiments, moved some eighteen miles from Brentwood to Franklin on March 2, 1863.[2]

Colonel Coburn was a native of Indianapolis and entered the military service as the first commander of the Thirty-third Indiana Infantry Regiment. He was a graduate of Wabash College and had spent a number of years in public service. Following the war, Coburn distinguished himself in Congress during four consecutive terms. Among other measures, his was a leading force in promoting the publication of the *Official Records*.[3]

His regimental commanders included Colonel Henry C. Gilbert, Nineteenth Michigan; Colonel James P. Baird, Eighty-fifth Indiana; Lieutenant Colonel James M. Henderson, Thirty-third Indiana; and Colonel William L. Utley, Twenty-second Wisconsin. Like most volunteer officers in the Civil War, Coburn and his regimental commanders were short on military experience. Coburn, Baird, and Gilbert had all been members of the legal profession prior to the war. "Utley was a veteran of political wars only." He had served as a state senator and adjutant-general prior to the war. Jim Henderson was teaching at the Morton Academy in Princeton, Indiana, when the hostilities began.[4]

The regiments they commanded were no different. Only the Thirty-third Indiana had experienced combat previously, and that was limited to a minor engagement at Wild Cat, Kentucky. The rest would be initiated shortly.

Henderson, at 26, was the youngest among Coburn's subordinates; Utley was the senior, having reached his 48th birthday at the time of Thompson's Station.

None would see the war to its end. Yet all but Gilbert would survive it. He was mortally wounded while leading his regiment in a charge during the Battle of Resaca in May, 1864. When Coburn's term expired in 1864, he returned to political life. Both Baird and Henderson resigned due to disability during the same year. Utley, too, ended his military service in 1864, following a bitter quarrel with his second in command, Lieutenant Colonel Edward Bloodgood.

Coburn's task force, as organized at Franklin, included his own brigade, the 124th Ohio Infantry Regiment, the Eighteenth Ohio Battery and cavalry detachments from the Ninth Pennsylvania, Fourth Kentucky, and Second Michigan. He reported his strength at 2,837.[5]

Early on the morning of March 4, Coburn's force marched out of Franklin with the Second Michigan Cavalry leading, followed by the Thirty-third Indiana, Colonel Coburn, staff and body guard, three guns of the Eighteenth Ohio Battery, the Twenty-second Wisconsin, Nineteenth Michigan, Eighty-fifth Indiana, the remainder of the battery, the wagon train and the 124th Ohio as wagon guard.[6]

Just prior to noon, Coburn's command met its first resistance as skirmishers clashed with Confederate cavalry four miles out of Franklin.[7] The rebel forces were those of General Earl Van Dorn's army then assembling at Spring Hill. Van Dorn's advance guard was also performing a reconnaissance mission. Coburn's task force began to deploy with infantry units as skirmishers and the Eighteenth Ohio, consisting of six pieces, getting into position. The Thirty-third Indiana and the Twenty-second Wisconsin filed off to the right of the pike, while the 124th Ohio and the Nineteenth Michigan came abreast on the east side of the road.[8] The artillery answered the rebel fire; and after a brief exchange, the Confederates broke contact and fell back to the next ridgeline. Coburn acted promptly to apprise General Gilbert of his situation while the brigade remained in position awaiting further instructions. The messenger returned with orders to proceed. Gilbert did, however, authorize Coburn to detach his forage elements. Colonel Coburn took advantage of the opportunity and released half of his wagons to the rear.[9]

Coburn's force resumed the march, pushing Confederate pickets for an additional two miles. Informed that a formidable cavalry force was threatening his left flank on the Lewisburg Road, Coburn ordered his command to halt, then to fall back in order to secure his flanks. The Union forces camped on ground previously held by Van Dorn's advance.

Further information of the supposed threat ahead became more apparent when two Negro youths entered the Union line and reported that Van Dorn's entire command was massed just south of Thompson's station. Coburn dispatched the Negro boys to General Gilbert's headquarters and asked "What shall we do?"[10] Headquarters was silent.

Van Dorn's biographer, along with General Gilbert, was convinced that Coburn was given considerable latitude in the execution of his orders. In a general sense that may well have been the case; yet, for certain, one option that Coburn did not feel at liberty to exercise was to retreat.[11] Coburn had filled thirty-nine wagons with forage, made contact with a force he could not handle, and he kept on going.

The battle tally for the first day of the engagement showed the Federals getting the best of it, inflicting some ten rebel casualties while suffering only three wounded among its ranks; two members of the Ninth Pennsylvania Cavalry and a corporal in Company F, Nineteenth Michigan Infantry. In addition, the Union artillery would be less one gun as one of the Rodmans was down with a broken axle.[12] Pickets posted, half-asleep Yankees waited for tomorrow.

The morning of March 5 broke cold and "Nary reb was seen."[13] With the 124th Ohio guarding the ammunition train, Coburn's force marched south in search of the enemy. The anticipation was short, for after marching about four more miles, the rebels were met in force. With a Confederate battery laid in on the pike, Coburn's lead infantry regiment, the Twenty-second Wisconsin, received the first round and it sent them digging for cover. "It was so near that the whole regiment involuntarily crouched to the earth, the command was immediately 'over the fence and lie down!' and that command was obeyed as quickly as any command ever was."[14]

Coburn ordered his brigade into action with the Nineteenth Michigan sent to the east side of the pike to anchor the left Hank, the Twenty-second Wisconsin abreast and also on the left, the Thirty-third Indiana deployed across the road from the Badger regiment, and the Eighty-fifth Indiana in line holding the extreme right.[15]

Coburn's infantry occupied a range of hills overlooking Thompson's Station from the north with the village, nestled midway in the valley floor below, separating the two armies. Coburn had seized the high ground flanking either side of a narrow gap through which passed the Central Alabama Railroad and the Columbia Turnpike before descending to the valley below. The Union commander positioned two guns of Captain Charles C. Aleshire's Eighteenth Ohio Battery right of the pike and alongside the Thirty-third Indiana, while the other section got into action just off the roadbed to the left occupying a slight rise. The Union cavalry were drawn up in the rear of the Nineteenth Michigan and less than a half-mile back on the pike, Coburn had located his trains under guard of the 124th Ohio Infantry.[16]

Although Coburn's information about the disposition of Confederate troops was incomplete, he was aware that the rebels held the commanding terrain on the south side of the valley to his front and that their artillery located along the pike and in the rear of Thompson's Station had found the range. Coburn unknowingly was cooperating with Van Dorn's plan.[17]

The Union commander first sent three companies of the Thirty-third Indiana forward to drive out rebel sharpshooters who had occupied Thompson's Station. The Hoosiers succeeded and Coburn next sought to remove a much greater threat by silencing the battery to his right front. Coburn again looked to his fellow Indianans as he ordered forward the rest of the Thirty-third and the Eighty-fifth Indiana. The Federals filed off their hill, formed into separate columns, and went for the guns. While opposing batteries exchanged fire, the Union offensive pushed forward through "an iron hail." The Hoosiers advanced to within a short distance of the depot when they were suddenly met with intense fire delivered point-blank from behind a stone wall. Colonel J. W. Whitfield's brigade had remained concealed behind the wall until the advancing forces were at close range. The advance of the Indiana regiments was stopped and thrown back.[18]

The retreating Yankees fell back toward their first position with Whitfield's and Brigadier General Frank Armstrong's brigades applying the pressure of a determined counterattack. Reaching the crest of the hill, they rallied to defend.

Across the pike, too, the Union position was being seriously threatened. The Nineteenth Michigan and Twenty-second Wisconsin had first gone into position on the reverse slope of a cedar-crowned hill mass east of the road. Here they had sought shelter from Confederate artillery fire as both regiments assembled behind a stone fence. During the early hours of the engagement, Coburn had assigned these regiments a reserve role. The rebels quickly jeopardized this position when Brigadier General Nathan B. Forrest, commanding the Confederate right, sent two guns of Freeman's Battery to occupy a hill about a half mile southeast and flanking the Union left.[19] The first round found its mark, ploughing up dirt among the ranks of E Company, Nineteenth Michigan. With his flank exposed, Colonel Gilbert, commanding the Nineteenth, ordered his regiment to march to the right and rear and occupy a position under the guns of the Eighteenth Ohio Battery. To meet this new artillery threat, the Union battery turned its guns to face the foe and the duel continued. Thus situated, both infantry regiments were immediately under the path of the artillery projectiles and the guns were "sending their demoniac-sounding missiles... so close to our ears that all those unaccustomed to such sounds would dodge their heads and involuntarily shrink closer to the stone wall as they went by."[20]

These were untried farm boys and there is little doubt that the Twenty-second Wisconsin, including its commander, Colonel Utley, was tense. They now held the Union left, they were pinned down by artillery fire, and they had been alerted that the Rebs were flanking them with a large force. They waited, searching the cedars at the top of the hill and suddenly "smoke... betrayed the enemy and a volley from almost every gun in the regiment greeted them."[21] The fire was returned, the regiment broke and in confusion reassembled behind the Nineteenth Michigan and near the original gun position of the Eighteenth Ohio Battery. Soon this position, too, became untenable as the rebels again threatened the left flank. The Nineteenth Michigan moved to the right, taking up a new position near the roadbed while the Wisconsin regiment withdrew to establish a position behind the railroad embankment.[22]

Now the Confederates pushed toward the turnpike and, if not denied, would soon divide Coburn's command. Again, the Twenty-second or at least part of it would move and here the chain of command would break down. Utley, the commander, was at the left of his regiment; Lieutenant Colonel Bloodgood, second in command, rode with the right. It is apparent that up until this point during the battle, Utley had issued orders through Lieutenant Colonel Bloodgood rather than assuming personal direction. Now in crisis, Bloodgood ordered the regiment up onto the pike, supposedly under brigade orders to extend the Union left; Utley interpreted the movement as a rout. With the enemy in their midst and unable to hear above the roar of battle, the regiment responded to two commanders; Company A and the larger part of D left the field while the remainder heard Utley's command to halt.[23]

This was only the beginning, for Aleshire's gun section of the Ohio Eighteenth posted east of the road had already withdrawn. Bloodgood and his part of the Twenty-second got out onto the road in time to meet the rest of the artillery also pulling back. Soon all of the cavalry detachments were detaching themselves and, along with the 124th Ohio that escorted the ammunition, began a self-styled retreat toward Franklin. Within minutes, Coburn's effective strength was reduced by more than 1,000 men and his ability to withdraw had been forfeited.[24]

Under heavy pressure the Nineteenth Michigan stumbled across the road in time to support the repulse of another Confederate thrust at the Union right. The line held, but now the greatest threat was being concentrated on the left, Hank and Coburn began reorganizing his defense. The Eighty-fifth Indiana was ordered to front facing the east as Coburn began organizing his new line parallel to the railroad. He brought the Nineteenth Michigan alongside and to the right of the Eighty-fifth. The Thirty-third Indiana remained the only regiment facing south as its left joined the Nineteenth Michigan on the right at a 45° angle to the main line. The Twenty-second Wisconsin was drawn up on the extreme left next to the Eighty-fifth Indiana.[25]

Now the Union position was severely tested. The Nineteenth Michigan was hotly engaged as the rebels "charged right in among us but our company had fixed bayonets and was determined to hold the hill."[26] "The brigade met several charges head-on, counter-charged, forcing them down the hill faster than they came up."[27] The fighting became desperate for "in one of the these charges a rebel fired at [a member of the Nineteenth Michigan], then threw down his gun and up with his hands; but the [Union soldier] said it was too late and bayonetted him."[28] Still the Confederates could not be discouraged. Stubborn resistance soon became hopeless.

Coburn's brigade began to break contact and started retreating, hoping to organize a stronger position on higher ground to the west. Coburn was flanked; and in a few moments, the rebels were also posted to the rear. With ammunition exhausted and after nearly five hours of sustained combat, Coburn's brigade surrendered.

Coburn's losses included forty-eight killed, 247 wounded, and 1,151 captured or missing. The Nineteenth Michigan and Thirty-third Indiana shared the infamous honor of recording the highest number of unit casualties. Those killed and wounded in the two regiments totaled 213. Van Dorn reported his casualties at 357.[29]

Following Thompson's Station, there was a sustained effort to fix the blame for defeat. Among infantry officers and privates, the consensus was clear: the fault lay with the supporting cavalry, the artillery, and Bloodgood's portion of the Twenty-second Wisconsin for cowardly retreating in the face of the enemy. No doubt, Coburn seriously missed these elements during the critical point of the battle; however, the die had been cast by others many hours earlier.

John Coburn clearly went beyond what he must have understood was the prerogative of a reconnaissance mission. His greatest error was to allow his command to become engaged in a pitched battle. Yet criticism of Coburn must be somewhat tempered by considering the failures of his commander, General Gilbert. Gilbert must be faulted for indecisiveness that set the stage for Coburn's dilemma. Seemingly, he had two alternatives: either clearly remind Coburn of his mission or support him. He failed to do either. Ironically, Gilbert had been under investigation for failure to support General Alexander McCook's Corps at the Battle of Perryville and on March 4, 1863, his commission expired; he was not reappointed.[30]

The outcome of the engagement at Thompson's Station had little impact on later military operations in the western theatre. It did, however, supply Rosecrans with information regarding the enemy's strength, although the price for obtaining it was high. Significantly, from Rosecrans's perspective, it served to confirm his grave concern over the superiority of Confederate cavalry. And for Coburn and his brigade, it meant their induction into the realities of war.

ᎶᏲᏦᏌᎤ

This article first appeared in the Winter 1970–1971 issue of the *Tennessee Historical Quarterly*.

1. This article also references Robert J. Hartje, "The Gray Dragoon Wins His Final Victory," included as the preceding chapter in this volume. William M. Lamers, *The Edge of Glory: A Bibliography of General William S. Rosecrans, U.S.A.* (New York, 1961), 244–56.

2. *The War of the Rebellion: A Compilation of the Official Records of the Union and Confederate Armies* (69 vols, and index; Washington, 1880–1901), Ser. 1, XXIII, Part I, 77, 85. (Hereinafter cited as OR. All references are to Series I.)

3. George Irving Reed (ed.), *The Encyclopedia of Biography of Indiana* (Chicago, 1899), III, 62–66.

4. Ibid., 63. See also Henry C. Bradsby, *History of Vigo County, Indiana, With Biographical Selections* (Chicago, 1891), 337; *American Biographical History of Eminent and Self Made Men* (Michigan Volume) (Cincinnati, 1878), 40; Frank L. Byrne (ed.), *The View from Headquarters: Civil War Letters of Harvey Reid* (Madison, 1965), xii; and Gil R. Stormont, *History of Gibson County, Indiana: Her People, Industries and Institutions* (Indianapolis, 1914), 211.

5. OR, XXIII, Pt. I, 86. Robert Hartje qualified this figure indicating that Generals Rosecrans and Baird differed with Coburn in reporting his strength at 1,845. Robert G. Hartje, *Van*

Dom: The Life and Times of a Confederate General (Nashville, 1967), 279. A closer examination of Baird's report indicates that the 1,845 men to whom he referred were only those representing the four infantry regiments of Coburn's brigade and that the Union force also included about "600 mounted men" from several cavalry regiments, the 124th Ohio and the Eighteenth Ohio Battery. OR, XXIII, Pt. I, 106. Lieutenant Colonel James Picklands, commanding the 124th Ohio, reported his strength at approximately 400. OR, XXIII, Pt. I, 106. Excluding the artillery, the composite of these troop strengths closely approximates the figure reported by Coburn. Since it is apparent that Rosecrans based his figure on Baird's report, it is safe to assume that he, like Robert Hartje, perpetuated the same oversight. OR, XXIII, Pt. I, 74. See also Charles P. Lincoln, "Engagement at Thompson Station, Tennessee," Military Order of the Loyal Legion of the United States, Commandery of the District of Columbia (1893).

6. Byrne, *The View from Headquarters*, 29–30. Hartje described the weather as "cool and favorable" and that "this was just another reconnaissance to them, and most of the men were happy to get away from routine garrison life for a few days." Hartje, *Van Dorn*, 280. Since Hartje's references are void of soldiers' accounts, it is difficult to understand his ability to recapture the attitude of the Union ranks. Coburn agreed that the weather was "cool and favorable;" yet, for Private Simon B. Shore, Company I, Thirty-third Indiana, 4 March 1863, was "cloudy... cold and... snowing." Simon B. Shore Diary, 4 March 1863, located in the Indiana State Historical Library, Indianapolis, Indiana. Corporal Harvey Reid, Twenty-second Wisconsin, described 4 March as "freezing cold." Byrne, *The View from Headquarters*, 29. And for a private soldier in the Eighty-fifth Indiana, "the morning [was] very cold snowing." Josiah M. Ephlin diary, 4 March 1863, located in Smith Library, Indianapolis, Indiana.

7. Hartje has concluded that both forces arrived at Thompson's Station "by midmorning" on 4 March 1863, and the action commenced there. Hartje, *Van Dorn*, 280. The distance between Franklin and Thompson's Station is nine miles. Every source examined states that Coburn's force first engaged the Confederates about four or five miles south of Franklin. Accordingly, Coburn did not reach Thompson's Station until the following day. See Colonel Coburn's Report, OR, XXIII, Pt. I, 86; Colonel James Henderson's Report, OR, XXIII, Pt. I, 100; Lieutenant Colonel Edward Bloodgood's Report, OR, XXIII, Pt. I, 111; William H. Mcintosh, "History of the Twenty-second Wisconsin Volunteers," 21. (Unpublished manuscript in Wisconsin Historical Society Library, Madison); Quartermaster Sergeant John A. Wilkins' letter located in Indiana Historical Society Library, Indianapolis, and others.

8. OR, XXIII, Pt. I, 86

9. Ibid., 86. Hartje's account indicates that Coburn initiated a feint to cover the release of the trains and that this operation met Confederate resistance to the point of only permitting thirty-nine wagons to escape. Hartje, *Van Dorn*, 282. Coburn in his report makes no reference to this difficulty, OR, XXIII, Pt. I, 86. Assistant Adjutant General Hamlet B. Adams explains that the wagons left with Coburn were loaded with baggage. Ibid., 94. Like Coburn and Adams,

the acting Assistant Quartermaster in charge of the wagons makes no mention of enemy pressure causing the release of the trains to be jeopardized. He, too, notes that the forty wagons that remained with Coburn's command "were loaded with other camp equipage and some ammunition." Ibid., 97. Colonel John P. Baird, commanding the Eighty-fifth Indiana and charged with guarding the trains, reported that his regiment "took no part in the skirmish of that day further than to watch the train." Ibid.,102.

10. Hartje, *Van Dorn*, 279; OR, XXIII, Pt. I, 77, 86–87.

11. OR, XXIII, Pt. I, 94, 98.

12. Ibid., 86, 97.

13. Byrne, *The View From Headquarters*, 32.

14. Ibid., 33.

15. OR, XXIII, Pt. I, 86, 104.

16. Ibid., 87, 88, 106, 107.

17. Ibid., 87, 116. See also John R. McBride, *History of the Thirty-Third Indiana Veteran Voluntary Infantry* (Indianapolis, 1900), 91. 18 OR, XXIII, Pt. I, 88, 94, 99, 101, 102. See also Wilkins letter, 7 March 1863 in McBride, *Thirty-Third Indiana*, 76.

19. OR, XXIII, Pt. I, 88, 104, 107, 112. See also Lincoln, "Thompson's Station," 7–8 and Byrne, *The View from Headquarters*, 33

20. Byrne, *The View From Headquarters*, 34.

21. Ibid.

22. Lincoln, "Thompson's Station," 9; Franklin G. Rice, *Diary of 19th Michigan Volunteer Infantry During Their Three Years Service in the War of Rebellion* (n.d.), 4; OR, XXIII, Pt. I, 88, 104, 107.

23. OR, XXIII, Pt. I, 107–108, 112. See also Byrne, *The View from Headquarters*, 36, 37.

24. OR, XXIII, Pt. I, 81–82, 89, 95, 99–100, 105, 108, 114.

25. Ibid., 89, 103, 104.

26. John S. Griffis's Letter, 11 April 1863, Michigan Historical Collections Ann Arbor. See also Lincoln, "Thompson's Station," 11.

27. Rice, *Diary*, 5.

28. Ibid.

29. OR, XXIII, Pt. 1, 75, 91, 119.

30. Ezra J. Warner, *Generals in Blue: Lives of the Union Commanders* (Baton Rouge, 1964), 174.

LIGHTNING AND RAIN IN MIDDLE TENNESSEE:

The Tullahoma Campaign of June–July 1863

⟨⟨⟨⟩⟩⟩

Robert S. Brandt

By the admirable disposition of our forces, we have gained all the fruits of a glorious victory with little loss. At every point the enemy has been surprised, and
in his irregular flight he has abandoned guns, camp and garrison equipage in
great quantities. Demoralized and beaten, he has fallen back beyond the Tennessee River: Middle Tennessee is freed from the marauding hordes by which it
has been overrun, and the Stars and Stripes now wave over it

Report of Brigadier General Richard W Johnson, Commanding,
Second Division, XX Corps, Army of the Cumberland, July 6, 1863.

Confederate Brigadier General Bushrod R. Johnson was startled by the news.
Federal troops were only a few miles away on the Murfreesboro-Manchester
Road at Hoovers Gap, a passage through the hills midway between the two
Middle Tennessee towns. Two boys, wet and covered with mud from hard riding, arrived
with the report at Johnson's brigade headquarters on the Garrison Fork of the Duck River.
Soon the report was confirmed by two cavalrymen who had struggled through the June
rain from the gap, four miles or so from Johnson's camp near the tiny village of Fairfield.[1]

Before long the nearby brigade commanded by a Tennessean, Brigadier General
William B. Bate, was ordered to the gap, near the crossroad of Beech Grove. Bate's

Brigade, mostly men from Tennessee and Georgia, ran into killing rifle fire from the Federals lodged in the hills.[2] They were the two thousand well-armed Illinois and Indiana men of a Colonel John T. Wilder's mounted infantry brigade. Earlier that day, before dawn in fact, Wilder's brigade had left its camp near Murfreesboro on the point of huge Union force headed for Manchester. Wilder's men were surprised to find that the Confederates were not in their fortifications at the narrow south end of Hoovers Gap, so they used the entrenchments for cover to fight Bate's Southerners.[3] The rain that began when Wilder was about half way to Hoovers Gap continued, as it would for the next two weeks, transforming the Tennessee dirt roads into troughs of mud and rendering swollen streams impassable.[4]

The fighting at Hoovers Gap on the afternoon of June 24, 1863, signaled the beginning of what came to be called the Middle Tennessee, or Tullahoma, Campaign. With a minimum of fighting and a maximum of stealth, it took just eleven days for Union Major General William S. Rosecrans's Army of the Cumberland to maneuver the Confederate Army of Tennessee under General Braxton Bragg completely out of Middle Tennessee.

No preserved sites or heroic statuary mark this campaign, only a few randomly placed historical markers. The contemporaneous events at Gettysburg and Vicksburg stole the public's attention then and have ever since. Yet those rainy summer days in Tennessee were decisive to the outcome of the Civil War. The campaign opened the way for the North to control the pivotal rail junction of Chattanooga, gateway to the Deep South, and it set the stage for the Atlanta Campaign one year later.

From a purely military standpoint, the December 31, 1862–January 2, 1863, Battle of Stones River at Murfreesboro was essentially a draw: Braton Bragg, the unpopular Confederate commander, feared that his army was about to be overwhelmed, so he ordered a retreat.[5] The Confederacy's principal Western Theater army moved about thirty miles south and settled along the Duck River where the Highland Rim rises above the Central Basin. Bragg's army remained there for the first six months of 1863, facing Rosecrans's larger Union army based at Murfreesboro. Except for considerable cavalry skirmishing, most of which proved militarily insignificant, the two armies remained inactive.

Bragg's January retreat from Murfreesboro was haphazard and unplanned as was the placement of his two infantry corps; they assumed their positions by accident, not by design. Lieutenant General Leonidas Polk's Corps located on the north bank of Duck River at Shelbyville. Lieutenant General William J. Hardee's Corps settled twenty miles southeast at Tullahoma, a rail junction where the branch line to Manchester and McMinnville joined the main line of the Nashville & Chattanooga Railroad.[6] In April, Hardee moved his command north into the Duck River Valley at Wartrace, parallel to Polk's Corps which was just to the west.[7]

In March, Bragg divided his large, reinforced cavalry command into two corps, one under Major General Earl Van Dorn, the other under Major General Joseph Wheeler.[8] Van Dorn, who had recently arrived from Mississippi, operated on the Confederate left out of Columbia. Wheeler operated on the right with McMinnville as his base. In all, the Confederate line extended for about a hundred miles in a large crescent across southern Middle Tennessee.

South of Murfreesboro a range of rugged, wooded hills separates the watersheds of the Cumberland and Tennessee rivers. The hills played a strategic role in the successful Union offensive. Gaps through the hills provided passage south to the Duck River valley and onto the Highland Rim that rises above it. On the east, the Murfreesboro-Manchester Road passed through Hoovers Gap, a three mile long passage through the high hills. Six miles west a road went over Liberty Gap to Bell Buckle and Wartrace. Two miles west of Liberty Gap, the Nashville & Chattanooga Railroad crossed a low point in the hills. Three miles southwest of the railroad gap, the Murfreesboro-Shelbyville Turnpike passed over Guys Gap.[9] West of the turnpike the hills gave way to largely open Central Basin farm country. An army attacking Bragg's Duck River infantry concentrations would have to pass through these gaps or take to the open country northwest of Shelbyville. Polk defended heavily fortified Shelbyville; Hardee defended the gaps.

With six months to recuperate from the violence at Stones River in a richly endowed land, sitting on a rail link back to the base at Chattanooga and to the Deep South, and increased to its greatest number yet through conscription and reinforcement, Braxton Bragg's Army of Tennessee should have been in a strong position to defend against an advance by Rosecrans's forces. But the Confederacy squandered this longest period of inactivity of any major army during the Civil War.

Bragg himself was the most significant of several factors conspiring to weaken the Confederate position along the Duck River. The forty-six year old West Point-educated Louisiana planter had led the army on his failed Kentucky invasion from Chattanooga the previous summer. Kentuckians did not flock to the secessionist cause, and Bragg missed several opportunities to inflict serious damage on the divided, disorganized Federals. After fighting to a standoff at Perryville in October, Bragg's ragged, hungry, and sick troops made a circuitous, demoralizing march back to Tennessee, settling at Murfrecsboro in November 1862.

The January 1863 withdrawal from the field at Stones River mirrored the Kentucky experience the previous October—first an acclaimed victory, then a retreat.

Bragg was already unpopular, but after Stones River, morale plummeted. Finding himself vilified in the Southern press, Bragg turned on his subordinate generals, blaming them for his unpopularity.[10] From then on he was in constant conflict with them, some of whom, most notably Polk, actively sought his removal.[11] Bragg proved to be his own worst enemy though. In a move that was not just unusual but bizarre, he sought a vote of confidence from subordinate generals, a vote Bragg unanimously lost.[12]

In late January, President Jefferson Davis dispatched General Joseph E. Johnston on an ill-defined mission to Middle Tennessee to investigate the discontent with Bragg. Davis had recently named the Virginian to command all forces in the west, but his role was vague and his authority uncertain.[13] Davis's correspondence to Johnston as he made his way to Middle Tennessee proved prophetic: "[T]hough my confidence in General Bragg is unshaken, it cannot be doubted that if he is distrusted by his officers and troops, a disaster may result which, but for that cause, would have been avoided."[14] Perhaps seeking to avoid the command himself, Johnston reported favorably to Richmond. Johnston left Middle Tennessee; Bragg remained in command.[15]

The discord continued. Johnston returned to Middle Tennessee in March with orders to relieve Bragg.[16] Johnston stayed with the Army of Tennessee until May, but he declined to take command.[17] Again, Bragg remained. Johnston not only failed to stabilize the command; the presence of this general senior to Bragg added to the leadership void.[18]

Bragg's own mental and physical health was not good. Lieutenant Colonel James Arthur Fremantle, a visiting British army officer, stayed with the Army of Tennessee during his 1863 sojourn through the Confederacy. In his diary Fremantle described Bragg in late May as "the least imposing of the Confederate generals. He is very thin. He stoops, and has a sickly, cadaverous, haggard appearance."[19]

During the Union advance, Hardee confided to his fellow corps commander Polk his fear for the army due to Bragg's "enfeebled state of health."[20] Bragg himself confessed to a clergyman that he was "utterly broken down."[21] And the troubles with the other generals continued to such an extent that by May there was a near total breakdown in communication.

One result of this turmoil and sickness was an absence of military planning. The storm clouds were gathering to the north, that was no secret, but about the only Confederate military plan was a vague proposal to move the two infantry corps around the Duck River valley depending on the route of the inevitable Union assault.[22]

Other factors contributed to the weakness of the Army of Tennessee as well. One was the constant struggle for food.[23] The Middle Tennessee land along the Duck River and its tributaries was rich and productive, described by the visiting Fremantle as "beautiful country, green, undulating, full of magnificent trees, principally beeches, and the scenery was by far the finest I had seen in America as yet."[24] Hardee, the Confederate general, described the place as "beautiful and rich in pastures."[25] But the Duck River area could not supply such a large number of men, and scarce resources were spent ranging as far away as middle Alabama in search of subsistence.[26] The plentiful stores in Atlanta, some of which were hauled south out of Middle Tennessee, were reserved for the army in Virginia; the army in Tennessee had to feed itself.[27]

The departure of nearly eleven thousand troops from the Confederate Duck River line within a month of Rosecrans's June advance also weakened the army. Hardee lost six thousand men and one of his division commanders when Major General John C. Breckenridge and most of his division went to Mississippi in late May.[28] Significantly, Breckenridge's division provided strength to the Confederate's right flank on the east of the front. The cavalry on the left flank was reduced by 2,500 troopers when they were sent to Mississippi.[29] Then over on the right flank, on the eve of Rosecrans's June attack, the flashy, impatient Brigadier General John Hunt Morgan took 2,480 valuable partisans on his wasteful raid north of the Ohio River.[30]

The Army of Tennessee's position was in truth something of a trap, a fact that had been pointed out to both Bragg and President Davis.[31] The Federals at Murfreesboro had several good options for out-flanking the Confederates concentrated along the Duck River. If the Confederate position was strong, it was strong only against a frontal attack on fortified Shelbyville or on well defended gaps. But the gaps were not even well defended.

By late June only the one Kentucky cavalry regiment protected Hoovers Gap on the east.[32] The nearest infantry brigades, Johnston's and Bate's, were camped four miles away near Fairfield. They were part of newly promoted Major General A. P. Stewart's small, recently thrown together division of Hardee's Corps. The route from Murfreesboro to Manchester, protected by Breckenridge's Division until late May, was thus largely undefended.[33] Six miles west of Hoovers Gap, only two Arkansas regiments of Major General Patrick Cleburne's Division protected Liberty Gap.[34] A small picket was stationed at the railroad gap just to the west.[35] By June, the evidence of the lack of planning for the inevitable Union advance would have been apparent to anyone who bothered to notice.

Misuse of cavalry seemed endemic to the Army of Tennessee through-out the war and the first half of 1863 was no exception.[36] Morgan's departure weakened the right flank, then Wheeler weakened it even further by moving west. With the Union advance imminent, Bragg ordered him to bring in his over-extended right flank Rebel cavalry to protect Hardee's positions, including Hoovers Gap. Instead the twenty-six year old major general moved most of his mounted men in front of Shelbyville.[37] This left hardly any cavalry to provide reconnaissance on the Confederate right or to cover the rear.

No such ineptness and chaos existed beyond the ridges to the north. The methodical Rosecrans, an Ohio engineer who finished West Point five years after his Confederate counterpart, had assumed command of the Army of the Cumberland the previous October. He proved to be a brilliant planner and meticulous logistical organizer. By June 1863, he had 96,010 troops compared to Bragg's 46,260.[38] Perhaps as important was the vast quantity of supplies and animals. His army amassed an enormous amount of food and had a total of 43,023 horses and mules at its disposal.[39] Rosecrans had a secure supply line, the railroad back to Nashville and Louisville.

Rosecrans strengthened and reorganized his cavalry under Major General David S. Stanley.[40] Colonel Wilder, who was to lead the advance on Hoovers Gap, conceived the idea to mount his infantry brigade. The young Indiana industrialist realized the benefit of speed after ineffectively chasing Morgan's rebel raiders around the Kentucky-Tennessee border on foot in December, 1862. Rosecrans authorized Wilder to obtain the necessary horses from the Middle Tennessee countryside. Needing quick fire power to match his quick movement, Wilder outfitted the brigade with the new Spencer seven-shot repeating rifles, financing the purchase of the repeaters himself through banks back in Indiana. Wilder had no pre-war military experience, but he proved to be one of the most effective Union officers in the west.[41]

As was his custom, President Abraham Lincoln, as well as his Washington bound General-in-Chief, Henry W. Halleck, constantly pressed Rosecrans to move against Bragg, partially out of fear that Bragg would send significant reinforcements to Vicksburg. At times seeming insolent, Rosecrans let Lincoln and Halleck know that he would move when he was good and ready. "Dispatch received. I will attend to it," Rosecrans tersely replied to Lincoln's prodding in late May.[42]

By late June Rosecrans was ready. His basic plan was simple: he would make Bragg think the attack was on the west toward Shelbyville, then attack the Confederates on the east through Hoovers Gap toward Manchester. Rosecrans wanted to destroy the railroad bridge across the Elk River in the Confederate rear and force the Army of Tennessee into a fight with its line of communication, food, ammunition, reinforcements, and retreat severed. At the very least, the Union commander hoped to force Bragg's army to retreat out of Middle Tennessee.[43] To accomplish this, surprise was essential; Rosecrans kept his plan largely to himself.[44]

It was equally essential to deceive the Confederates.[45] If they believed the offensive was coming on the west of the front, Polk's Corps would stay put at Shelbyville.

If the Southerners perceived a substantial threat to Liberty Gap, Cleburne's well-respected division of Hardee's Corps would move quickly to defend that gap.[46]

Rosecrans ordered a cavalry force under Brigadier General Robert D. Mitchell to advance through the open country as if to attack Shelbyville.[47] To further deceive the Southerners, Rosecrans devised another advance he hoped they would see as a feint, further strengthening their belief that the principal attack would be on the west. On the far east of the front, he would send Major General Thomas L. Crittenden with his XXI Corps and some cavalry in the general direction of McMinnville.[48]

To occupy Cleburne's veterans in the Wartrace-Bell Buckle area, Major General Alexander McCook's XX Corps was to attack Liberty Gap and the railroad gap, but with no intention to force the gaps. Rather, McCook was to withdraw and move east to Hoovers Gap where the main attack was to occur.[49] For that attack, Rosecrans selected his largest corps, the XIV, the workhorse of the Army of the Cumberland. It was commanded by the future "Rock of Chickamauga," Major General George H. Thomas, a Virginian who had remained in the Union army.[50] Thomas would push on to Manchester where eventually most of the army would gather to pursue its options: attack the Confederates, get behind them, or perhaps both.[51]

The Federal forward movement actually began before Rosecrans even explained his plan to his five corps commanders. On June 23, Mitchell's cavalry moved on Confederate outposts in the open country northwest of Shelbyville near the villages of Rover and Unionville, skirmishing that day and the next.[52] To deceive the Confederates into believing this was the main infantry attack on Shelbyville, the blue clad troopers were instructed to fill the countryside with campfires.[53]

At his Murfreesboro headquarters on the night of June 23, Rosecrans met with his corps commanders and gave them their assignments for the next day.[54] Wilder moved out first on the 24th, followed by the rest of Major General Joseph J. Reynolds's Fourth Division of Thomas's Corps.[55]

The Kentucky troopers that Wilder's mounted men ran out of Hoovers Gap alerted the Confederate infantry near Fairfield.[56] By the time Bate's Brigade moved up, Wilder's men were in the unoccupied rebel fortifications. With the superior fire power of the repeating rifles and Captain Eli Lilly's artillery battery, Wilder's Brigade held off the two brigades of Stewart's Division, Hardee's Corps.[57] By nightfall, Thomas's other units relieved the mounted brigade. When Thomas himself came up, he complimented Wilder: "You have saved the lives of a thousand men by your gallant conduct today. I didn't expect to take the gap for three days."[58] From then on, Wilder's men enjoyed the nickname, "Lightning Brigade."

Union General McCook struck thinly defended Liberty Gap, driving back the two Arkansas regiments.[59] Crittenden's Federal Corps, minus one division left to garrison Murfreesboro, headed in the direction of McMinnville on its transparent feint.[60] Major General Gordon Granger's Reserve Corps, along with Mitchell's cavalry, remained south and west of Murfreesboro threatening Shelbyville.[61]

On June 25, the fighting between Thomas's men in blue and Hardee's men in gray continued at Hoovers Gap.[62] Over at Liberty Gap, Cleburne hurried reinforcements from Bell Buckle, just as the Union commander hoped he would. There the two sides skirmished on the 25th.[63] On the east of the front, as Crittenden's men struggled through the mud up to the Highland Rim,[64] they heard the cannonading coming from the direction of Hoovers Gap, but they did not encounter any real Confederate resistance.[65] Over on the west, Granger, with Mitchell's cavalry, remained south and west of Murfreesboro.[66]

June 26, 1863, proved to be an important day. Some of McCook's troops staged a major demonstration at Liberty Gap to deceive the Confederates into believing this was a major attack, while Major General Philip H. Sheridan's division slipped around Liberty Gap to follow Thomas through Hoovers Gap and on to Manchester.[67] By the end of the day, the Lightning Brigade was leading the rest of Reynolds's Division to Manchester, flanking Bragg's entire army.[68]

The Yankee deception worked. Polk's two divisions held at Shelbyville for the attack that never came. Bragg, believing that the main Union strength was attempting to force Liberty Gap, developed a hazy plan to send Polk's Corps through Guys Gap on the Murfreesboro-Shelbyville Turnpike to attack the Federal troops he thought were massed north of Liberty Gap. Polk protested, but Bragg ordered that move for the next morning.[69] Later on the 26th, Bragg had second thoughts, apparently learning for the first time of the massive advance toward Manchester on his right flank. His army was about to be trapped. Close to midnight, the wavering commander ordered his whole army to retreat south to fortified Tullahoma on the Highland Rim.[70]

The two rebel brigades at Hoovers Gap began to fall back southwest to Fairfield.[71] To keep up the impression of an attack on the main infantry concentrations in the Shelbyville-Wartrace area, two of Thomas's divisions chased the Confederates toward Fairfield and Wartrace rather than following Reynolds's Division straight to Manchester.[72]

Early on June 27, the Army of Tennessee began its retreat to Tullahoma. Too many troops crowded on too few roads, nearly impassable roads at that. One of Polk's divisions coming from Shelbyville and Cleburne's Division coming from Wartrace crowded together to cross a single bridge over the Duck River.[73] It was a miserable march. The men of Hardee's Corps were soaked to the bone and exhausted from three days of fighting at the gaps. Many were without shoes.[74] Although it was only a short distance, it took some of the Confederates two days in the quagmire to reach Tullahoma.[75]

As the last of Polk's Corps left Shelbyville on the morning of June 27, twenty-two miles due east at Manchester, Wilder's Brigade surprised and overcame the small Confederate garrison.[76] The rest of Reynolds's Division soon followed.[77] Thomas's two other divisions, which had been chasing the two brigades of Confederates away from Hoovers Gap, abandoned their pursuit at Fairfield, turned, and marched to Manchester.[78] By the end of the day, most of Thomas's Corps was at Manchester.[79]

North of Shelbyville, Brigadier General William T. Martin's Confederate cavalry division, together with some regiments of Brigadier General John A. Wharton's Division, all personally commanded by the young Wheeler, guarded Guys Gap and the approaches to the Duck River town.[80] Major General Stanley took over command of his spirited Union cavalry and forced Wheeler's horsemen out of the gap into Shelbyville's recently abandoned fortifications.[81] With the brigade of Colonel Robert H. G. Minty of Michigan leading the way, the Yankees routed the Southerners, capturing 591 of them and forcing others to take to the flooded river where many drowned. Wheeler and Martin barely escaped.[82]

Brigadier General Nathan Bedford Forrest had assumed command of Bragg's left flank cavalry in May after a physician killed Van Dorn at Spring Hill in a shooting that has remained a mystery ever since.[83] When the fighting started south of Murfreesboro, Forrest's troopers headed east from Columbia. Laboring through the mud, they did not arrive in the vicinity of Shelbyville until Wheeler's men were being routed on the 27th. Forrest got his men across the Duck and headed for Tullahoma.[84]

Four days of fighting in and around the range of rugged hills were over, and the front moved south to the Highland Rim. Rosecrans did not waste any time at Manchester. On June 28, he sent Wilder's fast moving brigade further south with instructions to destroy the railroad bridge over the Elk River near Estill Springs, severing Bragg's line to Chattanooga.[85] At the same time, the rest of Thomas's Corps moved toward Tullahoma, twelve miles from Manchester.

At Tullahoma, Bragg remained as indecisive as ever. He formed his troops into a battle line and waited.[86] Back across the Duck River Valley at Liberty Gap, the remainder of McCook's Corps repeated the move of Sheridan's Division two days earlier; the men withdrew from Liberty Gap and moved through Hoovers Gap on the road to Manchester.[87] On the east of the front, Crittenden's force crawled through knee deep mud.[88] His troops abandoned their McMinnville feint, turned south and headed for Manchester.[89]

June 29 saw a consolidation of Union forces around Manchester. Stanley brought his cavalry over from Shelbyville.[90] The Confederate cavalry moved through Tullahoma to the new front, and the two opposing cavalry forces skirmished on either side of the Elk River for the next three days.[91]

After crossing the Elk near Pelham with some difficulty, Wilder's men on horseback were prevented from destroying the railroad bridge by a Confederate brigade rushed south from Tullahoma. The mounted infantry struck the railroad at Dechard instead, but some of Forrest's men, who had quickly moved across the Tullahoma front, ran them off.[92] The Lighting Brigade's raid did not destroy that much railroad track, but when Bragg learned of it, he became concerned about his line of supply and retreat.[93]

Indecision reigned in the Confederates' Tullahoma camp on June 29. Bragg sought the counsel of his detested corps commanders, but the lieutenant generals disagreed among themselves. Polk, the Episcopal bishop, favored immediate retreat; Hardee, the former West Point commandant, thought retreat was premature. Nothing was decided.[94]

On June 30, Bragg learned that a mass of men in blue was advancing toward his army from Manchester and that another force was moving to his rear toward the Elk River.[95] He decided to abandon his precarious Tullahoma position and ordered the army southeast ten miles across the Elk River.[96] Hardee's two infantry divisions left first, followed that afternoon by Polk's two divisions. While the Yankees edged toward Tullahoma, the Confederate infantry crossed the Elk on the two bridges near Estill Springs.[97] Wheeler's cavalry screened this move, then crossed the Elk and burned the bridges.[98] With the Elk at flood, the Confederates appeared to be safe behind it, for a while at least. Bragg set up his headquarters on the railroad at Dechard a few miles south of the Elk.[99]

The next day, July 1, three Union infantry divisions and a body of cavalry cautiously approached Tullahoma. To their relief, they found the fortifications abandoned.[100] Rosecrans again wasted no time. On July 2, he advanced his army on a broad front toward the swollen Elk. Sheridan's Division somehow managed to get across the Elk that day.[101] Bragg's position was not secure for long. He ordered another retreat five miles further south to Cowan.[102]

Cowan sits at the foot of the Cumberland Mountain where the Nashville & Chattanooga Railroad passed through a long tunnel.[103] The western Appalachian escarpment offered the Confederates protection against another flanking movement. The exhausted Bragg had to decide whether to fight or flee over the mountains to the Tennessee Valley. He wavered, then again decided on retreat.[104] The army started struggling over the mountain late on July 2.[105] In one final act of incompetence, Bragg did not order the Cumberland Mountain tunnel destroyed behind him. The Nashville-Atlanta rail corridor, backbone of the Confederacy, became a vital supply line for the enemy for the duration of the war.

The men and wagons labored in the mud across the rugged Cumberland while the Rebel cavalry covering the retreat skirmished with the enemy at the foot of the mountain.[106] As Forrest was making his way through Cowan, a woman yelled to him, "You great big cowardly rascal, you big cowardly rascal, why don't you turn and fight like a man, instead of running like a cur? I wish old Forrest were here. He'd make you fight!"[107] The Tennessean and his men headed on up the mountain.

Much of the Union infantry got over the Elk on July 3.[108] Worn out after eleven days of steady marching and skirmishing in knee deep mud and across swollen streams, Rosecrans decided to stop and give his men a rest.[109] The Middle Tennessee Campaign was over.

On Independence Day 1863, at Gettysburg two great armies rested on parallel ridges after three days of fighting the biggest battle ever in North America. Vicksburg surrendered on that day, too; the Mississippi River was now under Union control. And a wet, weary, and demoralized Army of Tennessee began crossing the Tennessee River headed for Chattanooga in East Tennessee.

The brilliantly executed Middle Tennessee Campaign resulted in only 550 casualties for the entire Army of the Cumberland, including only eighty-four men killed. The Union forces captured 1,634 Confederate soldiers.[110] Some Southerners, many of them Tennesseans, deserted rather than follow Bragg out of Middle Tennessee.[111]

The rain, of course fell, on both armies, but it hurt the Union cause the most. Rosecrans's first objective was to destroy Bragg's army, and the weather conditions slowed the Army of the Cumberland considerably.[112] Rosecrans was not able to get his army behind the Confederates before they fled, first to Tullahoma, then across the Elk, and finally over the Cumberland. Further, the conditions caused Rosecrans to halt the pursuit at the foot of the mountain. Better conditions likely would have permitted the Northerners to get their superior force behind the Southerners and engage them in a major battle, one in which the Confederates would have been separated from food, ammunition, reinforcements, and an escape route. As it was, Bragg barely did escape.

The Army of Tennessee under Braxton Bragg was back at Chattanooga, where it started a year earlier. Yet Bragg remained in command. He wasted an opportunity to strike Rosecrans's divided army below Chattanooga in September.[113] Then, through skill, bravery, and some good luck, his army won its only major victory—at Chickamauga on September 19–20, 1863. Bragg squandered that victory by letting the Northerners flee largely unmolested to Chattanooga, where he mismanaged the Confederate encirclement of the town.[114] The dissension among his generals grew worse, if such were possible, and even a visit by Jefferson Davis did not quell it. But Davis left Bragg in command.[115] In late November, a reinforced and reorganized Union force overran Bragg's army from its superior position on Missionary Ridge, driving it back into north Georgia.[116] Finally, Bragg left the Army of Tennessee, blaming his men for the Chattanooga rout. At Dalton, Georgia, nearly a year after he was urged to, Joseph E. Johnston finally took command.[117]

After Chickamauga, Lincoln appointed Major General Ulysses S. Grant commander of all forces in the west. Grant wasted no time getting to Chattanooga to prepare the breakout. The brilliance Rosecrans displayed in Middle Tennessee was overshadowed by the humiliation of Chickamauga and the desperate living conditions in the besieged town. Grant replaced Rosecrans with Thomas, who commanded the Army of the Cumberland in the November fighting around Chattanooga and for the rest of the war.

By the following spring, then-Lieutenant General Ulysses Grant was in Virginia commanding all Union forces, leaving Major General William T. Sherman in command of the west. The ultimate conclusion of the Middle Tennessee Campaign was Sherman's Atlanta Campaign in the summer of 1864.

It is widely believed that Atlanta's capture in September 1864 helped secure Lincoln's reelection in November, keeping the North in the war.[118] The burning of Atlanta and the March to the Sea are two of the best remembered events of the Civil War. Sherman became a hero in the North; Rosecrans was all but forgotten. But Sherman would not have been in Georgia, at least not then, except for the skill and strength exhibited by Rosencrans during those eleven rainy days in Middle Tennessee.

൪൜

This article first appeared in the Fall 1993 issue of the *Tennessee Historical Quarterly*.

1. *War of the Rebellion: A Compilation of the Official Records of the Union and Confederate Armies.* 128 Vols. (Washington, 188.5–1901), 602. Hereinafter cited as OR. All references are to Series I, Vol. XXIII. All references are to pt. 1 of Vol. XXIII unless otherwise noted.

2. Ibid., 611.

3. John T. Wilder, "The Battle of Hoover's Gap," in *Sketches of War History, 1861–1865,* Military Order of the Loyal Legion of the United States (Cincinnati, 1890), 168–173.

4 John Beatty, *Memoirs of a Volunteer, 1861–1863*, Harvey S. Ford, eel. (New York, 1946), 217.

5. See James Lee McDonough. *Stones River: Bloody Winter in Tennessee* (Knoxville, 1980).

6. Thomas Lawrence Connelly, *Autumn of Glory: The Army of Tennessee, 1862–1865* (Baton Rouge, 1971), 68; Peter Cozzens, *No Better Place to Die: The Battle of Stones River* (Urbana, 1990), 202.

7. Ibid.

8. OR, pt. 2, 701.

9. The gaps are still used today. I-24 and US 41 pass through Hoovers Gap, the south end of which was enlarged considerably by construction of the interstate. TN 269 crosses Liberty Gap between Christiana and Bell Buckle. The CSX Railroad (formerly the L&N) still crosses the range of hills at the same spot as did the railroad in 1863. US 231 crosses Guys Gap between Murfreesboro and Shelbyville.

10. Cozzens, *No Better Place to Die*, 208–209; Stanley F. Horn, *The Army of Tennessee* (Norman, 1941), 222.

11. OR, pt. 2, 729; Connelly, *Autumn of Glory*, 91, 95; Joseph H. Parks, *General Leonidas Polk, C.S.A., The Fighting Bishop* (Baton Rouge, 1962), 296.

12. Connelly, *Autumn of Glory*, 74–7.5; Cozzens, *No Better Place to Die*, 209; Horn, *The Army of Tennessee*, 223.

13. Connelly, *Autumn of Glory*, 77, 93; Gilbert E. Govan and James W. Livingood, *A Different Valor: The Story of General Joseph E. Johnston, C.S.A.* (Indianapolis, 1956), 164.

14. OR, pt. 2, 613–614.

15. OR, pt. 2, 624; Govan and Livingood, *A Different Valor*, 179.

16. OR, pt. 2, 674; Connelly, *Autumn of Glory*, 85.

17. OR, pt. 2, 745.

18. Connelly, *Autumn of Glory*, 77, 99.

19. James Arthur Lyon Fremantle, *The Fremantle Diary*, Walter Lord, cd. (Boston, 1974), 115.

20. OR, 623.

21. Connelly, *Autumn of Glory*, 71–72; Judith Lee Hallock, *Braxton Bragg and Confederate Defeat, Vol. II* (Tuscaloosa, 1991), 25–26; Charles Todd Quintard, *Doctor Quintard, Chaplain C.S.A. and Second Bishop of Tennessee, Being His Story of the War (1861–1865)*, Arthur Howard Noll, ed. (Sewanee, 1903), 87.

22. Connelly, *Autumn of Glory*, 116–117.

23 OR, pt. 2, 759.

24. *Fremantle Diary*, 109.

25 OR, pt. 2, 790.

26. OR, pt. 2, 647.

27. OR, pt. 2, 647, 680; Connelly, *Autumn of Glory*, 114; Govan and Livingood, *A Different Valor*, 187.

28. OR, pt. 2, 849; Connelly, *Autumn of Glory*, 97,110.

29. Connelly, *Autumn of Glory*, 97.

30. Horn, *The Army of Tennessee*, 233.

31. OR, pt. 2, 617, 760; Hallock, *Braxton Bragg and Confederate Defeat, Vol. II*, 13; Nathaniel Cheairs Hughes, Jr., *General William J. Hardee: Old Reliable* (Baton Rouge, 1965), 156.

32. OR, 406, 602, 611.

33. Connelly, *Autumn of Glory*, 118, 126.

34. OR, 588.

35. Ibid.

36. John P. Dyer, "Some Aspects of Cavalry Operations in the Army of Tennessee," *Journal of Southern History* 8 (May 1942): 210–215.

37. OR, pt. 2, 866; Connelly, *Autumn of Glory*, 126.

38. OR, pt. 2, 379, 873. The estimated strength of the two armies varies with practically each account of the campaign. Horn places the Union number at 70,000 and Confederate at 44,000. Horn, *The Army of Tennessee*, 231, 234. Hallock says 112,000 and 55,000. Hallock. *Braxton Bragg and Confederate Defeat*, 15. Shelby Foote fixes the numbers at 87,800 and 41,680, but notes that Rosecrans detailed large numbers to garrison duty, leaving 65,137 available for the offensive. Shelby Foote, *The Civil War: A Narrative*, Vol. II (New York. 1963), 665.

39. Foote, *The Civil War*, 664.

40. Stephen Z. Starr, *The Union Cavalry in the Civil War, Vol. III, The War in the West* (Baton Rouge. 1985), 211.

41 Glenn W. Sunderland, *Lightning at Hoovers Gap: The Story of Wilder's Brigade* (New York, 1969), 25–29.

42. OR, pt. 2, 369.

43. OR, 404.

44 OR, 405.

45 Ibid.

46. OR, 404.

47. Ibid.

48. Ibid.

49. OR, 466, 470.

50. See Freeman Gleaves, *Rock of Chickamauga: The Life of General George H. Thomas* (Norman. 1949).

51. OR, 404–405

52. OR, 543.

53. Foote, *The Civil War*, 667.

54. OR, 405.

55. OR, 454.

56. OR, 602.

57. OR, 458–459.

58. James A. Connelly, *Three Years in the Army of the Cumberland*. Paul Angle, ed. (Bloomington, 1959), 94.

59. OR, 465.

60. OR, 521.

61. OR, 535.

62. OR, 431, 455–456.

63. OR, 587.

64. OR, 521.

65. Theodore W. Blackburn, *Letters from the Front: A Union "Preacher" Regiment (74th Ohio) in the Civil War* (Dayton, 1981), 121.

66. OR, 536.

67. OR, 414; P.H. Sheridan, *Personal Memoirs of P.H. Sheridan: General United States Army* (New York, 1888), 263.

68. OR, 459.

69. OR, 618; Connelly, *Autumn of Glory*, 117.

70. OR, 618; Connelly, *Autumn of Glory*, 128.

71. OR, 608.

72. OR, 4:31; pt. 2, 465.

73. OR, 619.

74. OR, 587.

75. OR, 591.

76. OR, 459. The author's great grandfather, Lewis Washington Myers, was captured by Wilder's men when they overran Manchester on 27 June 1863. Myers, a second lieutenant in an independent cavalry unit, spent most of the remainder of the war in Johnson's Island Prison in Ohio. Myers was from Chickamauga, scene of the great battle in September 1863. When Wilder Tower was dedicated in September 1899 at the battlefield, Wilder and Myers encountered each other and discussed Myers's capture.

77. OR, 456.

78. OR 431.

79. Ibid.

80. OR, 539.

81. Starr, *The Union Cavalry in the Civil War*, Vol. III, 244.

82. OR, 557; W.E. Carter, *History of the First Regiment of Tennessee Volunteer Cavalry [U.S.]*

in the Great War of the Rebellion (Knoxville, 1902), 76–78; David Stanley, "The Tullahoma Campaign," *Sketches of War History*, 175; Starr, *The Union Cavalry in the Civil War, Vol. III*, 246–248; John A. Wyeth, "General Wheeler's Leap," *Harper's Weekly* 42 (18 June 1898), 601–602.

83. Robert G. Hartje, *Van Dorn: The Life and Times of a Confederate General* (Nashville, 1967), 307–327.

84. OR, 540; Robert Selph Henry, *"First with the Most" Forrest* (Indianapolis, 1944), 166–167; Stanley, "The Tullahoma Campaign," 178.

85. OR, 460.

86. OR, 621.

87. OR, 466.

88. John J. Hight, *History of the Fifty-eighth Regiment of Indiana Volunteer Infantry* (Princeton, 1895), 148.

89. OR, 521.

90. OR, 540.

91. I.W. Avery, "Patrick Ronayne Cleburne," *The Kennesaw Gazette*, Vol. II, No. 10 (Atlanta, 15 May 1887), 4; Henry, *"First with the Most" Forrest*, 167–168.

92. OR, 460; Andrew Lytle, *Bedford Forrest and his Critter Company* (New York, 1931), 185.

93. OR, 621.

94. OR, 622.

95. OR, pt. 2, 893–894.

96. OR, 623.

97. PR, pt. 2, 894; Connelly, *Autumn of Glory*, 132; Howell and Elizabeth Purdue, *Pat Cleburne: Confederate General* (Hillsboro, 1973), 194.

98. Alfred Lacey Hough, *Soldier in the West: The Civil War Letters of Alfred Lacey Hough*, Robert G. Athearn, ed. (Philadelphia, 1957), 104.

99. OR, 623.

100. OR, 453, 515; Benjamin T. Smith, *Private Smith's Journal: Recollections of the Late War*, Clyde C. Walton, ed. (Chicago, 1963), 79.

101. OR, 515; Sheridan, *Personal Memoirs*, 265.

102. OR, 624.

103. The tunnel is still used today.

104. OR, 625.

105. Ibid.

106. Ibid.

107. Henry, *"First with the Most" Forrest*, 168.

108. OR, 406; Chesley A. Mosman, *The Rough Side of War: The Civil War Journal of Chesley A. Mosman, 1st Lieutenant, Compamy D, 59th Illinois Volunteer Infantry Regiment*, Arnold

Gates, ed. (Garden City, NJ, 1987), 63.

109. OR, 408.

110. OR, 425.

111. Foote, *The Civil War*, Vol. II, 674.

112. OR, 404; Foote, *The Civil War*, Vol. II, 674.

113. Connelly, *Autumn of Glory*, 175–200: Cozzens, *This Terrible Sound: The Battle of Chickamauga* (Urbana, 1992), 61–100.

114. Connelly, *Autumn of Glory*, 253; Cozzens, *This Terrible Sound*, 519–521.

115. James Lee McDonough, *Chattanooga: A Death Grip on the Confederacy* (Knoxville, 1984), 20–40.

116. Ibid., 161–219.

117. Connelly, *Autumn of Glory*, 281.

118. James A. Rawley, *Turning Points of the Civil War* (Lincoln, 1966), 191.

THE LEGACIES OF FREEDOM AND VICTORY BESIEGED:

Stones River National Cemetery, 1865–1920

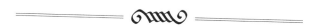

Miranda L. Fraley-Rhodes

I n 1865, the Civil War officially ended, and the state of Tennessee became the first rebelling state to rejoin the union. For the residents of Rutherford County, however, these changes only marked the beginning of the next stage in the conflict. The violence and hatred of the war continued. Freedpeople, including African American Union veterans, sought to support their families, educate their children, and exercise their new political rights. They wanted to build a good life for their families and enjoy the benefits of freedom in peace. A community of white Union veterans developed in Rutherford County as some of these men decided to stay and make this area their home. This group included officials employed by the federal government, and others who planned to be farmers. These two groups were inextricably linked in their efforts to preserve the memories of emancipation and Union victory and to realize the promises of freedom and prosperity under the protection of the federal government.

Although questions of political loyalty fractured the local white community during the war, the experiences of Union occupation and the end of slavery substantially reunited whites, who soon grew determined to reassert control over former slaves and to defy the Yankees who had killed so many of their loved ones and wreaked havoc on their communities. White and African American Radical Republicans dominated state and local politics from 1865 to 1869.[1] However, in 1870, when a new state constitution lifted suffrage restrictions on ex-Confederate voters, conservative whites throughout the state and in Rutherford County regained control of governments.[2] They began the process of excluding African Americans from electoral politics and constructing a system of legal segregation that culminated in the violent and tumultuous decade of the 1890s.[3] During these very decades of political turmoil, African Americans, white northerners, and some white Tennesseans worked to create an enduring tradition of pro-Union Civil War commemoration despite violence and harassment by angry southern whites.

For Middle Tennessee Unionists and African Americans, Stones River National Cemetery stood at the center of Union commemoration efforts from 1865 to the 1920s. They had created this sacred space to remember and honor the federal soldiers who had died at the Battle of Stones River. Closely associated with Union victory and African American freedom, the cemetery symbolized the persistent presence of the federal government within the local political landscape. These characteristics made the cemetery a target for repeated attacks by angry local whites who longed to gain control over this commemorative space and disrupt the biracial Union community of memory focused on the cemetery. Despite growing racial divisions within the Union coalition, as long as this group remained centered on the national cemetery as the primary space for commemorating the war, they were largely able to resist the myriad tactics Confederate partisans employed to disturb, discredit, and silence the legacies of Union victory in Rutherford County.

The federal government created the national cemetery system in response to the massive casualties of Union soldiers during the Civil War. Many of these men died and were buried in the rebellious territory of the South, denying most grieving northern families the opportunity to provide their loved ones with the customary care and burial rituals associated with death in their culture. According to historian Gary Laderman, the government's efforts to care for the Union dead that culminated in the national cemetery system fulfilled a vital political function for the Lincoln administration by helping to maintain civilian support for the war effort. The development of the national cemetery system during and immediately following the war represented a significant departure from earlier wars in which the government provided little or no care to the graves of its dead, and the public generally accepted mass graves on battlefields as the final resting places for soldiers. National cemeteries comprised a very early and important form of Union Civil War commemoration in which the federal government confiscated southern land to establish permanent and substantial cemeteries for Union war dead. These cemeteries served as persistent reminders of Union victory and federal authority within southern communities.[4]

The army issued its first regulations concerning procedures for burying, recording, and marking the graves of Union soldiers during the war. On September 11, 1861, General Order 75 charged the quartermaster with the tasks of providing military hospitals with materials for documenting soldiers' deaths and burial locations, marking soldiers' graves with headboards, and requiring military commanders to report soldiers' deaths and burial sites to officials in Washington. The federal government ordered military commanders on April 3, 1862, to select a site following each battle for use as a cemetery for Union soldiers, to prepare records of each soldier's burial place, and to mark each grave with a headboard. However, the chaos of battles and troop movements prevented many army officers from strictly adhering to these regulations during the war, and much of the quartermaster department's work of creating national cemeteries occurred after fighting had ceased.[5]

Major General George H. Thomas, who succeeded William S. Rosecrans as the commanding general of the Army of the Cumberland and was a veteran of the Battle of Stones River, founded Stones River National Cemetery in 1864 as a final resting place for soldiers killed in the Battle of Stones River and other engagements in Middle Tennessee. Captain John A. Means of the 115th Ohio Volunteer Infantry who was the assistant quartermaster at Fortress Rosecrans, the federal occupation fort at Murfreesboro, selected the site for the cemetery on the Stones River battlefield in an area where intense fighting occurred on December 31, 1862. This land lay between the Nashville, Shelbyville, and Murfreesboro Turnpike and the Nashville and Chattanooga railroad tracks. Means also created the design for the cemetery landscape.[6]

Chaplain William Earnshaw, a white northern Methodist minister, managed much of the early cemetery development during 1865 and 1866. He was a key figure in the development of this important commemorative space and in relationships between white northerners and local African Americans. Earnshaw participated in early emancipation celebrations held in Murfreesboro prior to the end of the war.[7] His efforts on behalf of Rutherford County freedpeople attracted attention within the local area and the federal government, and he received an offer to serve as the county superintendent for the Freedman's Bureau. On July 25, 1865, Earnshaw declined this appointment because the previous month he was assigned to be the superintendent of Stones River National Cemetery.[8] During his tenure as cemetery superintendent, Earnshaw worked with African American soldiers in the 111th United States Colored Troops (USCT) who provided much of the labor for early cemetery development.[9] By August 1867, he had left the army and accepted a position as the chaplain of the National Asylum for Disabled Volunteer Soldiers located in Columbus, Ohio, but Earnshaw remained engaged in efforts to assist

African Americans in Rutherford County.[10] During the early postwar period, the national cemetery was a sacred federal space constructed by African American soldiers and managed by a Union chaplain. Together they created a landscape where the bodies of white and African American Union soldiers would silently testify to their victory.

In the fall of 1865, Earnshaw and the men of the 111th USCT began the difficult and melancholy task of gathering the bodies of Union soldiers from throughout southern Middle Tennessee and reburying them in the national cemetery. By April 1866, most of the reburial work was completed. Earnshaw reported

> I was assigned to the position of Superintendent in June 1865, but did not get the help necessary until October and since that time we have taken up and re-interred nearly six thousand (6,000) bodies, beginning with Stones River battlefield, from thence to Hoover's, Guy's and Liberty Gaps, and, during the winter months, all who died in hospitals at this Post were removed to the cemetery. We have, since the close of winter, gone with wagons seventy miles, north east, east, and south east, and gathered hundreds who fell in skirmishes, were murdered by bushwackers, and some who were poisoned by eating food purchased of citizens....
>
> I left on the train...with one hundred and twenty men of the 111th U.S.C. Infy., leaving at each blockhouse from (6) six to (20) men and larger numbers at Wartrace, Fosterville, Normandy, Tullahoma, Estell Springs, Dechard and Cowan, and in the short space of four days disinterred near (600) six hundred bodies and on the fifth day we returned to the cemetery with the precious dust; without any disposition to claim the praise of any, you will permit me to say, that such a soul stirring sight was never witnessed on the earth before; nearly a regiment of dead soldiers, were borne on that train, men who had given their lives for the country and who passed over the same road, eager to strike the death blow to the rebellion, shouting and cheering as they passed to the front, where they fell in the van of the grand old Army of the Union, and now sleep beneath the green sod of our beautiful cemetery, on the immortal field of Stone's River. In three days we interred all these men.

While on this mission to retrieve the bodies of slain Union soldiers, Earnshaw related "in some places we have been very unkindly met by citizens, they trying by every possible means to annoy us, sometimes sending us to spots where others than our heroes slept."[11]

Earnshaw asserted that his staff worked diligently to establish the identity of each soldier buried in the national cemetery. Despite their best efforts, approximately twenty-five percent of the soldiers remained unknown. He clearly considered the ramifications of their labors on the families of the Union dead and sought to provide comfort to them. Earnshaw received "hundreds of letters and visits of those who have friends in this cemetery" inquiring about the final resting place of loved ones. The assurances Earnshaw offered to families testified to the devotion of the soldiers of the 111th USCT to their difficult work:

> Many persons who have dear friends buried here will be deeply interested to know whether the work of removal was done with that care actually demanded in such a holy cause. I can only reply that all that true men could do was done. All my assistants were brave soldiers who had served throughout the war—men who could sympathize with those far away who mourn the loss of their loved ones, but who could not be present to perform for them this last sad office. Long as I live I shall remember how tenderly they performed this work amid untold difficulties; how cheerfully they set out on long and toilsome journeys through rain and storm in search of fallen comrades, and the proud satisfaction expressed by them when the precious remains were laid in the new made grave.[12]

In addition to their other duties, the soldiers of the 111th USCT began construction on a stone wall designed to enclose the cemetery, and they completed approximately one-eighth of this structure prior to being mustered out of the army in 1866. Earnshaw repeatedly entreated the War Department for the funds to complete this structure. He emphasized the need of "*permanently enclosing* our national cemeteries of the larger class with stone or iron."[13] Historian G. Kurt Piehler noted that "in the South, the U.S. Army frequently decided to remove bodies from scattered locations and reburied them in larger cemeteries surrounded by stone walls so that they would not be desecrated by Southerners" and "made it a federal crime to vandalize a national cemetery."[14]

Several important themes emerged in Earnshaw's portrait of the cemetery's development. He clearly believed that their work honored the sacrifices of Union soldiers who died in their country's service and was committed to collecting their

bodies from the southern landscape and reburying them in the national cemetery. In his reports, Earnshaw presented the men of the 111th USCT in a very
positive manner and seemed highly pleased with their work. In contrast, he portrayed southern white civilians as potent enemies responsible for poisoning and
bushwacking Union soldiers during the war and later maliciously misdirecting the
burial parties to the graves of Confederates. Earnshaw clearly recognized the hostility of many former Confederates towards the federal government, freedpeople,
and the national cemetery, and he correctly assessed this group as determined and
formidable foes.

While Union soldiers laid their dead comrades to rest in the new national cemetery, the conflicts stemming from the war continued to rage in Rutherford County.
The demise of slavery fundamentally destabilized local social and economic orders. In
his study of this tumultuous time, historian Eric Foner emphasized "the centrality of
the black experience" to understanding Reconstruction because the changing status
of African Americans represented the most pivotal change caused by the war, and
African Americans' actions in claiming their freedom dramatically altered southern
society.[15] Freedpeople strove to claim their new rights with the aid of their allies
among northern Union veterans living in Murfreesboro—some employed by federal
agencies such as the Freedman's Bureau and others who had decided to move to
Middle Tennessee to live. In response, some embittered whites terrorized, assaulted,
and murdered freedpeople and northern migrants to reassert their control. Yet, despite
the real dangers, freedpeople and Union veterans persisted in their joint effort to
create a new kind of community based on the inseparable legacies of emancipation
and Union victory.

One anchor of their joint effort was the Freedman's Bureau.[16] The bureau had
a strong presence in Rutherford County, and through its Murfreesboro office, federal
officials continued the work of the occupying Union armies. Bureau superintendents
and agents typically were white Union veterans with deep commitments to protect-
ing the rights of freedpeople who were willing to stand up to hostile and sometimes
threatening local whites and recalcitrant county officials.

The bureau provided a variety of services to freedpeople in Rutherford County.
Agents assisted African American Union veterans and their widows with paperwork
to claim soldiers' wages and benefits. They helped freedpeople find employment, ne-
gotiate contracts, and resolve labor disputes.[17] Its agents joined with African Americans and northern benevolent organizations to help found and support schools.[18]
During its first years of operations, the office also supplied medical services and medi-
cines to freedpeople.[19] For the bureau office to function effectively, agents had to

work as partners with freedpeople, and the federal government had to be willing to support them with armed force as necessary.

Bureau superintendents in Rutherford County worked diligently to see that whites who committed violent crimes against freedpeople were prosecuted. Due to the reluctance of local courts and law enforcement officials to address these cases, bureau agents often found themselves in the difficult position of having to apprehend, try, and punish white offenders. For example, on April 1, 1866, John Seage, bureau superintendent at Murfreesboro, appealed to a Nashville superior officer for advice. African American minister Gabriel Simmons, who was held in high regard by Seage and others in the community, filed a complaint against a white man identified as Henderson who had hit him "on his head with a Blacksmith hammer fracturing his skull." Seage charged Henderson with "'assault & Battery with intent to Kill,'" and released him on bond. Simmons died as a result of his injury. No one else was present when the assault occurred, and Seage explained "Henderson confessed the crime but plead self defense & says Simmons was going to strike him." After speaking with character witnesses, Seage concluded that it was highly unlikely that Simmons, a respected minister, would have attacked anyone, and that Henderson, "reputed as always under the influence of liquor & 4 years in the Rebel Army," was probably lying. However, Seage requested additional federal officials to help him determine Henderson's fate because he was "very lo[a]the to sit in judgement alone in the case. It is too grave a matter." He had to appeal for assistance from other bureau agents because he maintained "it is no use to refer the case to the civil court."[20]

In February 1867, a violent incident occurred in which four local whites brutally attacked freedpeople and a white northern veteran. Freedmen's Bureau agent J. K. Nelson wrote to his superior to report these "outrages perpetuated in the vicinity of Murfreesboro on the evening of the 14th of February by a band of four desperadoes named Bill Allen, Ross Allen, (brothers,) and Wm White and John White (brothers)." This group began their spree of violence and terror in Murfreesboro where they were "partially under the influence of liquor and pretending to be very drunk and in leaving town shot at a Freedman on the side walk besides being very boisterous. These facts being known to the Policemen they made no attempt to arrest them."[21]

Nelson provided the following description of the Whites and Allen's violent assaults on local farmers:

> Bill Allen and his party reached the premises of Mrs. Johnson two miles from
> Murfreesboro on the [L]iberty Pike first about dark and while one of them held

the horses the others broke into a cabin occupied by Freedmen and presented their Pistols making threats to Kill the occupants and did seize upon the person of one of them named Henry Johnson and cut him severely about the head and neck with a knife inflicting three different wounds.

They then caught another John Suggs and cut him frightfully across the throat.

Mr. Wilson their Employer, a gentleman from Pennsylvania and highly respected by all who knew him hearing the disturbance, and not anticipating any serious trouble presented himself about this time, not knowing that any stabbing or cutting had been done (unfortunately for himself without arms) where he was addressed by Bill Allen as "Captain Wilson."Allen at the same time professing of friendship for him, under the cover of which he seized and commenced stabbing him, and before Wilson could escape from his grasp, a very severe wound was inflicted in his side, and a painful one in his arm.

They then declared themselves masters of the field and soon went on their way rejoicing that they had cleaned out the "Yankee Captain and his [freedmen]."[22]

Nelson noted that "the Allens and Whites belong to wealthy and influential families—intensely *"Southern"* and Bill Allen was a notorious guerilla during the war." Nelson diligently worked to induce the local law enforcement officials to take action, but his efforts were to no avail. He decided to exert federal jurisdiction over this matter because "every Union man and every freedman believe that it is simply because the outrages were perpetuated upon a Union man & freedmen, that nothing has been done. The feeling of insecurity among all Union men and freedmen is increasing daily."[23] With the help of a detachment of Union soldiers sent from Nashville, Nelson apprehended the Whites but failed to capture the Allen brothers who apparently fled the area.[24]

Individual attacks were dangerous enough; in addition, the Ku Klux Klan waged a campaign of terror against freedpeople in Rutherford County. The Klan was founded in nearby Pulaski, Tennessee, and Nathan Bedford Forrest, hero of a Confederate raid on Murfreesboro in 1862, was widely reputed to be its first Grand Wizard, where many members were Confederate veterans. "The first Klan incidents cropped up in 1867, when blacks gained the franchise and political excitement in the region intensified," concluded historian Stephen V. Ash. "These earliest manifestations were ostentatious (but generally nonviolent) processions of silent, hooded horsemen, intended to scare blacks and white Radicals away from the polls." According to Ash, when this tactic proved unsuccessful, the Klan resorted to violence.[25] In addition to the overtly political goals of the Klan, Eric Foner explained how white employers used this group to terrorize and coerce their African American employees. According to Foner, "the Klan sought to take the place of both the departed personal authority of the master and the labor control function the Reconstruction state had abandoned."[26]

In 1868, a Murfreesboro newspaper affiliated with the Republican Party named *Freedom's Watchman* reported that a local Klan parade was designed "to intimidate colored people, and if possible deter them from going to the polls." The author then issued a warning to the Klan that African Americans and white Republicans in Rutherford County were prepared to defend themselves and if necessary unleash the might of the Union army on their attackers, noting that "if Tennessee is again to be overrun with soldiers they have but themselves to thank." The article concluded with an affirmation of African Americans' political rights: "Every man in Tennessee is *free* and has a right to exercise that freedom in any manner he sees fit, provided he does not interfere with the rights of others. The law protects him in the exercise of his rights, and the law must take its course even if some of the Ku Klux dangle in the air."[27]

Despite the threat of federal intervention, Klan violence continued. In a 1930s interview, Hammett Dell recalled an encounter with the Klan. When the war ended, Dell decided to work for his former master Pleasant White. He described how he labored in the family's carpentry business for a share of the profits and learned masonry skills. Dell also related that White taught him how to read during this period. One night Dell was dragged out of his house by a group of Klan members that included Pleasant White, forced to perform tasks intended to be humiliating, and then made to watch them assault one of his African American neighbors. Dell related

> The [only] experience I had myself with the Ku Klux was one night fo' Grandma and auntie left. Somebody wrap on our cabin door. They opened it. We got scared when we seed em. They had the horses wrapped up. They had on long white dresses and caps. Everyone of them had a horse whoop (whip). They called me out. Grandma and auntie so scared they hid. They tole me to git em water. They poured it some whah it did not spill on the ground. Kept me totin' water. They they say, "You bin a good boy?" They still drinkin'. One say, "Just from Hell pretty dry." Then they tole me to stand on my head. I turned summer sets a few

times. They tickled me round with the ends of the whoops. I had on a long shirt. They laugh when I stand on my head. Old Mars White laughed. I knowed his laugh. Then I got over my scare. They say, "Who live next down the road?" I tole them Nells Christian. They say, "What he do?" I said, "Works in the field." They all grunt m-m-m-m. Then they say, "Show us the way." I nearly run to death cross the field to keep outer the way of the white horses. The moon shining bright as day. They say Nells come out here. He say "Holy Moses." He come out. They say "Nells what you do?" "I farms." They say "What you raise?" He say "Cotton and corn." hey say "Take us to see yo cotton we jess from Hell. We ain't got no cotton there." He took them out there where it was clean. They got down and felt it. The they say "What is dat?", feelin' the grass. Nells say "That is grass." They say, "You raise grass too?" He said, "No. It come up." They say "Let us see your corn." He showed em the corn. They felt it. They say, "What this?" Nells say, "It grass." They say, "You raise grass here?" They all grunt m-m-m-m everything Nells say. They give him one bad whoopin' and tell him they be back soon see if he raisin' grass. They said "You raise cotton and corn but not grass on this farm." They they moan "m-m-m-m".... I was sho glad to git back to our cabin. They didn't come back to Nells no more that I herd bout. The man Nells worked for muster been on in that crowd....[28]

Although Dell offered no speculation as to why the Klan molested him, he clearly saw their attack on Nells Christian as an effort to coerce Christian to tend his crops more carefully. Dell interpreted the Klan primarily as an institution for enforcing labor discipline reminiscent of slavery. African Americans' labor was essential to the local economy. Whites were determined to control this valuable resource and maintain white supremacy, and they drew on violence to do so.

The conflicts of Reconstruction shaped the later disputes among local whites, Unionists, and African Americans over the national cemetery. Control of African American labor and its value were early issues. Business arrangements between white cemetery superintendents and African American cemetery employees sometimes challenged the racial status quo in the labor market, creating controversies with local whites. In 1876, T. M. Robbins, a civil engineer with the quartermaster department, visited Stones River National Cemetery to observe the placing of the regulation marble known and unknown grave markers in this burial ground. Robbins's detailed report included recommendations about wages paid to African American cemetery employees who filled in sunken graves. Robbins concluded

Thirty dollars per month has been the customary wages; this is too much; $25 per month for the best men is all they are worth, and more than they can earn at any other place, or any other employment—while $20 per month for temporary men is first class pay. From 50 to 75 cents per day is the ruling price of farm laborers; or from $13 to $15 per month. The headstone contractors paid but 75 cents per day, and their work was heavy work—and during that time the neighboring farmers could scarcely get a colored man to work for them. The paying of high wages creates great local dissatisfaction, and on that account, as well as to make the limited appropriations for Cemeterial purposes go as far as possible should not be tolerated.

Shortly after Robbins submitted this report, Quartermaster General Meigs ordered that cemetery Superintendent Thomas Frame "begin Filling Graves as instructed by Engineer Robbins as soon as headstone work is finished, hire two extra men, pay twenty dollars per month." This incident highlighted the cemetery's practice of paying African American employees better wages than many other local employers that reduced white farmers' supply of potential workers willing to labor for little money. Unfortunately, the white farmers' anger over blacks being paid "too well" and the federal government's fiscal stinginess led to a reduction in cemetery employees' salaries in December 1876.[29]

Superintendent Frame later became a political target of local Democrats eager to tap into federal jobs and reward those more loyal to local political preferences. On May 15, 1885, James D. Richardson of Murfreesboro, who was a member of the U. S. House of Representatives, asked U. S. Senator Isham G. Harris to find out if the secretary of war would fire Frame. Richardson stated, "We want the Supt. of the National Cemetery here removed, and a citizen of our county appointed." Richardson explained Frame was "a bitter partisan, and always takes a hand in our politics." Interestingly, Richardson claimed that he had Frame's successor already selected, apparently a Union veteran living in Rutherford County with more pleasing political views. Harris submitted this request to the secretary of war's office, but it was denied. The quartermaster general affirmed that Frame had "discharged his duties faithfully and well," and pointed out that "the law requires that Superintendents of National Cemeteries shall be disabled soldiers, honorably discharged from the military service of the United States, and it has been the custom of the Department to remove them only for cause—dishonesty, neglect of duty, inefficiency, or intemperance." He also noted that superintendents' political views had never before been a factor in evaluating their fitness for duty. This time, the federal government resisted local pressure on the administration of the national cemetery.[30]

Controversy over the management of the cemetery and particularly over who was selected to fill the position of superintendent did not reappear for a generation. In 1911, Superintendent Thomas Shea faced the task of selecting a person to serve as acting superintendent during the period between when he left to take up his new post at another national cemetery and when his successor, John Thomas, would arrive in Murfreesboro. Shea recommended James Rucker, an African American cemetery employee. On July 7, 1911, Shea's superior officer, Joseph T. Davidson enclosed Rucker's appointment papers in a letter. In his reply on July 8, 1911, Shea assured Davidson that "matters will be attended to properly by James Rucker." He emphasized that "James Rucker has all the practical knowledge necessary for running the cemetery and there is really no one else in this neighborhood who will devote any real attention to the place." Rucker was officially appointed as acting superintendent for the pay of forty dollars a month.[31]

Local white reaction was swift and negative. In a Jim Crow society, African Americans would not be allowed to serve in positions of authority. On July 10, 1911, only two days after confirming Rucker's appointment, Shea telegraphed Davidson asking him to "please appoint Frank Ordway, of Murfreesboro, Tenn., Acting Superintendent to relieve me because of transfer. Will mail cause to-morrow…." In a letter, Shea explained

I received some indirect information late last evening that trouble would be probably made at this cemetery after my departure, by some disappointed aspirants for position here temporarily; and who might be surmised, but were not named; that the trouble would be based on the pretext of color—James Rucker, the laborer here, being a colored man. Getting the above data from a party who may be relied on, but who wishes to not be mentioned, I immediately went to town and telegraphed; it was too late to write and mail.

Frank Ordway, who I interviewed before telegraphing, is a civil engineer by profession; and had only come home yesterday; hence I could not have sent his name sooner. He is the son of Charles Ordway, mentioned in my letter of the 7th instant. The Ordways are one of the leading families of Murfreesboro educationally and socially. With Frank Ordway here, no one will dare to interfere, and he will not be absent from the cemetery at night. Rucker understands condition and does not want position.[32]

Shea's efforts to appoint the most qualified person to the position of acting superintendent came to naught because of the threat of imminent violence; he decided to rescind Rucker's appointment and install a powerful local white in his stead. Jim Crow triumphed over federal management of the national cemetery.[33]

Administrative control was just one of the issues making the national cemetery contested ground in Rutherford County. A more public issue was the Memorial Day celebrations at the cemetery. Local whites shrewdly avoided an overt campaign against these important commemorative events. Instead they focused on marginalizing these ceremonies and depended on white racism to assist them in this task.

The federal Memorial Day holiday was both the most important ceremonial occasion and the most controversial event held at the cemetery each year. Superintendents' reports and other accounts indicated that the majority of visitors to the cemetery on Memorial Day were African Americans, many of whom traveled by special trains on the Nashville, Chattanooga & St. Louis Railway from Nashville to the cemetery. African Americans from Murfreesboro and surrounding communities also attended. In addition to visiting the cemetery, African Americans created their own spaces for celebration on the lands surrounding this site where they set up booths selling refreshments. The Nashville newspapers advertised the Memorial Day ceremonies at Stones River National Cemetery as being specifically for African Americans while the services at the Nashville National Cemetery were for whites. For example, on May 30, 1907, the Nashville *Daily American* announced "There will be memorial services today at the National Cemetery near Nashville and near Murfreesboro [Stones River National Cemetery]. The exercises at the cemetery near Nashville will be attended by white people, and the exercises at the one near Murfreesboro will be attended by negroes." The Memorial Day event at Stones River became particularly associated with African American Civil War commemoration throughout the Middle Tennessee area.[34]

Other Memorial Day visitors included a Grand Army of the Republic (GAR) camp. The exact group of GAR veterans varied over time, but the GAR generally took responsibility for the formal program consisting of speakers and ceremonially decorating a soldier's grave. The Woman's Relief Corps (WRC), a female auxiliary of the GAR, participated in the formal program and assisted with decorating graves with flowers. Union veterans who had settled in the Murfreesboro area also attended. Although there were certainly African American Union veterans from the Murfreesboro area, the GAR and WRC groups involved in Memorial Day services at Stones River seem to have been predominantly, if not exclusively, white.

A third group of Memorial Day attendees included a few curious whites from the local area who would occasionally go out to the cemetery on this day to see the program. This would not have interfered with their participation in Confederate Memorial Day activities because throughout this period, federal and Confederate holidays were held on different days and locations. This group can be viewed as commemorative tourists—they were not intimately involved in the activities but were just interested onlookers. They also possessed comparative and often critical perspectives on the federal celebration that they inevitably contrasted with Confederate commemorations.

A fourth group of individuals present at Memorial Day services was, of course, the national cemetery staff including the white superintendent and African American cemetery employees. William Holland [sometimes spelled Harlan] was an African American Union veteran of the 111th United States Colored Infantry. After the war, he became a staff member at Stones River National Cemetery and bought a small farm next to the Hazen Brigade Monument. Unfortunately, the cemetery records offer little direct insight into the perspectives of African American cemetery workers like Holland on these events. Because the superintendents wrote the official reports, it is their perspectives that are most well-documented.[35]

Stones River Memorial Day ceremonies incited controversies because these groups often had very different ideas concerning the proper way to celebrate this holiday. Disputes concerning the activities at the national cemetery reverberated through the quartermaster department, the local community, and the GAR. At the center of most of these quarrels, which typically involved the cemetery superintendent and local whites or the superintendent and GAR members, was unease at the presence of large crowds of African Americans who tended to see Memorial Day as an occasion for celebration rather than formal mourning. Some controversies also involved confusion concerning who had authority over the Memorial Day events in and around the cemetery. Although the superintendent technically had charge of the national cemetery space, the GAR organized and conducted the formal programs. The superintendent's authority and federal law enforcement jurisdiction did not extend beyond the cemetery walls, and some who served in this position expressed frustration at their inability to control the crowds in the fields outside the cemetery grounds, whose activities inevitably influenced the atmosphere within the sacred space of the cemetery itself. Examining some specific Memorial Day events will demonstrate how these commemorative ceremonies evolved over time and provide insight into the disputes surrounding them.

The early Memorial Day ceremonies seem to have been relatively peaceful events, particularly during the tenures of superintendents Thomas Frame and R. C. Taylor. Interestingly, descriptions of these services and planning related to them do not include overt references to race, which become common after the mid-1890s. This silence may indicate that the writers considered the presence of African Americans less remarkable and threatening than their later counterparts. In general, relations between Memorial Day guests and program participants seem to have been less fraught with dissension during this early period. For example, in 1886, Frame wrote to his superior in the quartermaster department to "respectfully request that you Send me instructions in regard to Decoration day. This year the 30th of May falls on Sunday and the people here want to decorate the graves on Saturday the 29th as many of them do not think right to do so on Sunday please answer as soon as practicable that I may publish it in the Murfreesboro Weekly News so there will be no mistake." Frame was ultimately ordered to hold the Memorial Day observances on Monday, May 31, rather than on Saturday, May 29. However, his inquiry suggested a desire to honor the wishes of visitors and to work effectively with them.[36]

In 1887, Frame faced the problem of supplying sufficient water for the use of guests on Memorial Day. Little rain had fallen during that spring, and he wrote to his superior for permission to purchase barrels to haul drinking water from Stones River and noted "to make it drinkable there ought to be about $10.00 worth of ice bought and put in the water. Will you give me the authority to purchase the ice for this purpose [?]" Ironically, it began to rain on the approximately two thousand visitors attending the Memorial Day ceremonies causing "a great rush for shelter to the office and front Porch from the great number of people standing on the porch it broke down and is now a complete wreck."[37]

In 1891, a woman identified as Mrs. Miller attended and wrote an article documenting the Memorial Day services at Stones River National Cemetery for *The National Picket*, a journal published by the National Woman's Relief Corps. Her account presented a very positive portrait of this event. Significantly, she made no comments regarding the presence of African Americans at the ceremonies. She related

> The morning of May 30th was ushered in by the most brilliant array of sunshine, we thought, as a special tribute to the Ruler of All to the memory of the heroic dead. At 7:30 the train rolled in to the Nashville depot and Sheridan Post, No. 67, G.A.R., with its loyal friends to the number of two hundred boarded it and started on their journey of love and remembrance to Stones River Cemetery,

their destination. We were met by R. C. Taylor, who has charge of the cemetery and who was for many years a soldier in the regular army. We entered the lodge, registered, and then was handed the register of the dead, known and unknown. We found many names with which we were familiar, and missed many we knew had been in this engagement, for you must know this cemetery is the result of the engagement at Murfreesboro or Stones river.[38]

Miller offered the following description of the ceremonies at the cemetery:

Men, women and children assisted in the loving duty of placing flags at every grave. The glorious stars and stripes waved in its beauty over the graves of those who gave up their life that we to-day might have a free land. The scene will never be forgotten, thousands of our nation's banners waving in triumph in the sunlight.

After the decoration of this place was done, we were taken with the Post to a private cemetery some little distance from the above, where are buried the dead of Hazen's Brigade. Here is erected a monument of blocks of stone in the form of a pyramid....

The monument was adorned with flags, while flowers were strewn upon their graves and the flag placed at their head. I do not doubt that the friends of these soldiers, the comrades who marched by their sides will ever hold in grateful remembrance the members of the Sheridan Post, for so lovingly remembering their old Brigade.

I am back to Stones River where immediately after dinner the exercises were held. The Post accompanied by friends, marched to the graves of Redfern, Weitzel, Rooms and Kensel of the 21st Ill. Reg. and conducted the solemn exercises of the order. Perhaps you will understand something of my gratefulness, something of my feelings, when I tell you these soldiers were member of *my father's* regiment. Do you wonder when the silent salute for the dead was given by these old comrades, and I, the daughter of the Colonel of the dead, was asked to strew their graves with flowers, it was with deep emotion that I complied. After this we returned to the speaker's stand and listened to a most eloquent address from Hon. J. H. Pettibone, of the 20th Wisconsin. While I differ from him in some of his statements, as a whole the address was an eloquent tribute to the bravery of both the Blue and the Gray. His address was followed by others, all being appropriate and very much appreciated by the audience.

In this description, Miller noted the speaker's tributes to both Union and Confederate soldiers, which indicated that by this point in time, formal Memorial Day services at Stones River National Cemetery included appeals to reunionist sentiments. Miller depicted the Memorial Day ceremony at Stones River as a well-organized and decorous occasion providing her with an opportunity to honor the sacrifices of her father and other Union soldiers. Notably, she made no disparaging remarks concerning the behavior of visitors attending this event.[39]

Tensions concerning Memorial Day services and African American visitors began to erupt during the mid-1890s. This shift coincides with the crisis of southern race relations during the 1890s, a decade that witnessed the legal sanction of segregation, the defeat of Populists in the South through reactionary racial politics, and a growing epidemic of whites lynching African American men, women, and children.[40] In Tennessee, this decade was characterized by the rise of agrarian interests in politics and particularly bitter political contests.[41] Controversies concerning predominantly African Americans Memorial Day ceremonies coincided with the political uncertainty and worsening race relations of the *fin de siècle*.

In 1896, Superintendent Edwin P. Barrett requested the construction of an entrance into the national cemetery wall next to the railroad to discourage visitors arriving by train from climbing the wall and injuring the ivy covering its interior. In justifying the need for this expense, Barrett remarked "Memorial day there are trains run hourly from Murfreesboro, and on their arrival, unless there were some guards every few rods, the visitors (about 75 percent are negroes) will climb the wall."[42] The quartermaster department approved Barrett's request for the gate in the wall for visitors arriving by rail.[43]

The next year in 1897, the Memorial Day activities in and around the cemetery inspired an article in a local paper, the *Independent Banner*, and provoked a demand for an explanation from Barrett's superiors in the quartermaster department. In his report, Barrett first described his efforts to enlist the assistance of the federal marshal stationed at Nashville to assist with crowd control. The marshal did not reply to his letter. Perhaps even more frustrating to Barrett was the behavior of local law officers. He explained that "there was present County Officers Deputy Sherrifs and Constable but they made no effort that amounted to any thing to suppress the violation of laws (one or two serious offenders were arrested) but gambling (crap playing) selling liquor, drunkenness and other offences were condoned or overlooked." Barrett stated that crowd control had been a problem at the Memorial Day services in previous years as well. He asserted "while I have had good order maintained in the grounds, I will state that outside [where Barrett had no legal jurisdiction] the same disorder has been at every one." In this report, Barrett clearly attempted to present himself as a dutiful superintendent able to keep the peace in the actual sacred space of the national cemetery while other law enforcement officials failed to effectively contain the activities of the crowd outside the cemetery's walls.[44]

Barrett explicitly defined the crowd's activities which he, his superiors, and local whites found so upsetting as a racial problem. He specifically targeted the boisterous behavior of younger African Americans for criticism. Barrett reflected, "There are a few and a very few negroes (old slaves) who appear to respect the day and occasion, but nearly all the negroes make it a day of feasting, gambling, drunkenness &c." Significantly, Barrett attributed "bad" behaviors and challenges to racial etiquette to the fact that most participants had not been raised under the system of slavery and emancipated by the sacrifices of the soldiers buried there. Therefore, the "old slaves" supposedly knew how to behave properly, and respect the importance of the cemetery while the younger generation did not.[45]

Barrett seemed to regret that few local whites attended the Memorial Day services, and he blamed this on the African American visitors. Barrett reported "on that day the largest number of white visitors are the Members of the G.A.R. Post from Nashville, Tenn, a few old soldiers in this vicinity and their families. Citizens of Murfreesboro inform me that the reason why they do not attend is because of the negroes and their conduct." Surprisingly, it did not seem to occur to Barrett that local whites with Confederate ties might not want to attend a memorial service in a national cemetery that excluded Confederates in order to honor Union soldiers who killed their relatives and friends during the war. The local community definition of the national cemetery as a "black" and a "Yankee" space persisted.[46]

The furor over the 1897 Memorial Day services at the national cemetery may have been prompted at least in part by the publishing of a critical article in the June 4 edition of the Murfreesboro *Independent Banner* entitled "Federal Decoration." The author began with a description of the formal Memorial Day services within the national cemetery:

We attended the decoration of the graves at the National Cemetery near this city on last Saturday. As to the number present, there were not less than 2,000 nor more than 2,500. Of these not exceeding 250 were whites, the balance colored.

The memorial services were opened with a speech from Congressman Prince of Illinois, to which no one could object, as his praise of the Federal soldiers was not a denunciation of the Confederates, but a tribute to American citizenship, chivalry, and devotion to their country, irrespective of whether they wore the blue or the gray.

The memorial service of the G.A.R. was conducted over the grave of an unknown soldier near the centre of the cemetery, were very appropriate, not sectional, during which flowers were placed upon the grave.

To those who have never attended these services, we will state that at each grave a small U.S. flag is placed, and flowers are used only upon the grave where the memorial services are conducted by the members of the G.A.R.

After this service was over and the benediction pronounced, the audience were invited to the speakers stand, where the exercises were opened with a prayer, when a history of the cemetery was read, giving number of dead.

There was the best of order preserved inside of the cemetery inclosure, and we will do Capt. Barrett, the Superintendent, justice in stating that he did all in his power to make the occasion what it should be, one of solemnity and not festivity, frolicking, feasting and gambling, but outside of the walls of the cemetery he has no control.

We did not count the number present at the speaking, but 500 is a liberal estimate, while at the services at the grave by the G.A.R. there was more than two white persons present to one colored. We thought then and say it now publicly, this shows how much interest in the decoration services proper is taken by the negroes, and how much respect is shown by them to the dead. Any one present will admit that there were at least 1,500 negroes on and adjacent to the grounds while the ceremonies were being conducted, and if any one charges that the negroes predominated at these services on last Saturday, we pronounce it a FALSEHOOD, for there were only 46 of them present by actual count, while the service was being conducted.[47]

In this description, the author offered a detailed chronological depiction of the official ceremonies for his audience of local whites, most of whom had never attended this type of event. Significantly, the author endeavored to characterize the formal services as "white" events. He suggested that the many African Americans present in and around the cemetery during these services were not really participating in them. He placed particular emphasis on the ostensibly non-sectional tone of the services, pointing out that they would not offend local whites with Confederate sympathies. He also absolved Barrett, a white Union veteran referred to by military title, from responsibility for the behavior of the many African Americans present in the fields surrounding the national cemetery. Indeed, the author attempted to convince his audience that the Memorial Day services at the national cemetery were safe events, racially and politically, for local whites to attend.[48]

However, in another portion of the article, with the subheading "Outside of the Cemetery," the author offered a scathing account of the African Americans' activities around the national cemetery. He wrote

We will now state what we saw and no one told us, outside of the cemetery walls. On the East side there was a game of craps being carried on publicly, while a "dead drunk" was placed under a tree near by.

In the lane leading from the railroad to the turnpike, there was in operation publicly, one gambling device, five retailers of barbecued meats, cakes, et., and one lemonade (?) stand. The crowd was so thick in this lane, that we had to force our passage through it.

African Americans favored a more celebratory style of commemorating Memorial Day, and the author severely objected to their community festival, probably in honor of emancipation, since it spoke to equality, not merely the heroic sacrifices of Union soldiers. The large number of African Americans in the road by the cemetery was physically intimidating to the author. His complaint that they had to "force our passage through" the crowd indicated that the African Americans were not deferring to the whites by stepping out of their path, and that behavior was another sign that blacks at the ceremony were acting as equals.[49]

Not one simply to complain, the author proposed two solutions to remedy the conditions around the national cemetery that he found offensive. First, he suggested asking the state government to "make it a felony with imprisonment in the penitentiary for any one to run a gambling device of any kind, or to offer anything for sale to eat or drink within one mile of a cemetery on decoration day." Then, the author advocated

> Another remedy and one which we think more appropriate, would be to get Congress to allow the burial of the dead Confederates on the unoccupied grounds in the Cemetery, and let the blue and gray have the same day, the last Sunday in May, for the decoration day, and we guarantee that there will be a proper observance of the day, and the services attended by those who have a proper regard for the occasion.

Clearly, the author anticipated that if this became a joint event and sacred space honoring both Union and Confederate fallen, African Americans would no longer attend. With this plan, the author offered a means of physically reuniting the local Confederate sympathizers with the nation by including their dead in the national cemetery and through making Memorial Day at Stones River a "white" event. Lurking behind this reunionist suggestion, of course, was the implied menace that local Confederate supporters would exert control over the offending African Americans, probably through the threat of or actual violence. The Confederates were not interred in the national cemetery, and no evidence has been found indicating the development of a local political movement in favor of moving the Confederate dead from Evergreen Cemetery to Stones River National Cemetery during this period.[50]

The fourth and final section of this article, "A Question," provided insight into intersections of race, commemoration, and sectional identity in the Murfreesboro area. The author inquired

> Is there a man in Rutherford county who believes that a gambler would be permitted to operate his gambling devices within fifty yards of the Confeder-

ates graves on decoration day? If not, then we ask, why are they permitted to do so at the decoration of the federal dead in the national cemetery? Will not the same laws that debars gamblers from running their devices near Evergreen Cemetery on decoration day also debar them from running near the Federal Cemetery when the G.A.R. hold their services? If it does, we would like to know why it is prohibited at the one and permitted at the other.

The question that the author posed in this passage revealed that local whites, including authority figures such as the police, had little interest in trying to quell the African American celebration at the national cemetery on Memorial Day. They seemed generally content to allow the cemetery at Stones River to be racially marked as a "black" sacred space, which made some cemetery superintendents and probably GAR members uncomfortable. This state of affairs suggested that most local Confederate whites were less interested than their Unionist counterparts in creating joint reunion events at this time.[51]

In 1904, the cemetery superintendent complained about upcoming Memorial Day activities. On May 12, Superintendent Clayton Hart told his quartermaster department supervisor that the Phil H. Sheridan GAR Post based in Nashville had complete responsibility for the day's program. He acknowledged that "the residents of this community are not consulted in the matter, and the only knowledge I have of this years program is an item in a Nashville paper of last month which stated that the Post had appointed the usual committees for this years services." He also offered a description of the visitors who usually attended the services:

> The greater portion of the attendance here is from a negro excursion that has been coming here from Nashville for ten or fifteen years. (25 coaches last year loaded to the utmost limit). The picnic character of this crowd composed largely as it is of the worst elements of Nashville's negro population is a disgrace to this cemetery and a dishonor to the memory and graves of the brave men who are buryed here. Negro excursions to a National Cemetery are an evil that should be abolished if practicable.

> The character of the attendance here prevents the people of Murfreesboro from attending the Memorial exercises at this cemetery and there is usually less than twenty whites seen on the grounds that day. There is always some local

peace officers on hand to give any aid that may be desired. Very good order was maintained last year and we hope to do better this year.

Hart continued the pattern of decrying the behavior of African American visitors and lamenting the lack of local white support for the Memorial Day exercises. He passed blame to the GAR, not the cemetery staff, for the day's ceremonies. Hart and his staff continued to be responsible for making sure that the grounds were in excellent condition for this important occasion and for directing crowd control within the cemetery walls.[52]

In 1912, a complex public uproar about the Memorial Day services at Stones River National Cemetery took place. That year the Liberty GAR Post headquartered at Tullahoma conducted the ceremonies, and later protested its treatment by the cemetery superintendent John Thomas. The members placed complaining letters in the *Tullahoma Banner*, and sent a formal complaint to the war department. In their letter to the department, post members presented their objections:

First, we met there the 30th of May, 1912 and received very little attention…, and when it was time for us to spread our dinner we were prohibited from doing so, under the shade trees, as had been our custom for several years past; and was forced to use the speakers stand. There were several negroes who had the privilege of eating on the grass under the trees.

Second. The water conditions were very poor indeed, out of three wells, there were only one that was in a condition to be used, one was so infected and dirty that it would have been unhealthy for use, the other was out of repair to such an extent that it could not be used and from the only well that was fit for use was at the house, and the superintendent removed the handle from the pump and forbid our using the water, before he removed the handle he drew a tub full of water, to supply the large number of old soldiers which was far too little to supply the wants of all the old soldiers much less the number of visitors that were there, while a great number of them actually suffered for the want of water we remonstrated with the superintendent but to no avail, he was just as discourteous as possible in regard to all favors we asked him for.

Third. There are two sections or parts of the cemetery and I asked of the super-intendent whether or not he had decorated the lower part, and he replied that he had done so. I thought best to go down and see for myself, upon reaching there I found the gate locked, and was compelled to climb the high fence, so that I could inspect it, etc. There was no one on duty at the main cemetery gate, and teams, etc. could drive in at will, it seemed to be very loosely governed. We found the superintendent usually discourteous when approached upon the commonest act of privilege, that had heretofore been gladly extended to us, and to other old soldiers of our post we deem it nothing but Justice to us and other old soldiers that we should respectfully call this to the attention of this Department. These charges which seem very sever, can fully be substantiated by the old soldiers and the visitors that attended the memorial services there on the 30th of May.

One important aspect of the GAR's complaints is their particular fury over their perception that African Americans were allowed to eat their lunches in the national cemetery while they were not. Significantly, Thomas's superiors also closely questioned him concerning this portion of the GAR's charges.[53]

In response to these accusations, Superintendent Thomas submitted his own reports and solicited sworn affidavits from some local residents who visited the cemetery on Memorial Day. In addition to attempting to refute each of the GAR post's accusations, Thomas stated that he "was sorely disappointed with the members of Liberty Post who were here on Memorial Day. They were the only people who had no regard for 'Rules and Regulations' governing national cemeteries."[54] Thomas tried to enforce a regulation prohibiting picnicking on cemetery grounds that challenged the customary practices of the visitors who were used to eating their lunches in the cemetery on Memorial Day. He did purposely disable a cistern pump after members of the crowd broke the well pump. He argued that "it became necessary to remove the handle for the good of the service and for the protection of public property." Thomas also strongly protested against the GAR's contentions that the cemetery grounds were not well-kept and that he treated them rudely. One of Thomas's primary defenses was his assertion that he lacked sufficient staff to manage the large crowd effectively. He related:

There was 2500 to 3000 people on the grounds, among them was several tin type photographers who began their opperations and this crowd brought in a baseball out-fit and commenced practice. I was obliged to turn my attention to these violators as well and ejected them from the grounds. This took up a considerable of my time; this with the extensive amount of lawns give some of the negroes an opportunity to eat their lunch on the grass, which could not be prevented by a force of 3 laborers, 2 laborers were guarding the two main entrance gates, and the other laborer was on guard around the buildings.

From information obtainable this cemetery has been used by Nashville colored people for many years as their annual picnic ground, coming in by train loads every Memorial Day, and that heretofore no attempt has been made to prevent the colored people and the G.A.R. Post from littering up the grounds. To enforce the regulations on memorial day will require at least 15 to 20 men, for at least a couple of Decoration Days.

Significantly, Thomas noted that the GAR members were the only ones who objected when asked not to eat on cemetery grounds; when Thomas asked African Americans to take their lunches outside of the cemetery, they did so without complaint.[55]

Thomas enlisted the support of a group of prominent local whites and their African American chauffeur on his behalf in this dispute with the GAR. The presence of these white men at the services demonstrated that at least a few curious local whites visited the cemetery on Memorial Day to observe the ceremonies. Although the African American chauffeur Louis Proby's name was included on the affidavit it is reasonable to conclude that this account of the day's events more accurately reflected the views of his employer and his white companions. This group provided the following notarized affidavit:

We, the undersigned, Aaron Todd, a Justice of the Peace, aged 72 years; Richard Beard, Attorney at Law and Insurance Agent, aged 69 years; John A. Campbell, Real Estate Agent, aged 58 years, and Jesse W. Sparks Attorney at Law, aged 45 years, and Louis Proby, col., aged 24 years, Chauffeur for A. L. Todd, beg to make this statement relative to conditions and general management of the Stones River National Cemetery near this city on May 30, 1912, which statement is made at the request and instance of John H. Thomas, superintendent in charge.

We beg to state that on the day in question we drove out to the cemetery in a 5-passenger automobile in order to witness the ceremonies that were in progress at the place. Not knowing the rules of the cemetery we attempted to drive in through the gate at one of the entrances, and were politely told by Wm. Harland, col., one of the laborers at the cemetery, that we would not be allowed to enter with the automobile, which privledge was denied to others in our presence at the time. We therefore left the automobile on the side of the turnpike, and all of us went into the cemetery. **We frankly state we never saw a better behaved, more concentrated assembly of people, both white and colored, in a crowd of like proportions in our lives, and the best of order prevailed and was commented on by our party.** [emphasis added]

The cemetery was as clean and well kept as it was possible to make such a place, and there was not litter or paper of any kind scattered over the grounds; in fact, some of us heard various parties, all of whom were colored, denied the privledge of bringing into the grounds things that would make a litter, and we saw no picnic lunches or dinners spread on the grounds and no indication that anybody was partaking of lunch or drinking either intoxicating or soft drinks on the grounds.

There was provided on the outside, across the turnpike from the cemetery proper a number of eating stands, and also places where lemonade and soft drinks were served in abundance, and these places seemed to be well patronized, especially by the colored people, who were about 100 to 1 in the majority over the whites.

The keepers lodge, which we entered and where we registered, was full of ladies who seemed to be enjoying themselves resting on the porticos, and so far as we could see there was ample water to drink for everyone, as some of us found plenty of water there to drink, those who desired it.

At the time we were there the program was being carried out and speeches were being made, and we met the superintendent of the cemetery, Mr. Thomas, who was very attentive to us and very courteous and polite, and showed us around over the cemetery, and we went to the flagpole, which flag was at half mast, and the superintendent, not being pleased with its location, raised it a little higher while we were with him. Every grave, so far as we could see, was decorated with a small United States flag, and we begged him to give us a flag apiece, which he very courteously declined saying he was not allowed to do that.

After the speaking was over we met the main speaker, Hon. W. K. Crowell, from Shelbyville, Tennessee, who had quite an extended chat with us, and who complimented the management of the cemetery in the very highest degree in and out of the presence of the superintendent, and said that he had never in his life attended a decoration of the graves and he had been to a great many of them where he had seen such good order and behaviour and where he had seen things managed in such a painstaking way as on that day.

We met a number of old soldiers who were there with their families, and heard nothing but the very best expressions of how they enjoyed the day.

We have of our own knowledge of this orderly conduct on the part of the visitors, and that they were not permitted to throw paper or other litter on the ground, and no trees or shrubs or plants were cut or injured by any of them, and we saw no one or heard of any one being ejected from the cemetery for improper conduct or violating any of the rules, but we have been informed since then that after we left, which was about 3 o'clock, that some three or four negroes had been ejected from the cemetery for misbehaviour.

This group offered a portrait of the Memorial Day services that emphasized the maintenance of racial order. The crowd included a few whites, mostly associated with the GAR, and a large number of African Americans who were ostensibly subjected to a high level of scrutiny. The authors repeatedly emphasized that that the cemetery staff led by Thomas maintained strict control over African American visitors' behavior. They portrayed Thomas as a competent master of this sacred space. Strikingly, this group also does not seem at all offended by the celebratory character of the scene. This could be due in part to their conception of themselves as commemorative tourists rather than active participants in the Memorial Day services. This attitude may also reflect at least some of the local whites' construction of the federal Memorial Day holiday as an event to be celebrated by African Americans and Union veterans rather than a time to commemorate the experiences of all Civil War soldiers.[56]

In an atmosphere of violence and white supremacy, Stones River National Cemetery offered African Americans throughout Middle Tennessee a relatively safe federal sacred space to celebrate their freedom and Union victory. Even the boldest Confederate partisan would have hesitated to stage a violent assault against a Memorial Day service at a national cemetery for fear of federal reprisals. Some local whites may have attempted to marginalize the Memorial Day ceremonies and their participants by refusing to attend and presenting a racist portrait of the cemetery as a place associated with unruly African Americans, but they stopped short of employing violence as a means to fight these important Union commemorative events.[57]

African Americans and their white northern allies preserved and celebrated the memories of emancipation and Union victory during this period despite the sometimes violent hostility of former Confederates. Stones River National Cemetery served as a focal point for Union commemoration in the county, and in the minds of many local people, this sacred national space embodied the enduring link between African Americans, white northerners, and the federal government. Even as controversies over Memorial Day events at the cemetery and their predominantly African American audiences raged, the bonds between the federal government, African Americans, and northern whites forged in the horrible struggles of the war and its aftermath persisted in Rutherford County.

1. On the dominance of Radical Republican politicians in Tennessee in the late 1860s, see Robert E. Corlew, *Tennessee: A Short History*, 2nd edition, (Knoxville, 1990), 329–336; Kathleen R. Zebley, "Unconditional Unionist: Samuel Mayes Arnell and Reconstruction in Tennessee," in Carroll Van West, ed., *Tennessee History: The Land, the People, and the Culture*, (Knoxville, 1998): 186–194; and, specifically on Rutherford County, see John C. Spence, *The Annals of Rutherford County, Volume Two 1829–1870* (Murfreesboro, 1991), 1866, 258–259, 261; Spence, *Annals*, 1867, 263, 264–270; Spence, *Annals*, 1868, 271–275; Spence, *Annals*, 1869, 278–283.

2. On the decline of Radical Republicans in Tennessee politics after 1870, see Corlew, *Tennessee*, 342–345; Zebley, "Unconditional Unionist," 194–195; and, specifically in Rutherford County, Spence, *Annals*, 287.

3. See Corlew, *Tennessee*, 363–364, 372–387. For an excellent discussion of this issue in the South as a whole, see Edward L. Ayers, *The Promise of the New South* (New York, 1992), particularly 132–159.

4. On the origins and significance of the national cemetery system, see Gary Laderman, *The Sacred Remains: American Attitudes toward Death, 1799–1883* (New Haven, 1996), 117–

122; G. Kurt Piehler, *Remembering War the American Way* (Washington, 1995), 49–52; see also, Monro MacCloskey, *Hallowed Ground: Our National Cemeteries* (New York, 1968), 17–45.

5. Laderman, *The Sacred Remains*, 188–120.

6. William Earnshaw, "Extracts from a Report of Chaplain Wm. Earnshaw, U.S.A., in Charge of the National Cemetery at Stone's River, Tenn., *Roll of Honor No. XI: Names of Soldiers Who Died in Defense of the American Union, Interred in the National Cemeteries at Chattanooga, Stone's River, and Knoxville, Tenn.* (1866; reprint, Baltimore, 1994), 229.

7. John C. Spence, *A Diary of the Civil War* (Murfreesboro, 1993), 157–158.

8. William Earnshaw to C. B. Fisk, 25 July 1865, Selected Records of "Freedmen's Bureau," 1865–72 Letters Received, Office of the Assistant Commissioner, 1865, Registered Series (A–E), available on microfilm (M32, roll 25) at the Tennessee State Library and Archives, Nashville, Tennessee, hereinafter TSLA.

9. William Earnshaw to J. L. Donaldson, 25 April 1866, National Archives and Records Administration Record Group 92, available on microfilm at Stones River National Battlefield, Murfreesboro, Tenn., hereinafter SRNB.

10. William Earnshaw to Major [illegible name], 4 August 1867, Selected Records of "Freedmen's Bureau," 1865–72 Telegrams Received, Office of the Assistant Commissioner, 1866 & 1867, Registered Series (A–F), M32, roll 34, TSLA.

11. William Earnshaw to J. L. Donaldson, 25 April 1866, National Archives and Records Administration Record Group 92, microfilm, SRNB.

12. William Earnshaw, "Extracts from a Report of Chaplain Wm. Earnshaw, U.S.A., in Charge of the National Cemetery at Stone's River, Tenn., *Roll of Honor No. XI*, 228.

13. Ibid, 229.

14. Piehler, *Remembering War the American Way*, 51.

15. Eric Foner, *Reconstruction: America's Unfinished Revolution, 1863–1877* (New York, 1989).

16. The Bureau of Refugees, Freedmen and Abandoned Lands was commonly called the Freedmen's Bureau. For a general study of this agency, see William S. McFeely, *Yankee Stepfather: General O. O. Howard and the Freedmen* (New York, 1994) and see also Foner, *Reconstruction*; for discussions of this agency in Tennessee, see particularly John Cimprich, *Slavery's End in Tennessee, 1861–1865* (n.p.: 1985), 120, 124–129; Steven V. Ash, *Middle Tennessee Society Transformed, 1860–1870: War and Peace in the Upper South* (Baton Rouge, 1988), 192–224.

17. See entries in Selected Records of the "Freedman's Bureau," 1865–1872,Volume 186 Murfreesboro 28 October 1868–11 June 1869 and Volume 188 Murfreesboro 3 November 1868–14 June 1869, M32 roll 22, TSLA.

18. On the Freedmen's Bureau and schools in Rutherford County see for example, John Ogden to Superintendent at Murfreesboro, 15 March 1866; D. Burt to A. B. C. Douglass,17 October 1866; D. Burt to Maria M. Harrington, 24 April 1867; D. Burt to Stephen Burrow,

15 September 1867; and D. Burt to A. B. C. Douglas, 27 February 1868 each located in the Selected Records of "Freedmen's Bureau," 1865–1872 Letters Sent, Vol. 36 Supt. of Education, 26 February 1866–16 August 1868, M32 roll 5, TSLA.

19. For information on medical services provided by the Freedmen's Bureau office at Murfreesboro, see for example, John Seage to Clinton B. Fisk, 16 December 1865 and W. C. Kelley to Clinton B. Fisk, 16 December 1865 regarding a smallpox epidemic, and A. C. Smartfelder to Clinton B. Fisk, 22 December 1865 containing a medical inspection report located in Selected Records of "Freedman's Bureau," 1865–1872, Letters Received, Office of the Assistant Commissioner, 1865, Registered Series (P–W), M32 roll 27, TSLA.

20. John Seage to Maj. Genl. Fisk, 1 April 1866, Selected Records of the "Freedman's Bureau," 1865–1872, Letters Received, Office of the Assistant Commissioner, 1866, Registered Series (S–V), M32 roll 32, TSLA.

21. J. K. Nelson to S. W. Groesbeck, 19 February 1867, Selected Records of "Freedmen's Bureau," 1865–1872 Letters Received, Office of the Assistant Commissioner, 1867, Registered Series (G–P),M32 roll 35, TSLA.

22. Ibid.

23. Ibid.

24. J. K. Nelson to S. W. Groesbeck, 5 March 1867, Selected Records of "Freedmen's Bureau," 1865–1872 Letters Received, Office of the Assistant Commissioner, 1867, Registered Series (G–P), M32 roll 35, TSLA.

25. For Ash's discussion of the Klan in Middle Tennessee, see particularly. Ash, *Middle Tennessee Society Transformed, 1860–1870* , 203–206.

26. Foner, *Reconstruction*, 425–459, quote on 428.

27. *Murfreesboro Freedom's Watchman*, 26 February 1868, 3.

28. Hammett Dell, interview, conducted by Irene Robertson, *Born in Slavery: Slave Narratives from the Federal Writers' Project, 1936–1938 Arkansas Narratives*, vol. II, part 2, 144–146, *American Memory*, http://www.memory.loc.gov/ammem/amhome.html, spelling as recorded in the original.

29. T.M. Robbins to Quartermaster General, 16 December 1876, Museum Collection, SRNB; James A. Ekin to Thomas Frame, 20 December 1876, microfiche of original ledger Letters Received 1876–1881, Museum Collection, SRNB. All correspondence ledger materials cited below are also from the Museum Collection, SRNB.

30. James D. Richardson to Isham G. Harris, 15 May 1885, National Archives Record Group 92, microfilm at SRNB; G. B. Holland, 1st Endorsement on letter from James D. Richardson to Isham G. Harris dated 15 May 1885, 13 June 1885, National Archives Record Group 92, microfilm at SRNB; J. [last name illegible], Chief Clerk writing on behalf of the Secretary of War, to Isham G. Harris, 18 June 1885, National Archives Record Group 92, microfilm at SRNB.

31. Joseph T. Davidson to Thomas Shea, 5 July 1911, Letters Received 1890–1920; Joseph T. Davidson to Thomas Shea, 7 July 1911, Joseph T. Davidson to James Rucker, 7 July 1911, Letters Received 1890–1920; Thomas Shea to Joseph T. Davidson, 8 July 1911, Letters Sent 10 July 1890–3 August 1912.

32. Thomas Shea to Joseph T. Davidson, telegram, 10 July 1911; Letters Sent 10 July 1890–3 August 1912; Thomas Shea to Joseph Davidson, 10 July 1911, Letters Sent 10 July 1890–3 August 1912.

33. Thomas Shea to Joseph T. Davidson, telegram, 10 July 1911, Letters Sent 10 July 1890–3 August 1912; Thomas Shea to Joseph T. Davidson, 10 July 1911, Letters Sent 10 July 1890–3 August 1912.

34. "Observance of Memorial Day," *Nashville Daily American*, 30 May 1907.

35. For biographical information on William Holland (Harlan), 1834–1909, see the "Harlan Family Cemetery" file available at SRNB.

36. Thomas Frame to Rufus Saxton, 18 May 1886, Letters sent 27 July 1883–30 June 1890; Rufus Saxton to Thomas Frame, 21 May 1886, transcript of original ledger Letters Received 1885–1888.

37. Thomas Frame to Rufus Saxton, 23 May 1887, Letters Sent 27 July 1883–30 June 1890; Thomas Frame to Rufus Saxton, 4 June 1887, Letters Sent 27 July 1883–30 June 1890.

38. "Decoration Day at Stones River Cemetery," *The National Picket*, 1, no. 1 (July 1891).

39. Ibid.

40. For a discussion of racial politics in the South during the 1890s, see particularly Ayers, *Promise of the New South*, 132–159, 214–309.

41. Corlew, *Tennessee*, 383, 364; see particularly Ayers, *Promise of the New South*, 153–159.

42. Edwin P. Barrett to John L. Clem, January 1896; Letters Sent 10 July 1890–3 August 1912.

43. John L. Clem to E. P. Barrett, 14 March 1896, Letters Received 1895–1903.

44. Edwin P. Barrett to John L. Clem, 3 April 1912, Letters Sent 10 July 1890–3 August 1912.

45. Ibid.

46. Ibid.

47. "Federal Decoration," Murfreesboro *Independent Banner*, 4 June 1897, in Edwin P. Barrett to John L. Clem, 3 April 1912, Letters Sent 10 July 1890–3 August 1912.

48. Ibid.

49. Ibid.

50. Ibid.

51. Ibid.

52. Clayton Hart to C.A.H. McCauley, 12 May 1904, Letters Sent 10 July 1890–3 August 1912.

53. Samuel Main et al to the War Department, enclosed in G.S. Bingham to John Thomas, 14 June 1912, Letters Received 1890–1920. See also, "G.A.R. Members Say They Are Mistreated," Tullahoma *Banner*, 3 June 1912, also enclosed in G.S. Bingham to John Thomas, 14 June 1912, Letters Received 1890–1920.

54. John Thomas to Depot Quartermaster, Jeffersonville, Indiana, 29 June 1912, Letters Sent 10 July 1890–3 August 1912.

55. John Thomas to Depot Quartermaster, Jeffersonville, Indiana, 27 June 1912, Letters Sent 10 July 1890–3 August 1912; for quote, see John Thomas to Depot Quartermaster, Jeffersonville, Indiana, 14 July 1912, Letters Sent 10 July 1890–3 August 1912.

56. Aaron Todd et al to Depot Quartermaster, U.S.A., notarized affidavit, 15 June 1912, Letters Received 1890–1920. The William Harlan referred to in this affidavit was probably the son of Union veteran and cemetery staff member William Holland (Harlan), 1834–1909. The younger William Harlan, 1895–1979, was a World War I veteran. For information on this family, see the "Harlan Family Cemetery" file available at SRNB.

57. Mitch Kachun, *Festivals of Freedom: Memory and Meaning in African American Emancipation Celebrations, 1808–1915* (Amherst, 2003), see particularly 1–9, 175–206, 259–260. The theory that one of the reasons Stones River National Cemetery was a particularly attractive site for African Americans to celebrate Memorial Day was the relative safety of this federal site is very plausible considering the history of white attacks against African American gatherings in Middle Tennessee. For example, in 1868, the Klan violently assaulted many African Americans at a July Fourth holiday event in nearby Columbia, Tennessee. On this incident, see Zebley, "Unconditional Unionist," 193.

FORTRESS ROSENCRANS:

A History 1865–1990

══════════ ⚭ ══════════

Lenard E. Brown

A s the first full year of the Civil War drew to a close in the fall and early winter of 1862, the Union leadership had to look to the western campaigns for any evidence of continued success. The capture of Forts Henry and Donelson in February had opened up the Cumberland and Tennessee rivers to transport. In April at Shiloh, Major General Ulysses S. Grant had won another victory. By mid-year Federal forces occupied most of Middle and West Tennessee and parts of northern Alabama and Mississippi and were threatening the railroad center of Chattanooga. Even the Confederate campaign in August and September that resulted in the invasion of Kentucky and carried some of the Rebels to the banks of the Ohio was turned back at the Battle of Perryville in October. Although parts of Middle Tennessee and Alabama were lost, the Union was still in control. Grant, beginning his campaign to capture Vicksburg on the Mississippi, had his supply base at Holly Springs, Mississippi, destroyed by Confederate cavalry under Major General Earl Van Dorn on December 20.

The Lincoln Administration, which had experienced nothing but problems with the campaigns in the East, needed a victory at year's end for both political and psychological reasons. And the man they believed could secure it was the newly appointed commander of the Army of the Cumberland, Major General William S. Rosecrans. Rosecrans had moved his army into Nashville in early November and spent the month reorganizing and resting while gathering supplies. By early December, pressure from Washington was mounting for him to undertake a campaign against the Confederate forces under General Braxton Bragg located near Murfreesboro, Tennessee, some thirty miles southeast of Nashville. On Deember 26, 1862, the Army of the Cumberland moved out toward the Confederate Army of Tennessee with the intention of brushing it aside and capturing Chattanooga.

Four days later the two armies made contact at Murfreesboro. The Confederate line was on both sides of Stones River. The right wing was east of the river, while the center controlled the Nashville Pike and the Nashville and Chattanooga Railroad. The left was south of the Franklin Road facing west and extending beyond the right wing of the Union army. The Union right and part of the center between Franklin Road and Manson or Wilkinson Pike on the north was nearly parallel and about a half mile distant from the Confederates. However, the remainder of the center and the left veered away from the Confederate lines so that at the railroad and pike there was a distance of more than three-quarters of a mile. The left was anchored on Stones River near McFadden's Ford.

Both Bragg and Rosecrans planned to attack their opponent's right. The Confederates struck first, appearing out of the gray foggy dawn just after 6 a.m., catching some of the Union troops still at breakfast. They pushed the northern troops back to Wilkinson Pike where resistance stiffened and the Confederate advance was slowed by the division commanded by Brigadier General Philip H. Sheridan. However, the Rebel left continued to press the Union right, forcing it back until the Union line by late afternoon had the configuration of a backward or reversed "C." The left wing was still near McFadden's Ford on Stones River. The center was along Thompson Lane and bent back to run parallel but southeast of the Nashville Pike and the railroad. The right end of the line rested between the pike and the railroad, which were less than an eighth of a mile apart. The Union line, although bent, had not broken and the Confederates had not captured the road and rail line or cut them off from Nashville.

There was no major activity on New Year's Day, 1863, as both armies held their positions. Confederate cavalry under General Joseph Wheeler destroyed a Union wagon train near La Vergne. The Union gave up their position in Round Forest that they had defended so tenaciously on December 31 and the Confederates occupied it. Rosecrans moved an infantry division across Stones River to the high ground on the east side. If artillery could be emplaced on this position, the Union could shell Bragg's right and center. Bragg on the morning of January 2 realized the danger that this posed and ordered an attack on the Union lines by four brigades of Major General John Breckinridge's Division. If the assault were successful, the Confederates could shell the Union left and center. It was not. Begun about four in the afternoon the Rebels enjoyed initial success, but the Confederates pursuing the retreating Federals were slaughtered by the massed fire of fifty-seven cannon located on the opposite bank of the river. The Federal infantry counterattacked and the Confederates were driven back to their original line with a loss of 1,700 men killed, wounded, and captured.[1]

Rosecrans held his defensive perimeter on January 3. That night Bragg began his withdrawal to Shelbyville and Tullahoma. Rosecrans did not follow. Having displayed one of his character traits—a bull-dog tenacity in battle—he displayed another—slow methodical preparation and a reluctance to go to war. It would be late June before he would move to engage the Army of Tennessee again. However, the Army of the Cumberland had produced the victory that Lincoln sought.

During the five months that Rosecrans and his army remained near Murfreesboro, they constructed the largest enclosed earthen fortification built during the war. Located northwest of the town and named for the general, it was designed to be a refuge for the army after defeat, a supply base for the army in the field, and a means of controlling the rail line that linked Nashville and Chattanooga. Plans for the fortification were drawn up by chief of engineers of the Army of the Cumberland, Brigadier General James S. Morton. Morton no doubt based his plans on Dennis Hart Mahan's *Treatise on Field Fortifications*, the standard for earthwork construction by both sides during the Civil War.

Fortress Rosecrans was built on high ground about a mile and a half north and west of the Rutherford County Courthouse at the center of Murfreesboro. It enclosed about two hundred acres and measured 1,250 yards north to south and 1,070 east to west. The Nashville and Chattanooga Railroad and the main road from Nashville ran through the center of the fortifications. The fortress was composed of a series of lunettes linked together by a line of earthworks generally described as "curtain walls", or by abatis, trees and brush cut down to form an entangled obstruction. These lunettes were salient angles with two flanks but open to the rear or interior of the fort. Inside the fort were four redoubts (Schofield, Brannon, Johnson, and Wood) designed to be the final line of defense if the outer works were breached. Each redoubt was an enclosed rectangular earthwork and mounted artillery, a blockhouse in the form of a cross, and a magazine. These redoubts were located to control either the railroad or the Nashville Pike or both in order to deny their use to the Confederates. Their guns could also sweep the interior of the fort.

In front of the lunettes and curtain walls were ditches six or more feet deep. The area outside of the fortifications was cleared to give the defenders fields of fire. The artillery located in the lunettes and along the earthworks were ranged and sighted on points from 900 to 1,450 yards distant. The fortification was so designed that if attacking infantry were able to escape the rain of shot, shell, and canister from the artillery and approach the walls of the lunettes and curtains, they would be caught in a crossfire of musketry and rifles sweeping the ditches or abatis. The artillery pieces fired through embrasures or V-shaped openings in the lunette or curtain walls. A series of traverses or earthen walls set at right angles to the curtain wall protected the artillerymen from flanking or ricochet fire. In total it presented a formidable face to an attacker. [2]

Work began on the fortification on January 23, 1863. Labor was drawn from the 40,000 men encamped in the area. The soldiers were supervised by men of the Pioneer Brigade who were engineer troops skilled in the construction of fortifications, railroads and bridges. The work crews of soldiers were rotated in and out by brigades working on the fortifications for one or two days at a time. When not involved in the construction of the forts, the soldiers pursued other duties such as picket, duty to guard against surprise attack, foraging details, and patrols through the surrounding countryside that often included brief sharp skirmishes with Confederate patrols, and days in camp spending time "pretty much as they see fit." The weather was cold and rainy and there was considerable sickness in the camps. Desertion also was a problem for some units. Although roads were impassable, the railroad was functioning by the second week of February and supplies were sufficient. [3]

On February 22, General Rosecrans reported that the fortifications were rapidly taking shape. Five days later Rosecrans again wrote to Chief of Staff Henry W. Halleck reporting that the works were well advanced. On March 28, he requested that Halleck send him several companies of regular army artillery to man the heavy guns that were being located in the works near Murfreesboro, as well as those at Nashville. Halleck apparently ignored this request because no regular army units were sent to the Army of the Cumberland at this point.

From late January to early April, work went on 24 hours a day, seven days a week, and involved from four to seven thousand men. Then it was reduced to five days and on April 20 the "graveyard shift" was discontinued. In early June, the pace of work was increased to finish the fortress before General Rosecrans, responding to increasing pressure from President Lincoln and Chief of Staff Halleck, moved against Bragg and toward Chattanooga. When he took the field June 24, Rosecrans no doubt did not believe the fortification was complete. He left Brigadier General Horatio Van Cleve in charge of the fortress and a garrison made up of approximately two thousand light duty convalescents. Except for some minor construction the fortifications were not expanded. [4]

What Rosecrans left behind was an impressive engineering work. In addition to the 14,600 feet of rifle pits and lunettes and the four redoubts, there were four steam-powered sawmills to provide timber for the blockhouses, warehouses, depots, and other purposes. Because the fortress was designed as a point of refuge in which an army of fifty thousand could remain for sixty to ninety days, there were three commissary depots filled with rations, a quartermaster depot with supplies, two ordnance depots with weapons, and an engineer warehouse and depot.[5]

Stones River divided the fort into two unequal parts. Lunettes Negley and Stanley and Battery Cruft were located on the left bank of the river. Redoubt Schofield was located behind and in support of these strong points. The four sawmills and two commissary depots were also located on the left bank of the river. On the right bank or east of the river were seven lunettes (Palmer, Thomas, McCook, Crittenden, Granger, Rousseau, and Reynolds) and one battery, Mitchell. Lunettes Palmer and Thomas were south of Lytle Creek. The other three redoubts (Brannon, T.J. Wood and Johnson) and the remaining warehouses and depots were located east of the river. There were in addition three outlying works. Demi-Lunettes Davis and Garfield were located on high ground south of Lytle Creek and controlled Franklin Road, while an earthwork in the form of an inverted "V," Redan Van Cleve, covered the approaches to Nashville Ford from the east. Abatis consisting of felled trees with their branches pointing outward were located in marshy areas on both sides of the river and at strategic locations on approaches to the fort.

By the end of 1863, Fortress Rosecrans was in the backwater of the war. In October 1863, while the Union troops were bottled up in Chattanooga, Braxton Bragg sent Major General Joseph Wheeler and his cavalry on a raid into Middle Tennessee. Union troops were rushed from Nashville to Murfreesboro. Wheeler's Confederates, recognizing the strength of Fortress Rosecrans, burned a bridge, tore up some railroad tracks, captured a blockhouse, and retreated to Shelbyville. In November, Union troops under General Grant broke the siege of Chattanooga and forced the Confederates back into north Georgia. The two armies then went into winter quarters. During 1864 and for the remainder of the war, the fortress was garrisoned by convalescent soldiers and officers recovering from wounds or sickness and a variety of artillery and infantry units that remained there for brief periods before being moved elsewhere.

In November 1864 when Major General William T. Sherman left Atlanta headed for the sea, he detached Major General George Thomas and the Army of the Cumberland to engage General John B. Hood, who was moving back toward Tennessee. Again the garrison of Rosecrans was increased and five regiments, four thousand to five thousand men, were sent to Murfreesboro to defend the Nashville and Chattanooga Railroad by occupying blockhouses along the line. From the last week of November until the middle of December 1864, there were skirmishes in and around Murfreesboro and the fortress. The impressive works discouraged Confederates from any attack and they withdrew to rejoin Hood's main command. On December 15–16, Hood's Army of Tennessee was crushed by Thomas and driven south in headlong retreat.

Although garrisoned until the end of the war and mounting fifty-seven guns in March 1865, Fortress Rosecrans never was threatened again.

In April of 1866, a year after the war ended, the fortress was abandoned. By that date all the buildings within the fortification had probably been sold at auction. Most were removed by successful bidders, while others remained in place. A few may have survived into the first decades of this century.[6] The earthworks themselves were already melting down—a process that had begun by the end of 1863 as traverses eroded and the walls of redoubts left unfinished slipped into the ditches that surrounded them. General Zealous B. Tower observed in his inspection report in April 1865:

> It requires much labor to keep so large a work in repair; small portions of the parapets have sloughed off, due to frost and heavy rains. Some thirty feet of the parapet revetment of Lunette Thomas had fallen down, when I inspected March 10. Parts of the revetted traverses in Lunette Negley are badly broken down and I have been informed that the heavy and uncommon rains since have caused further damage.[7]

However, the earthworks did not disappear. Rain and erosion softened their outlines, portions of individual lunettes and batteries were lost, but evidence of their existence remained until the middle years of the 1950s. Then the growth of Murfreesboro, and development of motels and shopping centers along the new alignment of U.S. Highway 41, began to take its toll. In 1960 the National Park Service studied the possibility of adding Lunette Gordon Granger as a satellite of Stones River National Battlefield, but destruction of the earthwork ended that possibility. In the 1990s, Jackson Heights Shopping Center, the Goodyear Store to the northwest and the Murfreesboro Motel occupied most of the eastern side of Fortress Rosecrans.

Road construction, residential development, and other activities have destroyed areas on the north and south. A field hospital or convalescent camp shown in a sketch made from near Lunette Negley was destroyed by construction of a municipal golf course. A private home was built on top of Negley and the driveway cut through the earthworks.

The only portions of the fortress that remain in 2012 are Lunette Palmer, Curtain Number 2, the western half of Lunette Thomas, and some defensive works marked, "Unfinished Abandoned" on an 1865 map of the fort. Located south of Lytle Creek they are maintained by the National Park Service. Outside the property a small portion of Curtain Number 1 between Lytle Creek and the railroad still remains.

Brannon Redoubt, a part of the national battlefield, has also survived. Ownership of the property fell to the Nashville, Chattanooga, and St. Louis Railroad that developed it as a point of interest along its route and mounted three twelve-inch, bronze Napoleon cannons on the parapets. In 1928, a year after the national battlefield was established, the railroad transferred ownership of the redoubt to the government. The cannons were moved to the park in 1930 or 1931. A plan for restoration of the redoubt was completed in January 1941 by the National Park Service, which called for replacement of the original guns and development of a parking area. It was never implemented because of insufficient funds.[8]

In 1990, Lunettes Palmer and Thomas and Curtain Number 2 were overgrown with mature trees and underbrush. The back or eastern portion of Thomas was destroyed by construction of a power line in the 1930s and an access road at a later date. The unfinished or abandoned works bordering the golf course were more open. The remains of Curtain 1 were heavily overgrown. Redoubt Brannon that towers over the old Nashville Road had been partially cleared by the National Park Service, and in 2012 the site was cleared and open to visitors. The earthworks are still impressive in size, and interior details such as traverses, gun positions, and magazines are identifiable. [9] In all they represent between 15 and 20 percent of the original works.

That this portion of Fortress Rosecrans has survived can be credited in part to the ownership of the land by only three families in the last 150 years. Captain William Lytle, a Revolutionary War soldier was granted land in Rutherford County, Tennessee, as compensation for his service. When the county seat was relocated in 1811, Lytle offered sixty acres for the town and the site of the courthouse, suggesting that the new town be named after Colonel Hardy Murfree, a fellow soldier. Other lands on both sides of Lytle Creek and along Stones River remained in Lytle family ownership. In 1888, a tract of 278 acres was sold by Marion D. Lytle to C.N. Ordway.[10] The land remained in the possession of Ordway and his children until 1946, when three of his unmarried daughters sold sixty-four acres bounded on the north and east by Lytle Creek and on the south by Franklin Road to F. D. Bills and his wife. This land containing the remnants of Fortress Rosecrans was sold by the Billses to the City of Murfreesboro in June 1965.

In the twenty years that followed the city developed a golf course and other facilities on lands to the west, while preserving the two redoubts and curtain wall. These remnants communicated the impressive size and extent of the fortifications built during five months in 1863.

In 1989, one hundred and twenty-six years after the construction of the fortifications, the National Park Service began a series of studies to determine how to preserve the remnants of Fortress Rosecrans. As set forth in Public Law 100–205, upon completion of these studies and preservation of the remains, the City of Murfreesboro "shall operate and maintain the fortress." Work on the actual preservation of Lunettes Palmer and Thomas and Curtain Number 2 began in 1992. The earthworks were stabilized and severely damaged portions restored. Some of the trees and underbrush was removed and a trail was constructed through the site. In 1993, the city transferred the property to the National Park Servie.

Today, only 3,000 feet of the original 14,000 feet of earthworks remain, and of he interior forts only Redoubt Brannon survives. The preservation the fortress's remains as part of Stones River National Battlefield reflects the continuing commitment of the NPS to the nations heritage.

ꙮ

This article first appeared in the Fall 1991 issue of the *Tennessee Historical Quarterly*; it was updated for inclusion in this book.

1. This brief narrative of the battle was taken from several sources: Charles Spearman, "The Battle of Stones River: Tragic New Years Eve in Tennessee," *Blue and Gray Magazine*, Vol. 6:3 (1989); Mark M. Boatner, III, *The Civil War Dictionary* (New York, 1959), 803–808; and James McPherson, *Battle Cry of Freedom: The Civil War Era*, (New York, 1988), 579–583.

2. The preceding description is based on a report of Union Brigadier General Zealous B. Tower, Office of Inspector General of Fortifications to Major General George Thomas, 28 April 1865. *The War of the Rebellion: A Compilation of the Official Records of the Union and Confederate Armies*, 128 Volumes, (Washington, DC, 1880–1901), Series I, Vol. 49, Part 2, 502. Cited hereafter as OR.

3. Regimental histories of units stationed in the area during the first half of 1863 are very sparse on specific details regarding construction, noting often that they worked on the impressive fortifications during that period. The above was taken from the following sources: John Beatty, *Memoirs of a Volunteer, 1861–1863*, ed. by Harvey Ford (New York, 1946), 166–86;

Originally published as *The Citizen Soldier or Memoirs of a Volunteer* in 1879; Alexis Cope, *The Fifteenth Ohio Volunteers and its Campaigns* (Columbus, 1916), 177–80; Daniel Wait Howe, *Civil War Times, 1861–1865* (Indianapolis, 1902), 136–38; B. F. McGee, *History of the 72nd Indiana Volunteer Infantry of the Mounted Lightning Brigade* (LaFayette, Ind., 1882) 93–95. John Beatty commanded the First Brigade, Second Division of the Fourteenth Army Corps in the Army of the Cumberland.

4. David Wright, "Civil War Fortifications", Thesis in Support of Master of Arts, Middle Tennessee State University (1981), 195–98. Chapter 5 of Wright's study deals with Fortress Rosencrans. *Annals of the Army of the Cumberland: Comprising Biographies, Descriptions of Departments, Accounts of Expeditions, Skirmishes, and Battles* (Philadelphia, 1863), 190–91. Edwin C. Bearss, "The History of Fortress Rosencrans" Typescript (1960), 1–6.

5. The size of these support structures matched the size of Fortress Rosencrans. In a period of one month the First Michigan Engineers, a regiment of 800 men, constructed a magazine 140 x 30 feet and 12 feet high, an ordnance building 100 x 30 and 14 feet high, and a storage house capable of holding five million rations. *Annals of the Army of the Cumberland*, 195.

6. No evidence of the fate of the structures within the fortress was found during this research; however, based on what happened to other fortifications, it is fairly certain that the structures were sold to the highest bidder. General Order 42, 15 July 1865, recognized that property belonging to the Quartermaster's Department was being sold at auction and provided a form for recording the sale of food and forage, barracks and quarters, horses and mules, wagons and carts, and clothing and camp equipage. OR, Series 3, Vol. 5, p. 354–55.

7. OR, I, Vol. 49, 502–03.

8. Ann Willett, "A History of Stones River National Military Park", Types cript(1958), 75 and 97–98.

9. In 1976 Steven J. Fox, with funding from the National Park Service, Tennessee Historical Commission, and the City of Murfreesboro archeologically investigated Lunette Palmer. Evidence of this investigation is visible. His report, "Archeology of Fortress Rosencrans: A Civil War Garrison in Middle Tennessee" (1978) is available at Stones River National Battlefield.

10. Presumably the land appropriated by the Union for construction of the fort simply reverted to the Lytle family when the fort was abandoned.

STONES RIVER NATIONAL MILITARY PARK

Bob Womack

From 1767, when Uriah Stone first found the river that now carries his name, until the last day of 1862, Stones River was nothing more than a geographical reference point. Other men followed Stone and his hunting party into the area and once they caught a glimpse of the fertile land along the river bank the settlement of the country was assured. The territory was cleared of Indians in what now seems a savage and unfair manner, but history was moving rapidly and such savagery was dismissed as the necessary birth pains accompanying the founding of a new frontier. Men came and built their homes, made crude attempts at establishing industry, and watched with understandable pride as the area gradually assumed the appearance of the more developed places from whence they had come. But in all this transformation the river itself remained in the background, quietly making its way from its headwaters in the southern part of Rutherford County (and the east fork in Cannon County) to the point where it entered the Cumberland in Davidson County. Somehow it had not yet lent its identity to the people or the events around it, but that day would surely come.

By the time of the Civil War the land watered by Stones River and the lesser streams that fed it was in a high state of cultivation and formed the basis of a cultural environment perhaps unsurpassed in rural Tennessee. The town of Murfreesboro had grown from an obscure rural settlement to a business center of 4,200 people, but still the river that curved along its western border had not gained a distinguishable personality; it was merely another river in a land blessed with many rivers and it flowed northward in an unpretentious manner to lose its identity completely as it poured its waters in the Cumberland above Nashville.

The Civil War would change all this. War has a tragic way of changing an insignificant rise of ground into a national shrine, or converting the name of an unglamorous river into a synonym for heroism, and in such a way Stones River was destined to become a tangible symbol of those ideals held sacred by the people of this country. It would be as if the river and the land about it had waited patiently for their hour in history to arrive and at the appropriate time their heretofore hidden significance would blossom forth in the consciousness of a people who had previously accepted them merely as a matter of fact.

The people along Stones, River first saw an organized army immediately following the collapse of the Confederate defense line across southern Kentucky in early 1862. In February of that year General Albert Sidney Johnston brought the remnants of his army through Murfreesboro as he made his way south to what would eventuate in the Battle of Shiloh. At Shiloh this army tasted the bitter fruit of defeat, its general was killed, and the men learned that war was not nearly as romantic as it had been pictured by the politicians the year before.

By October this same army, under its new commander, Braxton Bragg, had regained its equilibrium and confidently turned its head toward Kentucky where both officers and men envisioned a glorious victory. But the fates once again dealt a stunning blow to southern hopes as the anticipated victory evaporated in a murk of confusion and indecision among the high command. Amid the disappointment of defeat and the gathering cold of approaching winter, the Confederate troops once again assembled at Murfreesboro in November, and the prelude to the drama that would be Stones River began. Soon the opposing armies would be arranging themselves for another battle. Substantially the same men in both armies would participate; only the scene and the casualties would be new.

As the Confederate army under Bragg made its way out of Kentucky, the Federal army under its new commander, William Stark Rosecrans, made its way to Nashville. During the last weeks of 1862 both armies occupied themselves with routine activities. The Confederates, in particular, believed they would see no further action until the break of spring. But Rosecrans had other ideas and, on December 26, he began moving his army toward Murfreesboro.

Most of the Confederate High Command was at a gala ball held in the courthouse at Murfreesboro when word reached them that the Federal army was approaching. The next few hours were hectic ones as Bragg sought to consolidate his men and align them in a defensive position. The terrain west of Murfreesboro is monotonously level and, other than the river, the Confederate commander found no natural advantages to offer help in repulsing the enemy. Knowing he had little time or choice, Bragg formed his army along a three mile line which extended across the level bottom land along Stones River. As the darkness of December 30 approached, the two armies faced each other in some places no more than fifty yards apart. In the cold, damp darkness the Rebel army lay sprawled like a giant serpent along the river bank ready to strike at the faintest sign of light. Stones River's hour of history was near at hand.

With the first dim light of December 31, the Confederate left slithered through the cedar thickets in its front and the Battle of Stones River was on. The Yankee line folded under the impact of the hard-driving Rebel attack and as Federal regiments down the line prepared to meet the onslaught they found themselves hit from the front, rear, and flanks. The Confederates were determined to win· their determination was evident most of all to the Yankees in their immediate path.

In the frenzied tumult of close-range fighting the Yankee line buckled again and again. At some places the Federals rallied and put up stiff resistance only to falter before the persistent Rebel attack. Long before noon the victory-hungry Confederates had bent the right side of the Federal line back until it was at right angles to the left. Behind what had been the Federal left, disorganized bands of Yankee soldiers searched desperately for a haven against the swiftly moving tide of Rebels that seemed sure to engulf them. Federal officers drew up lines of soldiers with drawn bayonets to stop the rout, but even this failed to check the retreat of many who fled to Nashville, thirty miles away.

The two flanks of the Federal army formed a hinge in a cluster of trees whose circular shape prompted the name "Round Forest." Knifing through this growth and parallel to the Federal right was a railroad whose bed cut deep into the ground and afforded a strong defensive position against further Confederate attacks. The forest and the railroad bed gave the Yankees enough protection to stabilize their lines, and here they took on new life.

Shortly before noon the Rebs concentrated their attack on the "Round Forest," and the savage slaughter of the early morning was resumed. But now the tables were turned, and it was the Confederates who saw their lines crumble before the concentrated fire of Yankee cannon and the stinging bullets of Yankee rifles. For hours the Confederates hammered at the "Round Forest," but to no avail. To the Confederate troops doing the attacking, the Yankee position was not called "Round Forest," but with the authority of men who had seen for themselves they called it "Hell's Half

Acre." In the late afternoon the Rebel generals saw the futility of further attack, and darkness soon forced a halt to the action of the first day.

The following morning Bragg expected to find the Yankees gone, but instead he found them standing firm in the position they had occupied the previous afternoon. Throughout the day both armies held their positions and watched each other like two wounded animals, ready on the one hand to fight if the occasion arose but on the other anxious to gain a reprieve from the bitter action of the day before. The day passed uneventfully, but by the afternoon of the third day the tension that told of impending action could be sensed by the men on both sides.

Late in the afternoon Bragg ordered a full scale attack on the Federal left by John C. Breckinridge's Corps. With a renewed burst of spirit, the Rebels struck just before sundown.

Once again the Confederates saw the Yankee lines crumble before their attack, and once again they envisioned a glorious victory. But what seemed so obviously an overture to victory suddenly became a prelude to disaster. As the retreating Yankees were pushed back toward the banks of Stones River they pulled the unsuspecting Rebels within range of some fifty-eight cannon masked on a hill behind a dense cedar thicket. In a moment it was as if the Confederates had opened the door of hell to be greeted by the devil himself. The soggy river bottom over which the Yankees had been driven became a death trap to the advancing Southerners who came within range of the concealed cannon. Like hunters shooting at trapped animals the Yankee gunners blazed away with deadly accuracy. In less than forty-five minutes over 1,800 Confederate soldiers fell before the Yankee fire. The impact of this crushing blow meant that Bragg had little chance of penetrating the Yankee line, and for all practical purposes the Battle of Stones River ended as the last Rebel soldier dragged himself out of range of the Yankee cannon.[1]

A few hours later the Confederates withdrew from Murfreesboro leaving a battered and bloody Yankee army in possession of the field. For the Federals it was another chapter in the history of an army that somehow always retained possession of the field but never won decisive victories. For the Confederates it was another chapter in the history of an army that almost won all of its battles but did not quite win any.

◠⥈⥊◡

During the days immediately following the battle at Stones River the battlefield needed no superficial markings to indicate what had happened there. The scattered bodies of the dead, trees split by savage cannon fire, ruts left by heavy guns, hundreds of dead horses, and thousands of bits of abandoned equipment told in a terrible language what had happened. But time and nature have a way of absorbing such evidence. They remove from man the evidence of his folly and offer him another chance to use the earth for humane purposes.

The deep ruts at Stones River soon disappeared under the plows of cotton farmers, wrecked equipment was picked up by the army or was carried off by souvenir hunters, blasted trees put out new growth to hide the ugly scars inflicted by gunfire, and gradually the battlefield regained its prewar identity and blended well into the unscarred countryside around it.

But man is a creature of symbols, even when those symbols remind him of his worst moments, and it is this symbolic longing that brings historical shrines into being. The Stones River Military Park is a case in point.

The first efforts toward marking the battlefield were a direct outgrowth of the battle itself. Surviving members of General William B. Hazen's Brigade, who had so bravely defended the "Round Forest," gathered their dead and buried them close to where they fell. A sturdy rock monument was erected, and the name of every fallen soldier was inscribed thereon. From this beginning, what is now the military park came into being.

The grim task of burying the dead, begun by Hazen's men, soon demanded the attention of almost every Federal unit that had participated in the battle. At first no effort was made to consolidate the graves. Such an effort was finally begun when General George H. Thomas, acting under the authority of a Congressional Act of 1862 establishing national cemeteries, directed that the Federal dead of Stones River be collected and reburied in a single plot of ground selected for the purpose. In keeping with this directive General Thomas appointed Captain John A. Means, 155th Regiment Ohio Volunteer Infantry, as first superintendent, and in this capacity Captain Means surveyed the site of the present cemetery and made preliminary plans for its establishment.

When Captain Means was mustered out of service at the close of the war, the superintendency was taken over by Chaplain William Earnshaw whose orders were to begin disinterring the dead from the battlefield area and to rebury them inside the new cemetery. This phase of the operation was begun in October, 1865.[2]

After the dead on the battlefield had been reinterred, all those who had been buried in the immediate vicinity of Murfreesboro were likewise moved to the national cemetery. This effort increased the number of graves in the cemetery to approximately 3,000.

Since in the course of the war Federal troops had been engaged extensively in Middle Tennessee, it was decided that the dead from a radius of eighty-five miles would be brought to Murfreesboro for reburial. Battle sites including Franklin, Hoover's Gap, Farmington, and the Battle of the Cedars were combed for scattered graves. Even former Federal camp sites and roads over which the army had traveled were searched for graves, and when such were found the bodies were brought to Murfreesboro. About 25 per cent of the bodies reburied in the national cemetery were never identified, but each grave was carefully marked with what information was available. At the end of this phase of the operation there were 6,124 graves in the cemetery. Of these, 2,307 are unknown.[3]

Although the cemetery was established in 1865, the deeds to the land it occupied were not made until 1868. By August of that year three deeds had been recorded by James M. Tompkins, Clerk and Master of the Chancery Court for Rutherford County. These deeds transferred to the United States title to 20.0 acres, 18.45 of which constituted the cemetery proper. The Hazen Brigade Monument reservation containing slightly more than an acre was purchased by the federal government in 1875. This plot of ground was ordered for sale through a decree of condemnation in 1874, and J. W. Sparks, Clerk and Master of the Chancery Court at Murfreesboro, bargained for the property and transferred it to the United States in May, 1875.[4]

Under the original act establishing national cemeteries for Civil War dead nothing was included to insure the maintenance of such cemeteries. This was taken care of by a subsequent act of 1867. Section 2 of that act directed the secretary of war to appoint a superintendent for each cemetery under his jurisdiction. The Annual Report of the Quartermaster General to the Secretary for the year 1868 records the name of one L. S. Doolittle as the first civilian superintendent of Stones River National Cemetery. From that time to the present the cemetery has been administered by civilian personnel acting within the framework of governmental organization.

For many years the cemetery and the Hazen Brigade reservation remained the only portions of the battlefield in the government's possession. The area over which the battle was fought remained in the hands of private owners, and other than two small parcels purchased by the N.C. & St. L. Railroad, no attempt was made to establish a military park.

When at last the veterans of both armies who had fought at Stones River became dissatisfied that nothing was being done to mark this memorable field, they took initial steps to bring the matter to the government's attention. In Murfreesboro the Stones River Battlefield and Park Association (SRBPA) was formed with the expressed purpose of persuading the government to buy all or at least part of the battlefield as a permanent reservation.

Through the insistence of the SRBPA, Congressman James D. Richardson of Tennessee introduced a bill in the Fifty-fifth Congress in 1897 that would have authorized the establishment of a national park. Reflecting the meticulous work of the association, supporting resolutions were sent to Congress from the national encampment of the Grand Army of the Republic as well as from the south-wide encampment of the United Confederate Veterans. In addition to these resolutions, 162 other groups from twenty-five states also petitioned the lawmakers to pass Richardson's bill. As originally drafted, the bill, H. R. 1647, provided for the purchase of the entire 3,100 acres of the battlefield and called for an appropriation of $125,000. The bill was reported favorably out of the Military Affairs Committees of the House and Senate but was vetoed by the Director of the Budget for reasons of economy.[6] The matter was not again brought before Congress until 1926.

During the first session of the Sixty-ninth Congress, Representative Ewing L. Davis of Tennessee introduced H. R. 6246 calling for the establishment of a military park on the Stones River battlefield. Senator Kenneth D. McKellar of Tennessee introduced a companion bill in the Senate. Although the Davis bill had the endorsement of President Calvin Coolidge it was passed over until the second session at which time it was passed without serious opposition. The bill was signed into law on March 3, 1927.[6]

Included in the act establishing the Stones River Military Park was the stipulation that a three-man commission be appointed by the secretary of war to inspect the field and make recommendations pertaining to its preservation as a national shrine. In keeping with this stipulation Major John F. Conklin, District U.S. Engineer at Nashville, John D. Hanson, a Union veteran from Shelbyville, and Sam H. Mitchell, a Confederate veteran from Murfreesboro, were appointed to the commission.

Upon investigation of the field the commission found little remaining evidence of the battle. There were, however, four places that had already been marked. Two of these, the cemetery and Hazen's Brigade reservation, were already in government hands, and the other two, a small plot of ground where the Federal artillery was concentrated during the last day's fighting, and Redoubt Brannon, a small section of Fortress Rosecrans erected after the battle, were offered the government by their owners, the N. C. and St. L. Railroad. The latter two plots were transferred to the government for the consideration of $1.00.[7]

In its report the commission recommended that a 324-acre tract of land be purchased as the park site. Although realizing this small acreage in no way represented the total battlefield area, the members of the commission believed it the best tract possible considering available funds. In addition to the main tract the commission recommended that two small plots outside the park be purchased since they represented the headquarters sites of the opposing generals. The commission's report was submitted to the secretary of war on July 17, 1928. It was approved on August 22, 1928, and the commission was directed to proceed with plans for establishing the park.[8]

The Stones River Military Park was ready for dedication in the summer of 1932. On the afternoon of July 15, the dedication program was presented from a rostrum in the cemetery to an audience estimated at 1,000 people. Adding a touch of drama to the occasion were veterans of both armies who had fought there during those three eventful days seventy years before. In a gesture symbolizing the unity that now existed between the former foes, the Honorable Sam Mitchell, a former Confederate soldier, raised the American flag over the Federal dead in the cemetery. The Stones River Military Park had become a reality.

Less than a year after the dedication of the park, all national military parks were transferred to the control of the U.S. Department of the Interior, which maintains and supervises them through the National Park Service.

The person who visited Stones River Military Park for the first time in the 1960s would have probably been disappointed in what he found. Although the park contains much of the area over which the battle was fought, there were no strategically located interpretive markers to explain the action. The markers that were in the park had no relation to the place where they stood and contained no information that could not be read away from the park as meaningfully as in the park. Many of the more interesting phases of the battle took place well outside the park area and are not marked in any way. Only a person intimately acquainted with the field and its history can point out to the visitor the historical significance of inconspicuous rises of ground, broad rolling fields, and an occasional structure that has survived the progress of time.

The cemetery in all its quiet dignity occupies the elevation from which the Federals aimed their cannon at the approaching Rebel line during the first day's fighting. Individual graves have tended to lose their significance after a hundred and fifty years but they remain as the vital element in what the casual visitor sees as a unified memorial to the Federal dead.

Less than a mile down the old Nashville turnpike toward Murfreesboro the visitor will find the Hazen Brigade reservation much as it was at the close of the war. The fence, gravestones, and the rock monument are still there but each in its own way reflects the uncompromising ravages of time. Perhaps the monument has suffered most. The lettering that tells of the exploits of Hazen's Brigade is almost illegible, but yet the monument remains a symbol of heroism. In this role it has lost none of its beauty. The thoughtful visitor will no doubt admire this fitting tribute to the Federal soldiers who so valiantly defended the "Round Forest" but he may wonder why there is no marker to commemorate the bravery of the Confederate soldiers who made this Federal heroism noteworthy.

Still further along the same road toward Murfreesboro the visitor will find Redoubt Brannon hovering above the bridge that crosses the river just outside the city. Existing now only as a ghostly image of its former self, this redoubt remains an imperfect symbol of the elaborate structure that was once Fortress Rosecrans.

Along this same road on either side of the cemetery can be found the location of the headquarters of the opposing generals. These square plots of ground are carefully kept, but the cannon balls that formed pyramids at each place have long since gone the way of the souvenir hunter, and only the concrete foundations on which they rested remain.

To the south of the cemetery and inside the park area can still be seen the limestone rocks that rear their ugly heads from the shallow soil over which both armies passed. Tangled among the rocks are the roots of scrubby cedars that remain today much as they appeared a 150 years ago. The informed visitor will remember how these rocks and scrubby cedars protected the wounded and slowed down the retreat of the Federal artillery and their ugliness will be forgotten in the thought that they in their own clumsy way helped to make the history that is now America's.

A mile to the northeast of the cemetery a white shaft marks the position of the Federal artillery that dealt the final blow to Southern hopes at Stones River. On its front it bears a tribute to the Confederate soldiers who charged into the death trap that fateful day. The area over which the Confederates came remains much as it was during the battle, and although it is outside the park the visitor can stand at the monument and get a panoramic view of the scene where this phase of the battle occurred.

Throughout the area the visitor will find trees and rocks that no doubt were there during the fighting, but such objects stand in a mute insolence and serve only to aggravate the imagination of one who sincerely wishes to understand what happened here so long ago.

In the 1960s, a building program was underway at Stone s River Military Park. New residences were erected for the superintendent and one other park employee. A visitors' center was also constructed to house a park museum. These additions came none too soon for a park whose potential has consistently been compromised in the name of economy. Efforts to acquire more battlefield land, to resist the encroachment of Murfreesboro's growth, and to maintain adequate interpretation at the park continued with mixed success into the twenty-first century.

The theater that once staged the drama of Stones River has changed its billboard to reflect other and perhaps more significant productions of a fast-moving society. The railroad that helped the Federals stabilize their lines during the first day's fighting is still there but interestingly enough it spurs off on the battlefield itself to bring in raw materials and take away finished products from a manufacturing plant that stands where the Federal left once was. Perhaps this plant is a more fitting tribute to the men who fought at Stones River than the monuments an economy-minded North and a self-pitying Southland failed to erect.

ᏪᏪᏪ

This article first appeared in the December 1962 issue of the *Tennessee Historical Quarterly*; it was updated for inclusion in this book.

1. *Battles and Leaders of the Civil War* (4 vols.; New York, 1887–88), III, 613–632.

2. Ann Wilson Willett, "A History of Stones River Military Park" (MA thesis, Middle Tennessee State College, 1958).

3. "Stones River National Cemetery, Tennessee," *Names of Soldiers Who Died in Defense of the American Union Interred in National Cemeteries*. Roll of Honor No. XXIII (Washington, 1869), 299.

4. Rutherford County Register's Office, Deed Book XV, 357; XVI, 30–32.

5. *Congressional Record Containing the Procedures and Debates of the Fifty-fifth Congress, First Session* (Washington, 1897), XXX, 112.

6. *Congressional Record of Proceedings and Debates of the Second Session of the Sixty-ninth Congress* (Washington, 1927), LXVIII, 4637, 5969.

7. Representative Ewin L. Davis to S. H. Mitchell, John F. Conklin, and J. D. Hanson, 18 April 1928 (Exhibit No. 1 to accompany Report of Commission, 17 July 1928).

8. Maj. Gen. B. F. Cheatham, QMC, to the Park Commission, 24 April 1929.

CONTRIBUTORS

WILLIAM A. ANDERSON has an MA in history from Michigan State University and a doctorate in education. His career in higher education culminated in the presidencies at Carl Sandburg College and West Shore Community College. In 2001, he became the first director of the Michigan Department of History, Arts and Libraries, a post he held until his retirement in 2009. Anderson is the author or editor of seven books.

EDWIN C. BEARSS was a research historian for the National Park Service, Region One, and stationed at Vicksburg National Military Park when he wrote his study on cavalry at Stones River. A WWII veteran with an MA in history, Bearss was chief historian of the NPS from 1981-1994. He is now Chief Historian Emeritus and a nationally-known speaker on the Civil War.

ROBERT S. BRANDT served as a chancery court judge in Nashville from 1976-1996 and still practices law. A former trustee of the Tennessee Historical Society, in addition to his work on Tennessee history Brandt has written numerous articles and books on hiking, the outdoors, and travel.

LENARD E. BROWN was Southeast Regional Historian for the National Park Service in 1993. He received an MA in history from the University of Arizona. He joined the NPS in 1964 and authored several research reports on historical sites for the park service.

MIRANDA L. FRALEY-RHODES is director of curatorial interpretive planning at the Tennessee State Museum. She received her PhD in history from Indiana University and is a former museum technician at Stones River National Battlefield.

ROBERT HARTJE received a PhD from Vanderbilt University and headed the history department at Wittenburg University in Ohio. He authored *Van Dorn: The Life and Times of a Confederate General* (1967).

TIMOTHY D. JOHNSON received a PhD in history from the University of Alabama. He is a professor of history at Lipscomb University and his specialization is the mid-nineteenth century American army. He is the author of five books, most recently *Liberty vs. Power*.

CHRISTOPHER LOSSON received a BA from Morehead State University and an MA from the University of Mississippi. He is on faculty at Bishop LeBlond High School in St. Joseph, Missouri. His books include *Tennessee's Forgotten Warriors: Frank Cheatham and His Confederate Division* (1989), and *Jacob Dolson Cox: A Military Biography* (1993).

BOB WOMACK was a professor in the Educational Leadership Department at Middle Tennessee State University, where he taught for more than 36 years. Womack earned his BS degree in 1948 and his MA in 1952 from Middle Tennessee State College. In 1956, he completed his Education Doctorate at George Peabody College. Womack was a recognized expert in two areas outside teaching, the history of the Tennessee Walking Horse and the history of the Civil War.

INDEX

Tennessee in the Civil War:
The Best of the *Tennessee Historical Quarterly*

The *THQ* has published 400 articles since 1942 on the Civil War in the Volunteer State. The best of these pieces are being reprinted in twelve thematic volumes from 2011-2015. The series includes:

- *Tennessee in the Civil War* (2011)
- *The Civil War in Appalachia* (2011)
- *The Battle of Shiloh* (March 2012)
- *The Battle of Stones River: The Fight for Middle Tennessee* (2012)
- *Forrest and the West Tennessee Cavalry Campaigns* (November 2012)
- *Emancipation and the Fight for Freedom: African Americans in the Civil War* (January 2013)
- *The Battles for Chattanooga* (September 2013)
- *Tennessee Women in the Civil War* (Late 2013)
- *Fort Pillow* (Spring 2014)
- *Eyewitness to the War: A Collection of First Hand Accounts* (2014)
- *Hood's Campaign: Franklin and Nashville* (2014)
- *After the War: Reconstruction* (2015)

This series is published with support from the Tennessee Civil War Sesquicentennial Commission.

To order copies of volumes in the series or to receive the *Tennessee Historical Quarterly* (a benefit of THS membership), please contact the Tennessee Historical Society at 615.741.8934, email the THS for information at info@tennesseehistory.org, or visit the THS website at www.tennesseehistory.org.